GOODBYE, COLUMBUS
HELLO MEDICINE

GOODBYE, COLUMBUS HELLO MEDICINE

Michael Meyers, M.D.

WILLIAM MORROW AND COMPANY, INC.

NEW YORK 1976

Printed in the United States of America.

1 2 3 4 5   80 79 78 77 76

Library of Congress Cataloging in Publication Data

Meyers, Michael.
    Goodbye, Columbus, hello medicine.

1. Meyers, Michael. 2. Medical students—New Jersey
—Correspondence, reminiscences, etc. 3. Actors—
United States—Correspondence, reminiscences, etc.
I. Title.
R154.M58A33   610'.92'4 [B]   76-15403
ISBN 0-688-03090-4

BOOK DESIGN CARL WEISS

TO PATTI,

WHO CONTINUES TO TEACH ME

TO LOVE AND BE LOVED

PROLOGUE

"I'LL READ the directions in the manual first, so you can cut."

"No, I'll read first and *you* cut; I was an English major in college, and I'm a real good reader."

As I proclaimed this brilliant piece of logic to the four other first-year medical students clustered about our cadaver on that first day of gross anatomy lab, we all sensed what was really going on. It was obviously very difficult to appear nonchalant about making the first tentative slashes with a razor-sharp scalpel on what was once a living human being, especially when it's the first dead body you've ever seen, much less touched.

It was unsettling enough simply walking into the ninth-floor gross anatomy lab on that first day of medical school and being assaulted not only by the sight of thirty shrouded bodies but also by the strange, pungent, acrid smell of formaldehyde reacting with dead tissue. I had walked around for the previous two days with a dull ache of apprehension in my gut, thinking about how I would react to this moment, and worrying as well about making the grade and not flunking out. I had been an English major as an undergraduate at Lafayette College, while the overwhelming majority of my classmates had been straight premedical majors, and although I had reasoned quite correctly that I wasn't going to get much Shakespeare in med school—and had thoroughly enjoyed my liberal arts training—my doubts at that moment caused me a great deal of uneasiness. But it was also a relief talking with my fellow classmates and finding out that I was obviously not alone in my feelings.

As we piled into the elevator at the end of that first three-hour session, I was proudly wearing the stains and odors of that first rite of passage to becoming a doctor. Surprisingly, I had found that not only was I able to cut and probe but that I was thoroughly fascinated by the ordered way the muscles, tendons, bones, and blood vessels were structured and fit together. We all were chattering excitedly about our experience when I began to notice the strange looks on the faces of our fellow elevator riders. It was only then that I realized how awful we all must have smelled. After being in the lab for so long, we had obviously begun to adjust to the strong odor, which had permeated my stained lab coat and clung to my hands.

It seemed that no matter how much I scrubbed, I could not get that smell off my hands. Perhaps some of it was psychological, in a sort of Lady Macbeth tradition ("Out, out damned smell") but I did finally hit upon a solution that worked. I still got strange looks in the elevator, but I found I much preferred the smell of Old Spice After Shave Lotion and reconstituted lemon juice (an equal amount of each was the best proportion), the only combination that would thoroughly mask the offending odor.

During that first year the medical school itself was located in Jersey City, New Jersey—hardly the garden spot of the Garden State. Hudson County politics has a reputation for corruption that made the Watergate situation seem like a Cub Scout jamboree by comparison, and as a matter of fact, during my year there, the mayor of Jersey City was actually thrown out of office after it was discovered that he was not even a legalized citizen of the United States. The motorcycle policemen are the biggest and meanest looking I've ever seen, and the same can also be said of the cockroaches, while the tap water leaves a curious purplish-green ring in every tub or basin. However, Jersey City was also the site of the only four-year accredited medical school in the entire state of New Jersey at that time. It was a state school as well, so that the tuition was at least reasonable compared with many other medical schools in the area. It also had a great view of New York Harbor and the Manhattan skyline.

By the second week of gross anatomy it was interesting to notice which members of the class really rolled up their sleeves and dug in (no pun intended—although one group of students

8

did nickname their cadaver "Ernest," so they could always say that they were "digging in Ernest") and which others were merely content to look over their classmates' shoulders and say things like "point out the radial artery" or whatever. My group had only one "watcher," but that still left plenty of dissecting to go around.

One of the more curious things that happened in those first few weeks was that I noticed I began to lose my taste for red meat. It became more and more unsettling to cut into a piece of roast beef and be acutely aware of the varied complement of tendons, fibrous tissues, and blood vessels (when you realize that a piece of roast beef or steak is actually part of the muscle of the animal, it is quite understandable how one could easily make the rather obvious association with the gross anatomy dissection). To compound the situation I had an instructor who liked to ask oddball questions during lab, and he made sure to tell us that because of the ratio of the proportion of fat to muscle, and its structure and composition, the human thigh muscle would taste the closest to beef steak if properly prepared. So it was plenty of fish for a while.

The same instructor once asked me what particular muscle group elicits the most male looks when a pretty girl walks by. I got the answer wrong because of personal prejudices—and because I forgot that the breasts are basically composed of fat, or adipose tissue. I could have protested that it was an unfair question because I had a male cadaver, but after seeing other groups struggle through the added layers of fat that every woman carries, even a thin woman, compared with a similarly built male, I realized I was fortunate, so I just shut up. The muscle he had in mind, by the way, was the gastrocnemius, which is the one that gives definition to the calf. Sense of humor notwithstanding, he did know his anatomy.

One late afternoon soon after classes began, we were huddled around the right shoulder of our own cadaver, delving into the mysteries of the axilla, or armpit, and I casually mentioned to my dissecting group that I had been in a movie that past summer.

"That's nice," one of my partners said, "but it's my turn to cut, so start reading the manual."

The same lack of enthusiasm was shared by the group as a whole, with the cadaver being the most visibly unimpressed, but my labmates weren't far behind. Their reaction, or absence thereof, was somewhat understandable, but I was still hurt to a certain degree.

"Hey, guys, I was really in a motion picture that was filmed this past summer. I had a big part, and it'll be out in the spring," I persisted.

"Sure, sure, and I lived with Brigitte Bardot all through college."

Obviously they thought I was either bullshitting entirely or that if I had been in a movie, I was either a spear carrier, a clothesrack, or some other kind of window dressing. Besides, they probably would have reacted much more strongly if I had told them I knew the questions on our rapidly approaching first practical exam, coming up in only a few days. . . .

Yet it was difficult to fault my classmates for their skepticism when I myself wasn't even sure of my own reactions to the unexpected chain of events that had transpired the previous summer, and which would ultimately result in some fairly significant changes in many aspects of my life in the months and years to come.

GOODBYE, COLUMBUS
HELLO MEDICINE

CHAPTER / 1

AFTER GRADUATING from college in June, I had planned on driving a truck for my father, in addition to teaching tennis, until medical school started in the fall. I certainly had no idea that radical changes in those plans were about to take place when I arrived at the Plaza Hotel one Thursday evening in early June for a wedding rehearsal. A friend of mine was getting married, and I had been asked to be an usher. Half-jokingly, I thought I would be expected to wear a white fur glove and clean off the seats as the guests arrived, since the only other ushers I was familiar with were either at Shea Stadium or RKO's. I was in a rather playful mood when I found the banquet manager's office.

As my friend Michael, who was to be best man, and I entered, two men I had never seen before gave me a quick but rather thorough visual inspection, talked excitedly between themselves, and then approached and made their introductions. We proceeded to make small talk, and one of the men asked me my plans for the summer. As soon as the word "tennis" was even half out of my mouth, he began getting rather excited, and he kept repeating, "Perfect, perfect."

"Okay, I'll bite," I said. "Perfect for what?"

"Well, this may seem like a put-on, but I'm a motion picture director making a film in New York this summer, and there's a part in it which I think you would be perfect for."

I thought the guy was putting me on, so I looked him straight in the eye and asked, "What have you done that would make you worthy to direct me, an unknown, in my first film?"

He said he had previously directed the movies *One Potato, Two Potato* and *The Incident* and had done some TV as well, and insisted that not only was he really a director but that I *had to* come down to Paramount the next day and pick up a copy of the script.

"Sorry, tomorrow is out of the question," I said. "United Parcel Service is on strike, I have twenty-eight deliveries to make in the Bronx and Manhattan alone, and the truck is already loaded."

Well, he just wouldn't take no for an answer, and he pleaded and cajoled to such an extent that I finally agreed to try to make it to the studio they were using in midtown Manhattan some time the next afternoon.

The following day I left New Rochelle at 7 A.M., completed most of my deliveries by midafternoon and finally pulled the truck up in front of the studio on West Forty-fourth Street as the rush hour was just beginning. I parked illegally, and dressed in my dungarees, work boots, and T-shirt, I entered the building, only to be stopped immediately by a guard who informed me, "All deliveries are made through the service entrance."

I had certainly had more than enough of service entrances by that time, and I indignantly told him, "I'm here to see Larry Peerce, the director."

This really cracked the guard up, and he asked me if he looked like he was born yesterday.

"You're the second guy this week who's tried the old delivery gimmick. The word must really be out that a hot part is open. You actors will try anything to get to see a director if you think there's work for you."

After a quick phone call settled the argument, I was ushered upstairs, where Larry then introduced me to Stanley Jaffe, the producer of the film. We sat around for several minutes and talked in general terms about Philip Roth, and his novel *Goodbye, Columbus* in particular. At college I had read the collection of short stories that had won Roth the National Book Award, and I felt secure that my comments displayed a certain level of comprehension and insight. Stanley finally asked what I had done in the past which made me think I could handle something like the third lead in a major motion picture. (I still wonder if there ever is such a thing as a *minor* motion picture.)

I sat there trying to come up with something, anything, for about thirty seconds, and then I blurted out that I had played Dorothy in a *Wizard of Oz* production in Cub Scouts when I was nine years old. I told him I had had two little-sock boobs, cute rosy cheeks, and everybody had thought I was terrific. I even volunteered to bring in the 8-mm home movies my father had taken of the "production."

Since the part obviously did not call for a six-foot four-inch Jewish Judy Garland in drag, this was surely not the type of background they had in mind. Nevertheless, they gave me a script and told me to go over my lines and be prepared to audition with Dick Benjamin on Monday.

"Monday is out of the question," I exclaimed. "My tennis job is scheduled to start at eight A.M."

Again, after much deliberation and debate, it was finally agreed that I was to meet them *after* tennis in Westchester, where they would be scouting locations.

As I was driving over from the tennis courts late that Monday afternoon, I was somewhat nervous. This was not going to be at all like the horsing around I had done with my family as we attempted to "rehearse" over the weekend. I was glad that they had not been privy to the scene of my mother, father, and brother as they attempted to coach me because as a family our aggregate acting talents seemed a lot closer to the Three Stooges than the Barrymores. I had a few butterflies in my stomach, but I wasn't all that anxious because I had reasoned that no matter how this thing would work out, I was going to enjoy my experience. Even if I didn't get the part, it would still make a good story—"Hey, guys, I was *almost* in a movie."

However, I quickly lost my resolve as I drove up and saw Dick Benjamin and Ali MacGraw, and the apprehensiveness persisted through the reading that I did with Dick. I was trying to "act" like an actor, and it was all too obvious as I gesticulated about the room. My voice was so singsongy that even *I* would have been hard pressed to say which was my real voice. But Larry and Dick were not only patient but professional, and they soon had me relaxed and "myself." I began to let my voice trail off at the end of sentences and talked, as I normally did, with many hand gestures. When we had finished, they were both quite excited and enthused.

The reason for their enthusiasm was not solely from my "performance" per se, as I was soon to find out, for it seemed that the film was scheduled to begin shooting in less than two weeks, and the role of the brother, Ron, had the third-largest number of scenes. They were becoming frantic about casting the part, especially after the frustration of auditioning and testing many professional actors over the previous months without success.

In my naïveté I assumed that everything was settled. But nothing in the entertainment business, as I was soon to find out, was ever simple and direct. I was told that I would have to do the same reading for Stanley, since, as the producer, he would have to agree with Larry's judgment. As they were frantically making arrangements over the phone to meet early the next day in New York City, I tapped Larry on the shoulder and told him I couldn't make it into the city until 6 P.M. because I still had my tennis commitment. It wasn't that I was playing it coy or hard-to-get, I was simply protecting my summer income, which I was counting on for tuition.

So Dick and I repeated the scenes for Stanley the following evening, and he concurred and immediately called the studio in California. It was only then that I let myself get excited, as I realized that at least for the summer, I was going to be in moving pictures, and not moving cartons. Naturally, I didn't have an agent, so I enlisted the help of an attorney friend of the family who negotiated the actual contract.

There was a stipulation in the contract that my filming commitment must be completed before the first day of medical school registration. As it turned out, we did just make it, as my last day of filming was on a Tuesday and I met my cadaver on Thursday.

The next five days were hectic and exciting. Besides the more obvious demands of wardrobe fittings, makeup conferences, and publicity sessions, there were also unexpected things, like going off to Central Park with my movie "family" for a mock picnic so that pictures could be taken which would then be hung on the set of our "house." I also had to rummage through the family photo album to find old pictures and clippings that could also be hung about to give the flavor of a real family with a past.

Larry is a director who believes in rehearsal, so we spent the majority of the remaining available time sitting around a large table reading through the script and discussing things like plot and character motivation and doing a lot of improvisations of how we felt the characters might react to certain situations.

The improvisations were a great deal of fun, and I was soon able to concentrate and enjoy them as well. At one point Nan Martin, who was to play the role of my mother in the picture, spontaneously cried during an emotionally charged improvisation, and this had quite an effect on me. I was impressed not only with her ability to bring herself to the intense level she felt the scene warranted but also with the way she was able to compose herself so quickly after the scene. It was most reassuring because I would not only be working with these competent people but I was counting heavily on them for help and guidance.

I got a hint, even then, of what was to be in store for me as my medical education would progress when I was introduced to the actress who was to play the part of Dick's typically Jewish aunt from the Bronx. As soon as she heard the words "medicine" and "doctor," she began a long dissertation about the terrible kink she had in her neck while at the same time writing out the phone number of two nieces in Queens that she insisted I call for a date. This naturally got a big laugh from everyone present.

The first day of actual filming was on a Monday, less than two weeks after my initial chance encounter with Larry at the Plaza. That morning, as I was finishing up in the bathroom, my father, who was then fifty years old, and who had worked hard all his life to support our family, stuck his head in the doorway to tell me, "The chauffeur is waiting." The look on his face said it all, and it was just as difficult for me to believe the things that were happening. I was excited, apprehensive and curious as hell about what was going to follow.

The character I was to portray was your basic, archetypal dumb jock. My hair had therefore been cut quite short, and I was even more upset at losing my hard-grown sideburns. This

17

was to turn out to be an area of continuing struggle between the hairdresser, the director, and myself throughout the ten-week shooting schedule; I was to repeatedly lose the battle of the creeping sideburns, which took place each Monday thereafter, when the snapshots that were taken on the first day of filming were brought out for comparison, and my hair and sideburns would then inevitably be trimmed so that I would "match."

This was an aspect of film making that I was totally unaware of until that time. It is related to the fact that almost all films, by necessity, are not shot in continuity, or sequence. For example, you may shoot all of the exterior shots during the first weeks of filming, when the chances for good weather may be the best, so it is quite feasible that you may actually shoot the final scene of the movie during the first week of filming. This allows for greater flexibility, as you generally can schedule standby indoor scenes so that you can be covered and not lose a day's shooting if the weather is fickle.

To further complicate matters, one particular scene may involve both an indoor and an outdoor locale. For example, there may be a meeting on a lawn, followed by a walk to a front door. The continuation of that scene indoors may not be filmed until you are scheduled to move to the studio or to inside the actual building, and this may involve a matter of weeks.

This posed a particular problem for me, as I am of somewhat fair complexion and get sunburned easily. Since makeup can compensate only to a certain point before looking like makeup on the screen, it was important that I keep the same general skin tone I had at the start of filming; consequently, I found I was basically sentenced to being indoors for the duration of the filming. It so happened that I was still needed by my father (Yes, United Parcel Service was still on strike!), and I continued to drive a truck when I wasn't scheduled to shoot. Also, as a result of my movie salary, I found it economically possible for the first time to be able to do volunteer work in the emergency room of New Rochelle Hospital, which I not only enjoyed very much but profited from as well.

Each night it became necessary to check my schedule for the following day so that when I awakened I would know whether to pull on my "whites" and go over to the hospital, or rehearse my lines as I waited for the chauffeur (fortunately, the character of Ron was not very verbal, to say the least, and since I already knew how to chew gum, shrug my shoulders, and eat sloppily, I didn't have much to memorize), or get into my work clothes to go pick up the truck and make deliveries.

At one point in the filming the irony of the situation really struck home. We were shooting a scene in a warehouse in the East Bronx, which was supposed to represent the family firm of Patimkin Plumbing. (Some actors go on location to Europe, the Caribbean, or some other exotic place; I went to the East Bronx. I guess you can't have everything.) At a certain point in the dialogue, after I have come up with what I consider to be a brilliant suggestion about sending the employees to lunch on a staggered schedule, Jack Klugman, as my father, mutters, "Four years of college and he can't even load a truck." It just so happens that my father had often made similar remarks when I would help him on the truck and do something silly, like stack the glassware on the bottom, "All that schooling and no common sense."

I think one reason that the film worked as well as it did was because people could relate to the family on the screen as a real family. This was due in part, I feel, to Jack Klugman being so similar to my own father, being a very warm, open, honest person. Nan Martin, Lori Shell, who was my little sister, Jack, Dick, Ali, and I all got along tremendously, and genuinely liked and respected each other, and I think that quality came across. I also feel that the fact that nobody was a real "star" or acted like one also helped to a large degree.

I was naturally at a certain advantage during the filming because I was an "amateur." However, I had great trust in Larry as a director (I had to have!) and, as importantly, in the other cast members as well. I surely didn't know my good side from my bad side, and I still don't know or care. Of course, I did have certain ideas about the character and how I thought he should come across, and my suggestions were given as much consideration as anybody else's.

It was my idea, for instance, to slap Dick on his rear end, a gesture that was very familiar to me from my own sports background, and although I only did it perhaps three times in the entire picture, it seems to be something that people always seem to remember. It had first come up when Larry told me to do something "jocky" at the end of a scene in which I had just walked with Dick to his room during a week's "visit" to our house. ("Visit" is certainly a euphemism, for even a dumb jock would have known the guy was sleeping with his sister every night.) Dick had deliberately not been told what was going to happen so that when I gave him a crisp right hand across both "cheeks," a great expression of surprise and disbelief crossed his face, which the camera caught perfectly.

There was also a growing realization on my part that everyone involved had a personal stake in making the movie as successful as possible, and since *they* were paying *me*, I generally went along with their judgment, even to the point of eating like a slob or jerking about on the bed like a puppet. I think the combination of that attitude and the relative absence of self-consciousness on my part made the total experience so enjoyable and successful, and this appreciation was heightened as well by my continuing to drive a truck and work in the emergency room, which played a significant role in permitting me to maintain a more realistic sense of perspective.

A good example of this occurred one Thursday during the middle of the filming. I had been on the set for the first three days of the week and then found myself the next day delivering a load of merchandise to a warehouse in Long Island City. I knew several of the other drivers and warehousemen fairly well, and since they all knew about the movie, I was the butt of some good-natured kidding as we settled down to eat lunch in the cafeteria. However, I was unprepared for the prolonged stares, giggles, and outright guffaws that accompanied my attempts to eat.

"Watch, he'll do it again. Just keep watching," one of the drivers said to another in a loud whisper. I had no idea what was going on, and they sure as hell weren't going to let me in on the gag. So I just continued to eat, although I felt like some kind of goldfish in a bowl, and soon there was another outburst around the table. This time I froze, and it then dawned on me what I was doing that was giving them all such a laugh.

It seems that I had been unconsciously dipping a corner of my paper napkin in my water glass and then daintily dabbing at

20

the corners of my mouth, a habit I had obviously developed on the movie set. I had experienced some difficulty adjusting to the wearing of makeup—since I'm in the habit of rubbing my hands across my mouth, I was always having to be "remade" because I would constantly be smearing the makeup all over my face. Consequently, I must have developed this pattern of dabbing myself, and it was this subconscious maneuver that drew the laughs from my fellow laborers, who took great delight in pointing out to me that if I wasn't careful, I was going to turn into a real movie fag, or something worse.

CHAPTER / 2

BUT ALL that glamour and attention seemed far, far away on that Saturday morning in early October as I bent over my cadaver and feverishly sought to identify the muscles, tendons, and blood vessels that make the human hand the wondrous thing it is. I generally spent each Saturday morning in gross anatomy lab reviewing the previous week's work, but this particular Saturday was more important than the others because the first practical exam was scheduled for the following Monday morning. There was to be a written exam as well, but the practical exam, with the face-to-face confrontation of just you and the examiner (and the cadaver, naturally) was a much more upsetting prospect.

Practically speaking, there was only time for approximately ten minutes with each student, but even that can seem like an eternity when you are expected to be able to not only identify every muscle group and tendon but to be able to also explain the actions of that muscle (Does it move the thumb away or toward the hand? Does it rotate the finger? And so forth.), know its origin and the insertion (where the muscle comes from and goes), as well as know which specific nerve makes that muscle work. Major blood vessels and other structures were also expected to be identified.

My examiner was a very soft-spoken Indian doctor, who mercifully understood the tension and pressure that we all felt and conducted a rather low-keyed examination, but included enough probing questions so that he could be sure whether or not we knew the material. This time was also used to evaluate the quality of the dissection; as it turned out, each individual member did well on his examination, and the group as a whole was commended for the obvious time and attention that had been spent working on the dissection. I was so relieved at passing that I didn't even resent the fact that the "watcher," who spent so much less time in lab than the rest of the group, passed as well.

There were no women in my immediate small lab group, but there were several in the class as a whole. They were the subject of a lot of teasing and ribbing, so it seemed almost inevitable when our talkative instructor contributed an appropriate story on the subject of female medical students in general, and in gross anatomy lab in particular. I later heard a slightly different version from a different source, so the story is probably apocryphal, and I hope it will be taken with a grain of salt.

It seems that three male students and one female were assigned to a female cadaver. The woman was a very aggressive student, who always was there early, worked very hard—and was as demanding on others as she was on herself. Her male partners could take only so much, and one evening after everyone had left, they managed to secure a penis from a male cadaver and proceeded to insert it into the vagina of their own cadaver, and then covered it all with the shroud. Word had circulated by next morning that something was cooking, so everybody was there early to see her reaction. As she drew the covering off and saw the penis neatly tucked into the vagina, she very coolly looked at her three grinning male companions and in an icy voice put them neatly in their place when she said, "Okay, which one of you guys had to leave in a hurry last night?"

However, I surely would not like to convey a one-sided impression as to what actually goes on in a gross anatomy lab. It is emphasized strongly, and frequently, that the student should never forget that the cadaver was once a living person and, as such, is entitled to be treated with appropriate respect. However, it is also imperative that there be a certain amount of levity and kidding around as well or else the morbidness of the situation could easily become overwhelming, and a functional balance is generally achieved. This sometimes takes time, however, and it is especially upsetting at the beginning when, for example, you are attempting to dissect part of the muscles of the neck and you suddenly realize that your elbow is resting on the cadaver's face.

Gross anatomy was only one of four courses that we were swamped with during those first hectic six months. There was a combined neuroanatomy and neurophysiology course, which encompassed not only the examination of the structure and anatomy of the nervous system as a whole but included a study of the normal vital processes involved as well. These ranged from the physics of what happens at a single nerve ending to the clinical interpretation of the signs and symptoms of neurological disease. There were a great many didactic lectures, with a large amount of complicated reading, and laboratory sessions as well.

One of the many vivid memories of that first year was my feeling as I held a human brain in my hand for the first time and ran my fingers along its twisted convolutions. I remember standing there for quite a long while as I tried to somehow comprehend that the gray mass in my hand was not only responsible for initiating and controlling innumerable vital human functions and physical activities in a way so complex as to seem like a cross between science fiction and magic but that it was also the seat of thought, language, behavior, and emotion. It was just as staggering when we proceeded to investigate which parts of the brain were responsible for what function; it all became quite vivid, and had the potential for real application, when you saw how a blood clot or hemorrhage in a blood vessel that feeds a particular, circumscribed area could cause any specific symptom of a stroke, such as loss of speech or motion. So not only was the experience exciting in itself but, in addition, it also had practical medical application in a way that seemed much more obvious, and dramatic, than a great deal of the other areas of study.

Histology, another field of study that first year, can succinctly be described as that branch of anatomy that deals with cells and the minute structure of tissue and organ systems, with special emphasis on the correlation of form as it relates to the function of the tissue being studied. A great deal of time was again spent in the lab looking at microscopic preparations. We learned different methods of preparation and staining procedures, and it was emphasized that various materials and stains were required in order to bring out the different features or highlights that were of particular interest. The stains were quite colorful, often strikingly so, but unfortunately, they also effectively stained your fingers at the same time, and seemingly on a permanent basis. There was a sense of quiet beauty present in many of the slides, not only from the actual pigmented physical appearance but as much so in the delicate ways the different cells and elements were combined. The realization and understanding that this beauty was also functional, in order to allow for the performance of vital functions that were essential for life, made it even more striking.

While studying, I would turn the slide box upside down and try to identify each cross section without looking at its label, and after spending so many hours poring over hundreds of slides, I was struck by the large numbers that uncannily resembled patterns in the day-to-day world around me. Even now, I can look up and see a particular cloud formation and immediately be reminded of a cross section of a liver or, other times, perhaps a spleen.

"Musical Microscope" was the less-than-affectionate term that we used to describe the practical examinations in neuroanatomy and histology. The lab was divided into anywhere from forty-five to sixty "stations," with a microscope at each, or in the case of neuroanatomy, a station might consist of a cross section of an actual brain, with three differently colored pins stuck in strategic locations. You then had one minute at each station in which to identify the specific structure under the pin, and its function. At the end of each minute a bell would ring. Everyone would then jump up and literally run to the next station, and then generally spend precious seconds desperately trying to remember what had been missed at the last station, thereby falling further and further behind. When I had left the lab at the end of that particular exam, it felt like leaving a battlefield where a tremendous struggle had taken place.

Actually the analogy is not that farfetched. There is a tremendous amount of pressure on the medical student not only not to fail but simply to do well. The competition for acceptance to medical school has reached such an absurd level that it places something of a burden on those who are accepted. With such intense competition on the undergraduate level it almost seems inevitable that an attitude would develop where it might seem almost a sacrilege and a sin to flunk out, and thereby not fulfill the expectations of one's undergraduate professors and counselors, one's own family, and even of society in general.

I subsequently have had numerous firsthand experiences that have served to reinforce my impression that these societal demands and expectations are real. For instance, I have had occasion to be at a party or some other social event when a total stranger, after hearing I was a medical student, has actually expressed indignation that I was out enjoying myself and not at home studying or shut up in a lab somewhere. "You're a medical student. Why aren't you studying?"

The strong drive to succeed and do well is deeply ingrained in the vast majority of medical students even before they get to medical school, and this is then generally reinforced as the process of medical education continues. This attitude can be beneficial, and even a great help at times, to someone who must sacrifice a great deal of his personal time and pleasure while the majority of his peers are already working at their chosen professions and have much more time to devote to their families. However, there is also an inherent danger, in that this drive is useful only up to a point before it becomes self-destructive. It is not difficult to anticipate how easy it could be to lose one's perspective, and although in the process some brilliant doctors might be produced, a high price would be paid by also getting some pretty screwed-up individuals as well.

Exams are therefore a very traumatic experience not only because of these built-in pressures but also because of the tremendous quantity of material that must be learned. There is the added dimension of the incredibly rapid growth of the body of medical knowledge, so that you may be taught something initially, only to have a professor come back in a few months, or even weeks, to say that the information is now obsolete due to recent advances and discoveries. Nevertheless, this still remains one aspect of medicine that is particularly appealing to me, as I look forward to the constant stimulation of new information. Yet despite the overall stressful atmosphere of tests and evaluations during those basic science years and the strain of the long hours spent in lectures and lab, there were still lighter moments and pleasant experiences. Our first and only embryology lab occasioned one of those times.

When the lab was first announced, there were naturally a great many quips and comments made concerning what the possibilities could be for such a lab. No one was disappointed, as we were able to see the actual merging of a sperm and egg under the microscope and observe the subsequent divisions of the fertilized egg up to the four-, eight- or even sixteen-cell stage before the process spontaneously stopped. Naturally, it was not feasible for human eggs and sperm to be available, nor was it necessarily desirable, and the easiest donor to use, without having to destroy the animal, was the sea urchin.

By attaching electrodes to certain areas and then applying mild electrical stimulation, the male and female urchins could be made to discharge their sperm and eggs into a solution. An eye dropper would be used to transfer the solution under the microscope, and the egg-sperm interaction would then be observed.

The session was conducted with much hilarity, guffawing, and giggling. It had all the trappings of an old Marx Brothers' movie, with the instructor standing in the front of the lab, appearing, for all practical purposes, like some madcap scientist intent on electrocuting those poor, defenseless creatures and then running quickly about the lab distributing the precious eggs and sperm, while suffering the slings of some not very witty cracks offered by the students. "How can you tell the male from the females?" "It doesn't matter as long as the sea urchins can!" or "I can think of much more pleasant ways to get a sea urchin to ejaculate!"

Microbiology and biochemistry were the two other basic sciences that were studied in the first two years. Microbiology deals with the study of microorganisms, such as bacteria, viruses, fungi, and protozoa, and their relationship to infectious disease, and as part of our laboratory experience we were introduced to the technique of "plating out." This diagnostic procedure involves applying a suspected infectious agent to a small plate of media, which contains the nutrients that are required by the organism for growth, and then, through various means, the organism can then not only be identified but its susceptibility to various antibiotics can also be determined.

The material to be tested is usually transferred from a sealed container to the plate by means of a pipette, which is simply an oversized eye dropper with a very narrow opening at one end. By applying suction with your mouth, a small, measured quantity of the material to be identified can thus be obtained, which can then be transferred by placing your finger over the open end and controlling the number of drops that are released by carefully alternating the amount of pressure applied with your fingertip.

There was a cotton filter in the end where you placed your mouth, ostensibly for your protection, but this was hardly reassuring. You quickly got the impression that if the bacteria you were sucking up decided to continue right through the cotton filter and into your mouth, there was very little you could do to prevent it. You kind of figured that if you knew it, and the bacteria knew it, why in the hell didn't the instructor (who had demonstrated it at the beginning of the lab with just water and not bacteria)? Or did he? However, there were never any instances of people infecting themselves and getting sick, but it would have been very difficult in the beginning to convince the majority of the class that this would be the case.

The pipettes were identical to the ones used in biochemistry lab if, let us say, you wished to run some tests on a measured amount of urine. Here, mostly through carelessness and horsing around, accidents did happen, and it was not uncommon to be working in a lab and suddenly hear a piercing scream, as if someone had just been shot, and then see that person making a mad dash to the nearest sink and begin furiously rinsing out his mouth. The only consolation, and it was a minor one, was that you usually tested your own urine, and the only saving grace was that it usually only happened to a person once—since generally, he never got careless again. It reminded me of that mouthwash commercial where they say, "Once in the morning is all it takes." Why can I say this with such authority? Because yes, it happened to me. Yes, it happened more than once, and yes, I'll tell you what it tasted like. It tasted exactly like piss.

I have indelible memories of some late afternoons in the microbiology lab, where I spent hours looking for the eggs of parasites in human excrement, since many of the parasites that infect man live in the intestines, and their presence can often be determined by carefully examining the feces for their distinctive eggs. It was hardly one of the more pleasant experiences to be sitting in a hot, stuffy lab with eighty fellow students, each of whom was assiduously examining his or her own little pile of shit. Several of my classmates were unable to work without covering their faces with a bandana or handkerchief, and they added quite a comic touch, especially when they got up to employ the obligatory can of room deodorant, without which the lab could not have possibly functioned.

There were two other biochemistry lab studies that stick in my mind. One was designed to demonstrate the effect of diet on the chemical composition of the urine. To accomplish this, we all did base-line studies on our own urine while maintaining our normal diets, and then we were placed on various special diets, such as high protein, or high fat, or low amino acid, and so forth, for a specified period of time. We then collected our own urine for twenty-four hours, and stored it in large brown jugs containing some preservatives, and then reran the studies. It was an interesting and effective teaching project, and although it was mildly inconvenient for me, it was obviously much more of a problem for the girls in the class, who not only had to lug the bottle around wherever they went but had to carry a funnel as well.

The other experiment entailed the preparation of a powdered substance, which was then to be spread on a flat surface and used to identify unknown chemicals through a process known as thin-layer chromatography. The powder itself took several hours to prepare, and was to be saved until the next lab, when it would then be used. After assiduously working for almost three hours, I had the finished product on a clean piece of filter paper on my workbench. I was in the process of cleaning and drying the glassware used in the experiment by holding it in front of a stream of air coming from a nozzle on the desk, when someone abruptly called out my name. As I turned to look, I inadvertently took the beaker out of the direct stream of air and proceeded to blow the filter paper, *and the powder,* over the entire room. My instructor, with powder all over the front of his lab coat, dryly remarked that he hoped I wasn't planning on going into research.

CHAPTER / 3

DURING THE course of that hectic year, I somehow managed to maintain fairly close contact with Dick, Ali, and Stanley, so I was somewhat aware of how things were progressing with the movie. The final rough cut was completed about the same time I said good-bye to my cadaver as gross anatomy ended, and I have to admit I was much more excited about passing all my exams than I was about learning that the movie was scheduled to open in New York about Easter time.

On my occasional Saturday night off I sometimes would go out to dinner and a play or a movie with Ali, and the darnedest thing always seemed to happen. Back in high school or college if I had a blind date who turned out to be physically unattractive, I would invariably run into several people I knew. But it seemed that each time we would go out, I would parade Ali all over New York City without bumping into a single person to whom I could show her off. It didn't seem quite fair, or maybe it really was.

Two weeks before the movie was scheduled to open, I attended a screening of the completed film. As I settled down in my seat, I had absolutely no idea what to expect. Larry had not let me see any of the rushes during the actual shooting of the movie because he told me he was afraid I might see a gesture or a mannerism that I didn't like and attempt to change it in the middle of shooting. I also think he did it so that I wouldn't become self-conscious after seeing how I came across on film. Whatever the reasons or rationale it was quite a shock to see myself on the screen. It's hard to imagine the feelings when your name first appears in the credits and then suddenly see yourself thirty feet tall on the screen.

When the audience began to laugh (and believe me, how they laughed) every time I came on the screen, I began to have very mixed feelings. It was difficult accepting the fact that the audience was laughing at the character and not at me, and those feelings of confusion were to be intensified as the reviews would come out. I had thought of the character of Ron as basically a good-natured, affable, albeit somewhat dense, jock, but in all honesty I was not prepared for just how dumb the character would ultimately come across.

Something else which struck me on that first viewing was how difficult it was for me to make any sort of objective judgment about the film or about any of the other characterizations. Frankly, it took two more viewings before I could even see who else appeared in any scene I was in, much less how they came across, because I couldn't stop staring at myself.

There was one exception at the first preview screening because seated next to me was Larry's father, Jan Peerce, the well-known opera singer. He had a small part in the scene in which I got married, and it was really something to watch this internationally acclaimed artist's face light up each time *he* was on the screen.

There were many congratulations when the movie ended, but I was still quite unsure of my overall reaction. To compound my confused feelings, we all went to a bar across the street, and while everybody was excitedly talking about flying out to California the next day for a Directors Guild screening, I couldn't share much of the enthusiasm. I had to excuse myself early and rush back to Jersey City because there was a practical exam scheduled for early the next day, and if I didn't know the material, it would matter very little to the instructor whether Judith Crist would, or wouldn't, like the movie.

Despite all the distractions I somehow managed to do well on the exam, and the grinding routine of lectures, labs, and long hours of study left little time for further reflection. Approximately a week later I was sitting at my desk in my apartment when the phone rang, and it turned out to be an agent from the William Morris Agency. I was quite flattered when he said that the agency wanted to represent me as a client, and this helped quiet some of my unsettled feelings, as well as gave my bruised ego a boost. Just realizing that someone had called me (and not collect!) from California made me feel important.

As I was to find out later, the agency had been trying to contact me ever since the Directors Guild screening, but Larry and Stanley refused to give them any information. They were being almost too paternalistic and protective, and the agency was finally able to get my telephone number from the Screen Actors Guild, the actors' union I had to join at the time I made the picture. I subsequently signed with the agency, but with the explicit understanding that I was to decide which offers I was going to accept and that I was not to have any demands made on my time which might jeopardize my medical education.

The movie was scheduled to open the Thursday before Easter, so with no classes on Good Friday, the timing was ideal when Paramount invited the entire first-year medical class to attend. There was just one stipulation—everybody was asked to wear their white lab coats so that publicity pictures could be taken. Everything went well as we gathered under the theater marquee, except for one unforeseen complication: after almost a year of gross anatomy, urinalysis, and various other laboratory experiences most of the lab coats were a bit on the gamey side, which led several passersby to remark that the scene looked and smelled more like a displaced butchers' convention than a movie opening.

Everyone was in good spirits and seemed to enjoy the evening, especially knowing that there were no classes scheduled for the next day. There was a loud cheer when my name appeared in the credits, and when Jack Klugman spoke to Ali during my wedding scene and said that he knew his son was not the brightest guy in the world, one of my classmates shouted out, "That's for sure," and everybody in the theater cracked up.

I was completely unprepared for what was to follow. Naturally, I had hoped the movie would be well received and get good critical reviews. As a matter of fact, I used to tease everyone during the filming by saying that since I was probably only going to be in one movie during my entire life, it had better be a hit. I don't think anyone was disappointed in that respect, as the movie received generally good reviews. As for myself I felt I would be more than satisfied simply by seeing my name in the New York press, *Time,* and *Life*—I had looked forward to getting a big enough kick out of reading such a straightforward statement as, "The part of the brother, Ron, was played by Michael Meyers."

But this was far from the way things ultimately turned out. Almost every review had something nice to say about my performance, at least on the surface, and it was obvious that many of the critics took great delight in drawing word pictures of both my appearance and my actions. Said one:

> Michael Meyers, as the dumb, dumb brother, is a delicious source of amusement who swoops into every handshake as if he was pumping for oil, thrashes into a room as though he was laying siege to a foreign country, makes conversation seem like a loping version of the St. Vitus dance, and all in all gives the definitive portrayal of the innocent, good-natured, slightly dense All-American Jock.

Another wrote:

> As Ron, Michael Meyers is hilariously all arms; in fact he is so much of an athlete that his arms continue to swing, even when he sits down, like a pendulum on a Grandfather Clock. He hits everyone he meets on the back as if he were about to dribble them towards some imaginary basket.

Yet another wrote:

> A terrifically funny portrait of Ron, a gangling jock strap of a brother who is such an incredible embodiment of the character in the book: tall, athletic, naive and Jewish, a new American edition of Adonis, that the audience roars with delight every time he ambles on the screen.

I was referred to respectively (surely not respectfully) as a lumbering rhino, a gum-chewing lummox, a human giraffe (comparisons with the animal kingdom were very popular), a personified ace bandage (my favorite), a grinning moronic Buddha (my least favorite), and a loosey, goosey house semipro, captured in all his gangling (most-used adjective) blandness.

Despite all the favorable things that were generally said, including the real mind boggler that I should get an Academy Award nomination (I didn't), I quickly became quite sensitized to certain other statements and inferences in which a great many people made the assumption that I was simply an example of perfect typecasting and was really a dumb jock who had been simply plucked out of a locker room somewhere, given some lines to memorize, and then set loose on the set.

As I've grown and matured, I can look back now and realize that a great deal of my uncomfortableness was due to my own insecurity. Four years of medical school, a year of being an intern in an inner-city hospital, hard work, and, most important, support and feedback from the people I love and trust have enabled me to become confident of both who I am and what I am, and I think that the experience of the movie and all that which followed from it played a significant part in that development. I learned a great deal about myself and about other people from my exposure to a wholly different life-style and value system, and though there were some unsettled times, it was really a tremendous learning experience, as well as a great adventure.

As the number of reviews, articles, and interviews began to mount, I became acutely aware of the existence of a situation of which I had previously only been vaguely conscious. It involved the frighteningly high proportion of half-truths and distortions that were blatantly apparent in many of the articles, and they were not all restricted to the "typecasting" business. It was a rude awakening when I realized that if the magazines and other news media distorted and manipulated the facts about me, for whatever reasons, then the same thing must be happening to truly important people and events. It was a very frightening realization, especially at a time when the public in general was just becoming aware of the existence of the so-called credibility gap.

However, some of the media experience was not all that serious or significant, and I am referring here specifically to the phenomenon of the movie fan magazines. There were numerous silly articles and vignettes that appeared in many of the so-called pulp magazines, such as "We Name for Fame . . ." or something gossipy under the banner of "The new young bachelor about town (I always took great delight that the "town" was Jersey City, New Jersey, truly the entertainment and swinger capital of the East!) who is singular, witty, and loves his new life of dating." What did they think I was before the movie, a monk?

My mother would go to the local stationery store and furtively leaf through all the fan magazines on the shelf to see which ones

I was in that particular month. She would then pay for them quickly and stuff them in her purse so that people would not see her buying a magazine telling all about Jackie O's leather fetishes or whatever. I could never figure out what Jackie Onassis had to do with movies in the first place, but I knew I had hit the big time when *Mad Magazine* did a takeoff on the movie entitled, "Oh, Boy, Columbus," and the artist included me in several scenes in which I didn't even appear in the actual movie.

From almost the moment the movie opened, and I began appearing on television and having interviews in the newspapers and magazines, I noticed a rather distinct change in attitude of the medical school faculty and administration. At the beginning I got congratulatory letters from the Dean of the school, and others as well, and several members of the faculty expressed delight at my apparent dual talents. As time went on, however, I began to notice a certain amount of resentment that I was involved in something other than a full-time medical education. This was not a response to any academic deficiencies, which I could see as a valid concern, but seemed to stem from a prevalent attitude among the faculty that if someone chooses medicine as a career, then medicine is supposed to be his entire life. The commitment is to be total and absolute, and I was rather surprised to find out not only how rigid such a belief might be—to the point of being almost doctrinaire—but also how widespread it was as well.

The head of the physiology department, for example, told me outright that the faculty was taking bets that I wouldn't return to medical school in the fall. This was not especially comforting or reassuring to hear, to say the least. I am still not sure how much of what transpired in this regard was because of jealousy or envy and how much stemmed from a sincerely felt conviction that in order to be a good doctor, it is imperative that one devote almost all his time and energy to the study of medicine, but whatever the individual motivations, the message itself was clear. There appeared to be an additional factor operating as well (which seems analogous to the tradition of pledging and hazing of various fraternal organizations) and this was an extension of the philosophy that "since we all went through the process in a certain way and under certain conditions, then you must do likewise in the conventionally accepted manner in order to join the fraternity of doctors." Regardless of its exact etiology this attitude continued to exist in various degrees throughout my medical education, including internship.

However, at the same time, I noticed a curious paradox, namely that it seemed that the two fields of medicine and entertainment appeared to have a strong mutual attraction and that the people involved in one area found the other to be both fascinating and glamorous. At the school and the hospital, for example, I would frequently get bombarded with questions concerning the celebrities I had met and what they were really like. And, surprisingly, this was not limited by any means to my classmates, but included many Ph.D.'s and M.D.'s on the faculty as well. It got so that when I was scheduled to appear on a talk show, several of my professors would ask me if I could do something special on the air, like touching my left earlobe at a certain point in the conversation or stroking my elbow, so that they could tell their wives and families that I was signaling them. If I had attempted to satisfy everyone, I would have ended up looking as if I were doing a ten-minute imitation of a hyperactive third-base coach trying to get a message through to a stubborn batter.

Conversely, the medical profession seems to hold a special fascination and attraction for a great many people in entertainment, who feel that medicine has much more real glamour than show business. I would frequently be asked good, probing questions from a real cross section of the people involved in the entertainment field, that covered every aspect of the practice of medicine and were not just attempts to get free medical advice about a rash or a bad back.

As the first year of medical school was about to end, I hoped to spend my two-month vacation in California. As luck would have it, I got an offer to go to Hollywood to tape a Saturday night show, *The Dating Game*. The show would not only pay my round-trip plane fare but would put me up in a hotel for several days, and I would also receive $250 for my appearance, since I was a member of the Screen Actors Guild.

My last examination of the year was in physiology and consisted of an hour-and-a-half session with three doctors, each of whom questioned me quite extensively on his own field of expertise, such as the physiology of the heart, the lungs, or perhaps the kidneys. After this rather grueling ordeal, I immediately got on a plane to Los Angeles, and that very evening, before a live audience, I was expected to answer, with whatever dignity I could muster, such inane questions as "Bachelor number two, if you were a housefly where would you choose to land on my body?"

Naturally, I was a bit nervous, but it helped a great deal to know that whatever silly question the girl was going to come up with next, it *had* to be a lot easier than attempting to explain the mechanism of water absorption in the kidney to a physiologist, especially when he could make me repeat the course if my answer wasn't satisfactory.

Suffice it to say that I was not chosen, and although it didn't do great things for my ego, it surely didn't ruin my summer. As a matter of fact, I had a chance to be vindicated (actually I had three more chances) at the end of the summer, when I was asked to do the show again. This time I knew what to expect, and I was somewhat more at ease. I gave myself a little pep talk before the show and concentrated on trying to keep calm and collected (a vestige of high school and college days—"Whatever happens, man, just be cool"), and if I wasn't chosen this time, I resolved that I surely wasn't going to walk around the screen and kiss the girl like the majority of the good sport losers.

I was bachelor number two again (watch out for that number two spot, it's a jinx), and the girl was Sue Lyon, the actress who played Lolita in the movie of the same name. At one point she asked bachelor number one what was the first thing he had ever loved, and why, and this timid mousy-looking type in a three-piece suit and moccasins proceeded to take off on a rhapsodic tale about being in love with a furry white bunny rabbit when he was a child. He described how he cuddled it, and slept with it and so forth ad nauseum, and I just sat there looking at him, absolutely dumbfounded. When he finally finished, Sue Lyon threw me a curve (unfortunately, not one of hers) by asking me the very same question.

I was still staring in disbelief at bachelor number one, and I slowly turned and answered, "Well, I'm not sure if I've ever been really in love yet, but I'm dying to meet number one's rabbit." Everybody in the studio broke up and started laughing and applauding, but sure enough, she chose bachelor number one. As I trotted around the corner and saw Sue Lyon, all my previous resolve suddenly went right out the window, and I laid a big, fat, wet kiss on her because I figured you never know when you are going to ever get another chance to kiss a Sue Lyon.

Over the course of the next two summers I was to have the dubious distinction of becoming a four-time loser on the program. Each time I just tried to be natural and funny and not go in for any of the cheap jokes and double entendres that were so often prevalent, but I was never chosen. It must have been that number two jinx. However, I did receive four very interesting, or at least varied, booby prizes in addition to the fee. I eventually was to receive the following: a portable typewriter with a radio in the cover so you could "type to music" (which I subsequently sold for $75); a wrist watch (I only could get $50 for it); a $75 gift certificate for slacks and two shirts, which turned out not to be manufactured in my size, so I got cash instead; and finally, a 150-pound hibachi stove (which I surely wasn't going to take back on the plane with me to New Jersey). I mustn't forget to mention the four home versions of the dating game, all of which were subsequently given to the pediatrics unit of the hospital with their cellophane covers still intact.

The summer in Los Angeles was quite a welcome change of pace from the pressures of medical school. I had many magazine and newspaper interviews, appeared on some local radio and TV shows to help promote the movie (which was still in its first run), auditioned for several guest spots on television, and generally enjoyed a life of relative leisure. My circumstances allowed me to indulge in such a wide variety of activities that it almost seemed like going to a camp for grown-ups. For example, one morning I might have an interview or a reading, then perhaps lunch at Paramount Studios, and in the afternoon either play basketball or tennis or perhaps go over to the emergency room of the UCLA Medical Center and try to make myself useful. Evenings might be spent in the company of some young lady (if I was lucky), and I got to do the whole Hollywood discotheque and party scene (grossly exaggerated and overrated).

During that summer, and even more so subsequently, I naturally came in contact with many celebrities, and I usually enjoyed meeting them, especially those people whose work I admired.

When I was introduced to Alan Arkin, for example, I was taken completely by surprise when before I could finish telling him how much I'd enjoyed his movies and how many hours of pleasure he had given me, he proceeded to interrupt and tell me he thought I was absolutely hilarious in *Goodbye, Columbus* and that I had him rolling in the aisle. This would not be the only time something similar to this was to happen, and on each subsequent occasion I couldn't get over the fact that the actor or actress seemed as pleased to meet me as I was to meet him or her.

I was particularly struck by the large number of people in Los Angeles who read the "trades" (the trade papers of the entertainment business, such as *Variety* and *The Hollywood Reporter*) and yet who are not connected to show business in any respect. I received my share of "planted items," and on several occasions I was told to get hold of a certain copy because of the presence of an item such as "Michael Meyers, *Goodbye, Columbus* and Marie Latuche, up and coming young actress, were seen dining intimately at Cyrano's on the Strip last evening," when in actuality I had never even heard of, much less met, my so-called date. I was particularly floored when a gossip column referred to me as "B. F. Michael Meyers" in relation to some actress, and I was later relieved to find out that the "B. F." stood for boyfriend, in Hollywood jargon, and not what it meant when I was in college, when a "BFer" was someone who stole your date at a fraternity party.

Since I did very little actual work that summer, I was naturally concerned about finances for the upcoming year. Because of the money I had made from the movie, I had not had to apply for any additional bank loans the previous year, as I had been forced to do all through college, and I was actually in the process of applying for such aid for the second year of school when I was selected to appear in a commercial for little cigars. The financial prospects were both immediate and long term, as there was to be a series of these commercials shot over the next several years, and it couldn't have happened at a more opportune time, financially.

The first commercial was to be shot in Central Park in New York City, and it was to be a direct takeoff on the movie. I portrayed a jogger, and I actually appeared on camera for only seven seconds, just long enough to jog up to the young stud who is smoking the product, hit him on the arm a la *Goodbye, Columbus*, and then jog out of sight. For this arduous and time-consuming task I was flown first class from Los Angeles to New York, and then back to Los Angeles, put up in a luxury hotel, and made as much money for this seven seconds of "work" (over the next twelve months) as I did from the entire movie.

There were several other projects that necessitated my flying coast to coast, and I actually ended up making five transcontinental flights over a two-month period, all at someone else's expense. None of the projects ever came to fruition, but since I enjoy flying, especially when someone else is paying, it was not a chore. In addition, I found I was often able to switch the ticket from first class to tourist and bank the difference for the upcoming year, and besides, I got to see a lot of Grade B movies on the plane, as well as acquire a real taste for macadamia nuts.

CHAPTER / 4

WHILE I was spending my summer commuting between Los Angeles and New York, the medical school did some moving of its own. For a variety of reasons, the majority of which are still not entirely clear to me, the school was relocated to the Central Ward of Newark. Suffice it to say, and far from unexpectedly, politics was a prime factor, not only in the decision to move out of Jersey City but also in the choice of Newark as the new site. The basic science courses were to be conducted in specially constructed, portable, interim "semipermanent" facilities—which turned out, in actuality, despite the attempt at official-sounding designations, to be simply another example of political double-talk, as for all intents and purposes they were nothing more than glorified Quonset huts. The clinical in-hospital portion of our training was to be conducted in the Newark City Hospital, which was to be taken over by the medical school and the state and renamed the Harrison S. Martland Medical Center.

The interim facilities were constructed across from the hospital, with much additional land being taken over by the college for eventual construction of the permanent basic science facilities, library, and a new university teaching hospital. It was this issue, namely the amount of land secured and the subsequent displacement of many families from their grossly inadequate housing, which had played a substantial role in the tragic riots of 1967 that had raged about the hospital, and from which the neighborhood still bears raw, ugly scars to this day.

After a summer in the Xanadu known as Southern California,

it was quite a shock to find myself in the Central Ward of Newark. The inner city of Newark is, quite frankly, a very frightening place. It has been said, and I wholeheartedly agree, that whatever is going to happen in the next decade or so to the larger cities of America is already taking place today in Newark. The statistics are staggering. Newark ranks shamefully high among U. S. cities in rates of unemployment and percentage of welfare recipients; it has some of the highest incidence of tuberculosis, venereal disease, narcotics addiction, and infant mortality of any city in the country. Much of the housing in the inner city is criminally inadequate, the educational and job opportunities are woefully poor, and there is a legacy of corruption, which pervades the local government on virtually every level, including, and especially, the very top. The poverty, squalor, and pervasive attitude of hopelessness and despair of so many of the people is overwhelming, and combined with the general atmosphere of racism, with its inherent components of ignorance, prejudice, distrust, fear, and hate, it all seemed almost like a bad dream or a nightmare.

I was so struck by what I saw around me, especially after my experiences of the summer, that I wrote down some of my impressions in an article for the school literary publication. Unexpectedly, when I began to write, I found a surprising number of similarities between my Hollywood experience and the Central Ward, and though some of the observations now seem to me to be a bit pretentious, I think a great many of the points have validity. It was entitled "Hollywood and Vine, South Orange Avenue and 18th Street, A Study in Contrast."

Greetings from the land of plywood windows. (A staple of post riot architecture), white vigilante groups, Black Panthers, indicted city officials, and one semiretired actor returned to medical student. After two months in Southern California, it was quite a step to go from the unreal world of Hollywood to the surreal world of Newark. Although it seems much farther than 3,000 miles, from the blue-tiled 50-yard official olympic-size swimming pools of Beverly Hills to the cesspools of Newark, the apparent ends of the spectrum appear to have a surprisingly great deal in common.

It is ironic that the world which the people of the Central Ward are trying to escape *to,* through the needle-size holes in their arms, or better still under their tongues, or even in the dorsal vein of their penis, so as to avoid the telltale track marks, is quite often the stereotype image world of the beautiful people they see on TV, or read about in the magazines. Yet, it is the very same world the "beautiful people" themselves are trying to escape from, with their acid trips and snorts of gorilla, "fairy dust" tranquilizers. There is a difference, though, in that Hollywood is a world of their own making; the people there choose to create and walk through their own illusions, whereas the eleven-year-old black girl, whose deserted mother is on welfare, and whose three older sisters are shooting heroin, has far less opportunity to make any real choice.

Is there any more respectability in sitting around a friend's pad in West Los Angeles, watching the tube while waiting for your welfare or unemployment check, than there is in hanging around waiting on the corner of South Bergen and Fourteenth Street? One is simply more obvious and visible than the other. Just as the liquor sales are sure to go up the day the checks are delivered in Newark (so-called "Mother's Day"), the Westwood hash dealer is just as likely to have an above average amount of sales that corresponding day. It's the same inactivity, stagnation and waste of human talent, only in Newark the lament may focus upon a white union boss and his lily-white union, and the all too real fact that there just aren't enough respectable jobs in which one could derive any sense of personal pride open to a black with an eighth-grade education, whereas in Hollywood the copout is usually concerned with a casting director. In the field of entertainment, you can always rationalize that you are going through a dry spell creatively, and you can be fairly certain of relative ease in being able to save face and take refuge, at least among your peers, by simply stating that you are a professional writer or performer, etc., since most of the other so-called "creative people" are in a similar predicament, and they will never demand any recent credentials because that, in turn, would give you the right to destroy their own myth, so you both just play the game.

Sunset Strip and Clinton Avenue, one similarity is strikingly obvious, and that is the number of people who just seem to hang around. It is more apparent in Newark in the morning as you rush to class, whereas the Strip doesn't really come to life until well after dark, but even there, during the day, you can wander up and down and invariably meet a group of willing "conversationalists." A beaded, bearded hippie, and a black cat with an Afro and a dashiki, both "doing their thing," 3,000 miles apart.

There are many people in Los Angeles who would never think to go out for a cheeseburger and a milkshake unless they could somehow be organically grown or processed. Exotic dishes, like peanut butter chops (rye bread base with pureed peanut butter sauce), eggplant and sea kelp, and herb tea and honey all abound at the health food restaurants. In Newark, it may be barbecued ribs or ham hocks and blackeyed peas, or maybe just down to almost any street corner for a chili dog. Take it from me, you have not eaten a genuine chili dog until you have had one, "with the works," from a street vendor in Newark.

When you are first introduced to someone in Los Angeles, it is not at all uncommon for the person to inquire, not, as might be expected, *who* you are, but rather, what you are. This is not to be taken as some deep, existential philosophic inquiry about your place in the universe, but merely reflects a desire on the part of questioner to ascertain under what sign of the zodiac you were born. This is imperative, as it might very well determine the future extent of the relationship.

Muhammed's Mosque No. 17, the new Euphious Baptist Church, The Second Pentecostal Church of Christ, etc. In Newark, the storefront church is almost as plentiful a commodity as the liquor store. Again, as in astrology, much of the appeal seems to involve the concept of escape; a comfort in the unknown, with fate as the scapegoat.

How much difference is there, really, between the hooker in Newark, who at least guarantees physical satisfaction for your investment, and the sweet young aspiring atcress, who won't let you, or anybody, for that matter, in the front door, much less the bedroom, until the score of the game (How many dates? Where is he taking me? How much has he already spent on me?—or else, What can he do for my career?) is tallied to her satisfaction? I venture to guess that the only true difference is in degree and honesty.

However, as a second-year medical student, I was still somewhat removed from Newark, and the day-to-day struggles that had to be met just to survive in the Central Ward. I commuted to school every day, either by means of rides from friends or on the bus, and I was still somewhat insulated by the cloister of the classroom and the safety of hypothetical situations in textbooks.

Consequently, the mounting sense of impatience and eager anticipation that would gradually escalate throughout the course of that second year was augmented and heightened by the excitement of new surroundings and the prevailing atmosphere of an almost pioneering spirit. The courses were still didactic, with many hours of laboratory, but the areas of infectious disease, pathology, and pharmacology were easily recognized as being strongly related to the clinical practice of medicine. I finally felt that I was learning material that would directly prepare me for that long-awaited moment when I would put on that short white coat and enter the hospital as a clinical clerk.

However, before that moment would arrive, there was still a great deal of new material to learn, as well as reviewing all the previous year's work, so as to be prepared for Part I of the National Boards, which was to be given in the spring. Despite this prospect, the mood was generally more relaxed than during the first year, and this was helped by the general knowledge that for each successive year of school, a smaller percentage of students flunked out due to academic difficulties. There was also relatively more free time, and even an opportunity to take an elective course in an area of interest. Contributing as well to the somewhat more relaxed atmosphere was the aforementioned frontier quality, secondary to attending classes and labs in those ridiculous huts, which turned out to be unbearably hot in the early fall and late spring—due to the ventilation system not functioning properly—and uncomfortably cold and drafty in the winter, so much so that several of the lab facilities were actually unusable.

Throughout the course of the year there was quite a spirited and colorful graffiti war in constant progress between the construction workers and the medical students, who shared the same bathroom facilities. I could hardly wait each day to go in and see who had struck a blow for his respective side with his words of wisdom. The students often used esoteric and technical terminology, which had to go over most of the construction workers' heads, whereas the workers used words and phrases that left little doubt as to their exact meaning and implication. I have to give the workers an additional edge because they were also much more graphically oriented and drew some very nice, anatomically explicit diagrams to accompany their prose.

For example, a typical med student graffiti scrawl might be:

"All hard hats are Kleinfelters" ("Kleinfelter" being the medical designation for a situation involving a genetic abnormality wherein the masculinity of the male is in doubt). The retort would usually be something of the genre: "He who write on bathroom walls rolls his shit in little balls; he who reads these words of wit eats those little balls of shit." Even though my loyalties naturally lay with my fellow students and I myself was an occasional contributor, I had to concede at least this particular battle, if not the war, to the workers.

CHAPTER / 5

THE OVERALL atmosphere of excitement, generated as a consequence of both the relocation in particular, as well as the expectations of what was to follow, was accentuated even further on a personal level when, soon after classes resumed, I began receiving fairly frequent phone calls from my new agency. For the most part they involved feelers and offers for my services, running the gamut from a rather well-known theatrical producer inquiring as to my availability for a role in an upcoming Broadway musical (Him—Of course you sing and dance. Me—You sure you know who you're speaking to? My God, I'm not even sure I act.) to requests for appearances on the network talk shows and auditions for commercials. And with somewhat less formal demands on my time, I realized that even with the still considerable amount of lab work and lecture material involved, I had the opportunity to be able to make some sorely needed expense money and not only have some fun in the process but, most important, be able to continue with my medical studies.

Of course, I had to be on guard not to let my education suffer to any significant degree, and I found that if I scheduled and budgeted my time efficiently and was willing to work and study at odd hours, I could indulge in some of these "extracurricular activities" and still keep up with my work. And actually, in my somewhat shaky financial position, it was not really an indulgence at all but represented a means with which to enable me to get through school without going even further into debt and without having to resort to working long hours in the hospital laboratory or as an orderly, as some of my classmates were forced to do.

So that is how it came to pass that one afternoon, after spending two bleary-eyed hours looking at microscopic sections of a diseased liver in pathology lab, I took the bus into New York to audition for a commercial. The product was a new men's cologne, to be called Roman Brio, and the bulk of the audition consisted of a one-hour "necking session" with a sultry-looking, dark-eyed model. We kissed for almost the entire hour in all sorts of costumes and poses (with the entire sequence being videotaped), and at one point I told them that they had the makings for a very good X-rated commercial. As I was leaving the session and the producer said that they would "let me know" (a variation of the old "Don't call us, we'll call you" routine) I mentioned, only half in jest, that I wouldn't mind coming in once a week for this kind of reading. It sure beat hell out of staring at an inanimate, diseased piece of liver.

After two weeks of "Maybe yes, maybe no," the client decided I didn't look old enough to sell his cologne, so we repeated the entire audition. I wasn't very disappointed at the prospect, to say the least, but this time they made me up with lines along the corners of my mouth, crow tracks around my eyes, and silver-gray streaks in my hair and sideburns in an attempt to make me look older. However, what it did instead was to make me look like some sort of closet queen, and after seeing myself in a mirror, I cracked that if this particular commercial didn't work out, maybe Andy Warhol could use me in one of his freak movies—a sort of *Midnight Doctor*. Needless to say, no one liked the end result, except maybe the makeup man, who kept giving me some strange looks, and it was finally decided that I would be able to do the character without the aging process.

Consequently, the next week I found myself standing in the lobby of a luxury high-rise apartment building, dressed like some cheap Italian gigolo in suede coat, driving gloves, and scarf, waiting for my cue to rush out and hop into a white Ferrari, which was to be the first scene of the commercial. As it would appear in the finished version, as I pull away from the curb, an announcer is intoning, "Today's young man about town, like his ancient Roman counterpart, has a flair for living," and the scene then abruptly changes. Through the miracle of editing I am suddenly attired in a short skirt, a huge copper breastplate, and a headpiece that looks very much like a football helmet with a huge brush on top and I'm ferociously driving a sporty little chariot with elaborate purple and gold ornaments.

Actually, I was not driving at all, but rather I was desperately clutching at two reins that led not to a horse but to the rear bumper of a station wagon, to which the chariot was connected by means of wooden supports that acted as a towline. The cameraman was strapped onto the beams in such a way that he could shoot up at me and create the illusion that I was actually being towed by a horse. I, in turn, was supposed to look about the countryside and occasionally use the whip in my right hand in such a way that the effect would be that of the whip coming right at the camera lens. The only pathology that I could think about at that moment was my own, as I barreled along on a deserted road in Central Park, busily surveying my domain while desperately holding on to the reins (there were no seat belts— besides, I had to stand) and whipping the poor cameraman.

In the following scene I'm again miraculously transformed into my modern-day gigolo outfit and I am being greeted at the door by a beautiful woman, who proceeds to lead me to a couch. As she reclines and I bend over to kiss her, the setting again changes abruptly and—you guessed it—we are back in ancient Rome. She is now wearing a diaphanous gown with a Roman coin-type top, and I'm all decked out in my full-length, wrap-around, formal-type toga, and the set is adorned with numerous flaming cauldrons.

As we began to film this particular shot, the director didn't think my outfit was flashy enough and figured I needed some ornamentation. After much searching and discussion, it was decided that a doorknob on the next set was just what we needed, so they simply removed it from the door, took some double-faced masking tape, and proceeded to smack it on my shoulder. The scene was finally completed with me grinning sillily into the camera, dressed in a toga, with a doorknob stuck on my shoulder.

After another instantaneous time shift there was the obligatory bathroom scene, with me stripped to the waist, liberally applying the product and looking pleased and smug, and then my date and I set off in the car. This last bit of filming had its own traumatic moments, as I attempted to follow directions being shouted from a bullhorn in the camera car, which was traveling at thirty-five miles per hour only ten feet or so off my left bumper. It was very difficult trying to keep the proper expression on my face (snide, cocky, and a bit bored) while driving an unfamiliar foreign sports car, with a girl I barely knew stroking the back of my head and nibbling on my ear. All in all, however, even with a few near misses, it's really the only way to travel!

The last shot was to be of the both of us dressed in our Roman togas, with my date slung over my shoulder in the fashion of a conquering Roman hero, as we clatter off into the sunset in my chariot. Filming that sequence necessitated some long, hard minutes with the model (who was no lightweight in her own right, and don't forget to take her coin top into consideration) slung over my shoulder, and every time we would hit the smallest bump (there obviously are no shock absorbers in a studio-built wooden chariot) my breastplate would ride up and pinch some skin against the bottom of the helmet. It hurt, and by the end of the day I had quite a red neck, covered with large, angry welts.

The following day, back at school, I happened to meet one of the deans in the corridor on my way to class. We stopped to chat for a moment, and the Dean noticed the condition of my neck and asked if I had had some sort of an accident. As I began to explain about the perils of driving a chariot, especially with a girl slung over your shoulder, and how the breastplate pinches against the helmet, he just slowly shook his head, mumbled something about "students in the good old days," and walked on.

There were several other commercials I was involved with over the course of the year, but I was insistent that the auditions and actual filming be scheduled so that I missed as few lectures and labs as possible. I certainly had an advantage in that although I could have surely used the money, there were still extensions available on my education loans so that I was not frantically desperate and could therefore be selective and turn down offers that would have taken too much of my time or energy.

My agent at William Morris deserves credit for understanding the situation and being insistent, in his own right, that I do nothing which might possibly jeopardize my medical education. I was able to accomplish what I actually did by conscientiously borrowing the lecture notes I had missed and putting in extra hours in the lab to make up for time lost.

It was during this period that I began appearing on various network talk shows, and this, too, turned out to be quite an experience. Since I didn't have any vested interests to push—my career was not dependent on how well I came across—I did not feel pressured, which certainly did not appear to be the case with so many of the professional guests with whom I came in contact. It was a good opportunity to pick up some welcome money, and I enjoyed meeting a great many of the other people involved. Of course, there was also the ego gratification of seeing myself on television, and maintaining my tenuous quasi-celebrity status.

One of the first of the talk shows I did was with David Frost (I eventually appeared on his program a total of four times over the course of the year). It actually got to stage where the staff was so familiar with my background and experience that they would contact me directly rather than through the agency when they felt I could contribute to a particular program. So I was not really surprised when one late afternoon around 4:30 P.M. (after I had returned to my apartment after a full day of classes) the show's producer called to ask if there was any chance I could possibly make it to the studio by 5 P.M. He explained that they were just starting to tape a show that very moment with Alan Funt and Phyllis Diller, and since the discussion was scheduled to center around Alan Funt's new movie *What Do You Say to A Naked Lady?* and nudity in entertainment in general, the staff felt I could certainly add a different dimension to the discussion.

I borrowed a car from a classmate who lived upstairs, grabbed a suit from the closet, and quickly drove to Manhattan. I left the car illegally parked in front of the theater while a page sat inside (he must have loved me for that job), quickly changed clothes, and the producer filled me in as I sat in makeup. I was all put together with four or five minutes to spare, and was introduced after the next station break. I was on camera for the last fifteen minutes of the show, and after suffering through as the butt for several Phyllis Diller doctor jokes, I joined in the general discussion and told some anecdotes from my somewhat limited hospital experience. Several of the band members were originally from Newark and so could really relate to some of the stories, so much so that the laughter and shouts from backstage were at times louder and more raucous than those from out in the audience.

As soon as the taping was completed, I socialized for a few minutes, then hopped into the car and was soon back in Newark, literally three hours after the initial phone call. I was about $260 richer, and had a little something extra to daydream about while I sat at my desk and attempted to read the next day's assignment.

After having done several of the other talk-interview shows over a period of time, I was particularly impressed by how intently David Frost seemed to listen to what his guests had to say, whereas some of his colleagues appeared to be just going through the paces, seemingly without giving a damn about what was actually being said. Frost would ask a question and then sit there with his chin cupped in his hand and bore in on you with those piercing eyes with such apparent genuine interest that you felt obligated to say something quite profound.

Around that time I also was a guest on the *Merv Griffin Show;* it was then a network program and not syndicated like David Frost. On this occasion I found myself literally wedged in between a South American sex symbol plugging a new soft-core pornographic movie and Harrison Salisbury from *The New York Times,* who was plugging a new book. I wasn't plugging anything, so I could really enjoy the somewhat incongruous position of having all that breast tissue on my right and all those brains on my left. The show went well, as I told some medical school stories and related some show business experiences, and I particularly enjoyed asking Harrison Salisbury about his recent trip to China.

I did have some previous experience with talk shows, having done *The Steve Allen Show* the previous summer in California shortly before returning to school. I was immensely impressed at that time with his multifaceted talents, but it really was only after I appeared on other people's shows that I truly appreciated his awesome talent. On the particular show in which I was involved, he proceeded to compose an impromptu piano piece from notes selected at random by members of the audience, sang a ballad, played a toy instrument along with the band, and really had me laughing at his unique humor and wit. I also felt quite comfortable with him, even though I was never sure what surprise was going to come out from under, behind, around, or through his weird desk and bookcase, but I could take some comfort in the realization that he was never 100 percent sure either. In addition, he had a son who was attending medical school at the time, so we also had some common ground.

As my involvement in show business became broader, I became more and more aware of my unique position. I knew that this was not going to be my life's work or the main source of my livelihood, and I especially began to appreciate this fact when I saw the incredible levels of frustration that had to be tolerated in order to stand even a chance of success, as well as the enormous amount of self-deception that seems to permeate almost every facet of the industry. It is one of the few professions where someone else makes a highly subjective decision as to whether another individual can work at his trade or not. It would be one thing if the decision was limited to whether the person had the ability and talent to do the job, but unfortunately, this is rarely the case, especially in the area of commercials.

You can go in and do the greatest reading for a particular part, but if you just happen to have the misfortune to look like the producer's brother-in-law, whom he despises, then most likely you are not going to get the part, no matter how good you are. The same result is likely to occur if the producer happened to have a fight with his wife that morning or is just in a bad mood for any other reason. I don't mean this to be a blanket indictment, but I have seen far too many people in charge of casting who inject their own personality or problems into a decision where it has absolutely no relevance. Of course, a forty-year-old white man cannot realistically be considered for a role written for a twenty-year-old black man, but situations are usually not that clear cut, and too many fine actors and actresses are simply not working, and for the wrong reasons.

I therefore began to look upon my rather fortuitous position as somewhat analogous to being "In Jail" on the Monopoly board, but in that fringe area marked "Just Visiting." I was involved to be sure, yet I could get out any time I desired without having to roll a double or pay anyone off. I had the dice in *my* hands, and it was truly "my roll."

CHAPTER / 6

As MY medical training and show business experiences began to increasingly intertwine, with the concomitant excitement and increasing periods of almost frenetic activity and rescheduling, the year naturally went by very quickly. By the spring almost everybody else in my class was also in good spirits, as the final exam in pharmacology signaled the completion of the basic science courses. It was now time to learn to be a clinician and how to treat sick people, and for most of us this was the long-awaited moment when we would finally be in the hospital and see firsthand what medicine was really all about.

However, before we could actually begin taking care of patients, and learn diagnosis and treatment, it was necessary to be trained in such basics as eliciting a complete history (a true art, and unfortunately often sorely underemphasized) and conducting a thorough physical examination, as well as to become familiar with the fundamental "tools of the trade": the stethoscope, the otoscope and funduscope (for examining the ears and the eyes), and the sphygmomanometer, or blood pressure cuff.

This material was to be covered in an eight-week course known as physical diagnosis. For the first week, before we actually approached any patients, the class was split into small groups, and we alternated between being the patient and the examiner so that we could practice on each other. We were given reading assignments nightly to prepare us for the areas that were to be covered the next day. Each small group had its own instructor, and rather fittingly, I was assigned to the same comedian

I had in gross anatomy lab. He was somewhat more subdued, but there were occasions, such as when we were learning the proper technique for conducting a rectal exam, when he ran true to his previous form. His blithe comment was designed to serve as a consistent reminder of the importance of the thoroughness of the exam. After inserting the lubricated gloved finger, while pushing down gently until the muscle relaxed, he said we should then "dial operator," since this familiar motion would insure that the entire rectum would be examined. After having been the "patient" in the rectal exercises, most guys in the class were disappointed when we were told that we would wait until we were on gynecology before being taught how to do a pelvic exam.

The next seven weeks were then spent going to affiliated hospitals in the area and working with an individual tutor who instructed us in the examination of his particular area of expertise. For example, the sessions on the heart might be spent in a cardiac care unit, where you would be assigned a patient and told to examine his cardiac status and describe the findings to a cardiologist. Similarly, an afternoon might be spent on the respiratory service listening to the chests of known asthmatics or patients with emphysema.

I remember the very first time I walked into a patient's room and introduced myself as Dr. Meyers, and wow, did those words feel both wondrous and strange. The particular patient involved was a seventy-two-year-old veteran at the nearby VA Hospital, and as I proceeded with the history taking, I knew I was procrastinating by not asking some vital questions because I was just too embarrassed to do so. I was thinking how I could possibly ever ask this gentle, soft-spoken man, who easily could have been my grandfather, whether he had ever had any venereal disease. I finally somehow mustered up the courage, and when he paused for what seemed like an interminably long time, but in actuality was probably no more than a few seconds, I thought he was really going to tear into me for asking such a personal question.

He slowly turned, faced me squarely, and said, "Three times, sonny boy, three times. Once before World War I, once in France after the war, and once in 1943, but I'd appreciate you not mentioning the last time to anyone," and at this point he dropped his voice, "because my wife doesn't know about it, you understand,"

and gave me a conspiratorial little wink. I never again had any hesitation about asking anyone that type of question.

It was during this time that I encountered my first ticklish patient. She was a teen-age girl, and no matter where I touched her, she would start giggling to such an extent that it was impossible to examine her properly. To further compound things, her laughter was so infectious that it was equally impossible not to laugh along with her. I realized that I was expected to report my findings to my instructor, as well as maintain some degree of professionalism, but it turned out to be very difficult to do either, since the patient would roar with laughter every time I touched her. This, too, turned out to be a worthwhile educational experience because when I realized the futility of my efforts and told the instructor about my difficulty, he gave me some valuable tips involving certain techniques for distracting such patients so they can then be examined. The experience also taught me an additional important lesson, which was that if I was unsure of the proper approach to a situation or didn't know the procedure, the best thing was to admit to it and be taught the easiest and most efficient means and not try to fake it, as some of my colleagues were inclined to do.

My close friend was assigned a very pretty, very statuesque lady to examine for his first patient. It turned out that she wasn't wearing a bra, and when Paul asked her to unbutton her blouse, so he could listen to her heart, and then saw the situation (he saw her breasts is what he saw!), he became so flustered that the only thing he could think to do was to immediately place his stethoscope on her chest. After about five seconds the woman politely tapped Paul on the shoulder and said, "Excuse me, Doctor, but wouldn't you be able to hear a lot better if you put those things in your ears?" Paul became so totally embarrassed that all he could do was mumble something about being able to compare the sounds better that way and run out of the examining room; he was so chagrined that he couldn't go back to finish the examination.

One technique that is difficult to master, but which is of great importance, is the examination of the eye grounds. The eye is the only place in the body where the blood vessels can be viewed directly, and much valuable information can be gained regarding such things as the presence of a chronically elevated blood pressure, the systemic effects of diabetes, and the presence of increased pressure in the blood vessels, which might be suggestive of a tumor or the consequence of a blow to the head, as well as other important clues. However, it is difficult to perfect the actual technique, in which both eyes are kept open and you do not have to squint with one eye while focusing in with the other.

When it is done properly, you and the patient are literally touching nose to nose as you position yourself to get the best possible view. At the beginning of physical diagnosis I was very self-conscious of this intimacy, to such an extent that I actually would hold my breath while conducting this part of the examination. An incident occurred that although embarrassing at the time, I was later to appreciate. I was examining the eye grounds of an elderly woman who was quite perceptive as to what was going on, and she finally said, "Gee, Doc, you don't have to hold your breath while you're doing this. You don't have bad breath." As a result I was subsequently able to devote a longer amount of time to this particular part of the examination without being self-conscious, and thus became proficient much sooner than if I had continued to try to do it each time with one big breathful of air.

As part of your final evaluation in the course, you were given a patient to examine thoroughly, and then you had to review your findings with your instructor. Martland Hospital has no private rooms, and drawing the curtains around a bed on the ward does not afford a great deal of privacy. The particular patient assigned to me for this purpose was quite obese, and I was trying very hard to differentiate the type of heart murmur I felt was present so that I could describe it accurately. Unfortunately, at the same moment, in the next bed, a patient was being visited by a female minister of some small Southern denomination, who turned out to be a real holy roller, fire-and-brimstone type. I was trying to listen intently to my patient's heart on my side of the curtain and give her instructions on how to breathe while from the other side emanated some rather loud exhortations of the nature, "Can I get an Amen for Jesus?"

It soon became impossible to concentrate when the woman

in the bed across the room got caught up in the fervor as well and joined in, and I was forced to wait fifteen minutes for the "Hallelujahs" to be finished before I could even hear the woman's heart again, much less try to describe the murmur. It made for an exciting and, as I was soon to find out, quite appropriate introduction to my future clinical experience.

CHAPTER / 7

BEFORE SETTLING down to what was sure to be a much more intense, personally challenging, and stimulating year as a clinician in training, I got involved in a rather light-hearted experience that was to prove to be quite a fitting finale for that still-quite-exciting second year. It occurred at a time when the movie was just ending its first run, and it came about as a consequence of a friend suggesting that we double-date, and I would take out a friend of his wife whom I had never met before. No one had told her anything about my having been in a movie, and the four of us subsequently met one evening at one of those Upper East Side New York bars with a name that sounded like a flower or a fruit.

As we were getting acquainted, my date asked me all about medical school and college, and when she inquired about my summer activities, I left out any reference to show business. In the course of the conversation my friend Ritchie casually mentioned that he would like to see *Goodbye, Columbus* as he had heard it was a good movie. My date got very excited at the prospect because she, too, had been an English major in college, and admired Philip Roth as an author very much. I said it sounded fine with me.

We then went over to the theater and took our places on the line waiting for the next performance. As the show broke and I realized that people might possibly recognize me, I noticed we were in front of a shoe store, and I conveniently developed an instantaneous fetish for shoes. I proceeded to peer intently into the display window while delivering such profound remarks as, "Wow, look at the great pair of shoes with buckles," and "Ritchie, catch these wild boots," while the line inched forward.

If my date thought my antics queer while on line, she was surely unprepared for what happened as we rounded the corner and I detected several publicity pictures and reviews on display. I immediately ran over and covered a picture of myself with my backside, and hurried everybody inside. I made sure to get a large box of unbuttered popcorn, and when my name was just about to appear in the credits, I emptied the entire box down the front of my date's dress. I further proceeded to position the empty box in front of her face so that she couldn't possibly see the screen, but this turned out to be unnecessary, as the poor girl was distracted enough just trying to get the popcorn out of just about every crevice of her body.

The first time I actually appeared on screen, my date gave me a very quick sideward glance, and when I turned to her to ask if everything was all right, she gave a little jump as if she half expected me to spill my soda on her or something equally disastrous. However, she didn't say anything until there was a close-up of me for several seconds, and then she slowly looked from the face on the screen to the face in the seat next to her and said, "You son of a bitch. That's you up there, isn't it?" I confessed, and she turned out to be a real good sport, and we all had a big laugh. She enjoyed the rest of the picture, although every time I subsequently appeared, she did quickly look back and forth from me to the screen.

When the movie ended, we all went back to the bar to meet some friends. I'm not sure if it was the excitement, the effect of the alcohol on an empty stomach, or a combination of both, but we were standing at the bar for no more than five minutes when my date suddenly fainted and slipped to the floor, totally unconscious. To compound the situation she was wearing a fall (unbeknown to us at the time, but not for long), and when she hit the ground, she fell on one side of the bar stool and the wig landed on the other. As she lay there prostrate on the floor, my friend calmly announced, "Don't panic. It's okay. He's going to be a doctor, and he knows what to do. She'll be fine in a minute."

Well, at that point I surely was not a doctor but just a second-year medical student with no clinical experience. I knew from my physiology course *why* she might have fainted, and could probably have explained the mechanism if anyone was interested, but that surely would not have helped my date at that moment. The only first aid I knew was from the Boy Scouts, and that had been a long time ago, but with everybody crowding around and looking expectantly in my direction, I realized that I had better do something.

I had no reason to believe that she was pregnant, so I knew there wasn't any point in asking for boiling water, but for some strange reason I called out for a bowl of ice cubes and some vinegar. The French bartender was hilarious as he ran around frantically screaming, "Ze Doctor wants ice cubes and vinegar. Ice cubes and vinegar for ze Doctor, *toute de suite*."

I kneeled down next to her and started rubbing ice on her wrists and neck, basically stalling for time and hoping that she would come to on her own. After about two minutes of this with no appreciable response, I became a bit panicky, and I took the vinegar and started flicking it on her face in an attempt to revive her. This, too, was having no apparent effect when a well-dressed man in his mid-thirties approached and immediately began to massage her neck while at the same time feeling her pulse. He handled himself like he knew what he was doing, but I wasn't quite sure. For all I knew he could have been just some dirty young man who hung around bars waiting for this sort of thing to happen so he could "grab a feel or two." I therefore rather hesitantly asked for his credentials, although at that point I would have been happy to hear that he was a veterinarian, and I was overjoyed when he said he was an oral surgeon.

As he continued to feel for her pulse, he looked up at me worriedly and said that poor circulation might be the cause of her fainting, since her extremities were ice cold. I sort of stage-whispered to him that it was probably because I had rubbed her wrists with ice, and could he please not talk so loudly. He then proceeded to bend down closer to examine her, and as he did, he sniffed quizzically about her face and finally could contain himself no longer. "My God, this poor girl smells like a tossed green salad. What's going on?"

I then began to give him a quick, embarrassed explanation,

and as I began to do so, my date started to revive. We supported her and made her comfortable, and I went on to explain what had happened. At that moment she must have unconsciously reached up to straighten her hair, and when I glanced over and saw the look on her face as she realized that her fall had come off, I thought for sure she was going to faint again. Fortunately, she didn't faint but reacted by quickly scooping up the fall and running off to the ladies' room, with my friend's wife in hot pursuit. After everything, and everybody, calmed down, we went elsewhere for a snack, and fortunately the girl retained her sense of humor.

It was to be the last situation in which I would find myself having to bluff my way through as an inexperienced doctor-to-be, for in a few short months I was to begin my third year as a clinical clerk in surgery.

CHAPTER / 8

"FIVE FULL minutes on each hand, *by* the clock, and no cheating. And don't forget your fingernails!

"Scrub means just that—SCRUB, not dab or pat or wipe. All the way down to the elbows—like this. You're about to go into an operating room, not sit down to dinner!

"You, the tall one with all the hair. Go back and get a nurse's scrub cap, for God's sake, you'll contaminate the whole room."

As I trotted back to the doctors' locker room to change my cap, it was a welcome relief to get away, even for only a few minutes, from the head OR nurse. It was the first week of my general surgery rotation, and I was already self-conscious to begin with because I couldn't find a scrub suit that fit properly. The extralarge bottoms were only extralarge at the waist, and they barely came down to the tops of my ankles—I felt like Little Abner in a pair of green pajamas that were about three sizes too small. Although some of my classmates had previously worked in the operating rooms, there were several other members of my group who were neophytes as well, so at least there was some consolation in that I wasn't the only one being bullied by the nurse in charge of our orientation.

As I caught up with the group, they were holding their arms out in front of their bodies in such a way that the water would run off their elbows and not drip back onto their hands. They waited as I finished scrubbing, and we all backed into the operating room itself. The nurse proceeded to demonstrate the proper technique for drying each arm with a sterile towel, emphasizing that we were to start from the hands and work down each arm, being careful not to retouch an arm that was already dried. We were then shown how to get into our gowns without contaminating ourselves, and everything was going smoothly until the nurse asked me what size glove I took. Everybody laughed when I answered, "A large," as I had no way of knowing that the sizes are graded numerically. It is very important that the glove fit properly, and it was only through trial and error that I arrived at my proper size—a perfect seven, as they say. The gloves made a very satisfying snap when the nurse released them as I plunged my hands in, and I was somewhat relieved to notice that several of my colleagues were also having difficulty getting all the right fingers to go into the right holes.

We were finally all put together, and it was a rather pleasant sensation to stand there, arms folded across my chest, with everything about me so glistening clean, and feeling, at least physically, like I belonged. However, my grandiose pretensions were soon dispelled when the group split up and an intern and resident arrived to begin the actual operation. The patient was already anesthetized and on the operating table, and my fellow classmates and I were eagerly looking forward to participating in our first operation, even if it was simply a routine hernia repair. Obviously, I didn't expect to do any actual cutting, but I was disappointed when I realized that my role was to be basically that of observer rather than assistant. However, it was fascinating enough just to be close and watch, and I remember being particularly struck by the initial incision. After pointing out the landmarks on the patient's body, such as the pubic bone and the crest of the pelvis, and explaining how they are used to approximate where the initial incision should be made, the resident placed the scalpel on the skin and cut firmly and deeply in one sure stroke. I projected that if I was holding the scalpel, I would have been much more tentative out of concern that the cut would be in the proper location and not be too deep. I was also surprised at the absence of a great deal of blood and noted that the intern did not have to be told to locate and clamp off the several small blood vessels that were cut and bleeding but simply picked up the proper instruments and quickly performed the task.

As I stood there, or more correctly stooped there (it seems that the operating room table is adjusted to the most convenient height for the surgeon, and not his assistants, and since the resident was a rather short doctor from India, I was forced to bend over) holding a retractor (an instrument that is used to give the surgeon better exposure by pulling the surrounding tissues away from the immediate area he is working on), I began to appreciate what it really meant to be a third-year clinical clerk getting his in-hospital training.

I quickly realized that this was going to be a radical departure from the previous regime of didactic lectures and labs of the first two years as I would now be directly involved in the care of patients. Naturally, there was to be a great deal of supervision, as well as scheduled lectures, conferences, and reading responsibilities, but I was soon to find that on the clinical level, medical training is basically an apprenticeship.

Our first day on the surgical service each student was assigned to a particular intern or resident. The class itself had previously been split up into smaller-sized groups, and certain groups would then rotate through the different services at different times, so that perhaps only ten students would be assigned to any specific general service or subspecialty at any one given time. My particular resident turned out to be a very soft-spoken, very intelligent (and very short, as previously noted) Indian doctor who, after graduating from medical school in his own country, had come to the United States for further training. Unfortunately, his command of the English language left a great deal to be desired, and this was to prove to be a handicap both to him and to me, specifically in regard to my medical education.

As a third-year student I was expected to shadow him as he went about his daily routine—in addition to attending the lectures and conferences designed specifically for students—and learn through observation, dialogue, and experience. The resident has a responsibility to teach the student, as he himself was taught by his intern and resident. It is through this structured hierarchy, or ladder system, that a student is supposed to receive the largest proportion of his teaching and practical experience, complemented by the didactic lectures and readings.

This concept is specifically enunciated in the opening paragraph of the Hippocratic Oath:

I swear that according to my ability and judgment, I will keep this oath and stipulation: to reckon him who taught me this art equally dear to me as my parents, . . . to regard his offspring as on the same footing with my own brothers, and to teach them this art if they should wish to learn it. I will impart a knowledge of the art to disciples bound by a stipulation and oath, according to the Law of Medicine, but to none others.

The quality of education received, therefore, depends a great deal on the qualities of the person on the next higher rung of the ladder, and it is dependent not only on his knowledge and experience but, as importantly, on his ability and willingness to communicate the information to the student. So in my particular case, even though my resident had a good, sound medical background and seemed eager to teach, the language problem would prove to be a severe handicap. He could be the most brilliant doctor in the world, but what good would it do me if I couldn't understand half of what he was trying to tell me?

This situation is hardly unique to my hospital and may be found in any other similar institution where a large proportion of the house staff (the interns and residents) are foreign born and foreign trained. The general situation exists partly as a consequence of the fact that each year, American medical schools graduate only about half the number of doctors that are required to fill the available number of internships. The deficit is then made up by these foreign graduates, many of whom come to this country to get better-quality postgraduate specialty training and who then return to their homelands to practice after their training is completed. Prestigious university hospitals (a university hospital is one that functions as a teaching hospital of a medical school), such as Massachusetts General or the UCLA Medical Center, have their choice of American graduates to fill their needs, but the vast majority of other hospitals, especially the smaller community hospitals that are not affiliated with a medical school, and therefore whose teaching and training programs are naturally not at the same level, must fill their vacancies with foreign-trained personnel.

There is a written qualifying exam in English that must be successfully completed before a foreign graduate is accepted for an internship or residency in this country, but many people, including my particular resident, can pass those exams and not only be less-than-fluent but almost unintelligible. However, I would not like to give the impression that these graduates are therefore necessarily poor doctors, as the vast majority of them are more than competent medically. My experience has been that many of them are equal, if not superior, to many Americans educated in this country in regard to their medical expertise, but their poor English language training is obviously a tremendous handicap in many other areas besides their ability to teach their medical student.

The implications obviously extend to the much broader context of the general practice of medicine, which depends so much on the ability of the doctor and the patient to be able to freely and openly communicate. In addition, there is also the consideration of the staggering cultural differences that exist between someone who was born and educated in the upper social strata of India, Pakistan, Korea, Japan, or wherever and a black person who was raised in the deep South and is currently living in a big city ghetto.

With my own white middle-class background, I quickly became aware of the difficulties *I* would have in relating to the culture, mores, and even slang of the general patient population of an inner city, and I soon saw how absurd it was to expect any real level of common ground between these foreign doctors and their patients. As early as that first week I realized that in addition to my own educational needs, I was going to have the burden of acting as a sort of interpreter between two people who were ostensibly attempting to speak in the same language, but who were miles apart in their understanding and comprehension of each other. The frustration and feelings of exasperation experienced in struggling to understand what a patient is trying to express in the highly unique vernacular of the inner city is understandably compounded even further if, at the same time, you are forced to cope with trying to comprehend what your resident is attempting to teach you in his broken (more often fractured) English.

As a consequence of this situation there is often a great deal of resentment from the community to the presence of those doctors. I had become aware of this during my physical diagnosis course, when there had been an incident involving a young lady who was scheduled to be seen in the clinic. I was waiting for another doctor at the same time, and I observed her telling the nurse as she was being led to her examinining room, "Look, I don't want any of those foreign doctors taking care of me. I want an American who knows what he's doing."

As fate would have it (along with the law of averages), just as the nurse was attempting to calm the woman by telling her that the foreign doctors are just as qualified as the Americans, who should enter the cubicle but a Japanese resident. This was all the woman had to see, and she stormed out of the cubicle, screaming at the top of her lungs, "Get that slanty-eyed bastard away from me. I don't want no foreigners experimenting on me. I want an American, and I want him now." (P.S., she got one.)

"Michael. Michael. MICHAEL! Do you want to sew up the incision?"

Startled, I looked up from the operating table, and since this was the loudest tone of voice I had heard my resident use all week, I realized that I must have been daydreaming.

"Sure, of course," I answered quickly, "but I've never done it before, except on a dog, so I'll need some help."

Since the patient had only received a spinal anesthetic and was merely groggy from his preoperative sedative, I was careful not to speak loud enough for him to hear me. The patient probably wasn't aware that medical training is basically a form of apprenticeship, and it would not have been too comforting for him to have been made aware of this fact at the time. As we bent over the patient and I was being shown the proper technique for suturing, I remembered an oft-quoted saying in this regard, "See one, do one, teach one." This applied mainly to the numerous small procedures and techniques I first had to master, such as suturing for example.

As we were changing back into our civvies in the locker room, I realized that in another respect, I was fortunate to be working with my particular resident, language difficulties notwithstanding. For on that same morning it seems that a classmate had stood for four and a half hours holding a retractor during a major stomach operation, and even though he had had some previous surgical experience, including suturing lacerations in the emergency room, the South Korean resident he was working with (or perhaps, more appropriately, against) insisted on closing up himself. Of course, after a long procedure the surgeon is naturally fatigued—and tiredness is a valid consideration, as the inexperienced student will naturally take appreciably longer to complete the task—but even so, a compromise could have been reached under these circumstances so that the student would have been able to receive at least some much-needed experience.

This illustrates an additional factor that operates to affect the quality of education received under such a system, and it is directly related to the degree of aggressiveness of the intern or resident. By this I mean that an intern or resident, for a wide variety of reasons, may attempt to do as many of the technical procedures as possible, as well as handle all the practical aspects of patient management. These reasons may include impatience with the longer time that the student may take to perform the task, general feelings of insecurity, or perhaps not having had enough opportunity himself when a student (which can obviously lead to a self-perpetuating cycle), but whatever the motivation it is unfortunately done at the expense of the student, who must then actively compete for experience with the intern rather than have the two work together. The student consequently has much less opportunity to develop his skills or exercise his own judgment (still under supervision, of course, but not merely functioning solely as an observer), and, therefore, to develop his own confidence.

There is also the other end of the spectrum, where a student, again for a variety of reasons, is delegated too much responsibility, without sufficient tutelage and guidance, and this situation does a disservice both to the patient and the student. However, these are the extremes, and I found on the whole that the system functions fairly well, although there is room for much improvement.

The general surgical service is divided into three separate teams, with each team on duty or on call every third night. This means that all teams are present from 7 A.M. until approximately 6 P.M. during the week, but the team on call each day remains at the hospital throughout the night. This team is then responsible for not only all new admissions during that twenty-four-hour period but has responsibility for the primary care of *all* the general surgical patients on the ward as well. If a scheduled rotation falls on a Saturday or Sunday, then that on-call team works that day and night, although all the teams have had to make rounds on their patients at least once each weekend day, or holiday, as well. What it boiled down to was that every third day you were on for thirty-six hours straight, and at an institution such as Martland the prospects were good that you were not likely to get any sleep at all.

The very first night my team was on we were called by the emergency room to inform us that a gunshot victim was being brought in by ambulance and that he had been shot in the gut at almost point-blank range with a double-barreled shotgun. We got downstairs just as the ambulance pulled up, and it was not a very pretty sight. It took all my strength not to let my face mirror the sickening feeling in my own stomach when I saw the man's mangled abdomen, with his bloody guts literally hanging out. Incredibly, he was still conscious when he was first brought in, and he kept muttering over and over, "Don't let me die before I get that motherfucker. Don't let me die."

Intravenous lines were started in both arms, and a line was placed in a vein in his neck as well. I was given the job of catheterizing him, which involved placing a small tube up his penis into his bladder, and although I had observed the procedure, I had never done it myself. Everybody was preoccupied with trying to keep this man alive until we could get him to the operating room; he had already lost consciousness by the time I had finished.

Once in the operating room, the chief resident, assisted by my resident and several others on the team, worked for almost six hours removing fourteen damaged portions of his intestines and then meticulously sewing each healthy section back together. I was very impressed with the total team effort, and especially the skill and dexterity of the chief resident, who happened to be Egyptian, and who had had several years of previous surgical training in England.

He was an excellent teacher, as well as surgeon, and spoke impeccable English (with the slightest hint of a British accent) so that despite the length of the operative procedure and the fact that it was 4:30 A.M. when we finished, I got a great deal of teaching in return for my aching back, feet, and fingers (I had not done any more than my fair share of holding a retractor). It was not until I was helping push the patient into the recovery room and the chief resident asked about the urine output that I stopped to think about my small contribution. Small though it was, it gave me a good feeling.

The patient, who did fairly well the first few postoperative days, was naturally being cared for in the intensive care unit (ICU). He was maintained on intravenous therapy (IV's), as it would have been damaging for him to take anything by mouth until his gastrointestinal tract was healed sufficiently to allow normal functioning. He was a big, extremely well-muscled black man, and I found that I got along well with him on a personal level. He never really bitched or moaned about the pain, which at times must have been severe, and I spent a great deal of time attending to him.

On the sixth postoperative day our team was again on call, and when I went by to check on him in the early evening, he kept incessantly asking for water. He tried entreating, cajoling, and ultimately threatening me, and I told him I understood how uncomfortable he must be, especially with the presence of a tube that went down his nose all the way to his stomach. I carefully explained how the tube suctioned out all the secretions that were present and that if he drank any fluids, he could easily become violently ill with excruciating cramps, diarrhea, and vomiting and, in general, do much damage to his already severely stressed intestines.

I was alone at his bedside at this particular point, taking a blood sample so I could monitor if he was bleeding inside his intestine, when he rather violently, and with a great deal of strength, grabbed the lapels of my white coat and pulled my face down close to his. "Look," he hissed into my ear, "for the past two nights I've been slipping the cleaning man a couple of bucks, and he's been sneaking me in some soda and candy bars, and the cramps I got have been more than worth it. So just cut the shit, give me some water, God damn it, and stop bullshitting me." With that effort, he let go, and fell back on the pillow. He proceeded to offer me money, and I did give him a small piece of ice to suck on, but this did not placate him, and since further discussion appeared futile, I turned and walked away. I was feeling really lousy as I left the ICU, not only because someone was helping the man do a great deal of potential damage to himself but, just as importantly, because it made me feel that the man would never again really trust anything I would tell him.

I informed the chief resident about the incident, the patient naturally denied everything, and the cleaning man was reported to the administration, but nothing ever came of it. After that I avoided being alone with the patient as much as possible, although there were several times when it couldn't be helped. Nothing regarding the incident was ever mentioned by either of us, and we barely communicated. Soon after, however, he began to exhibit signs of a massive infection (quite common after such extensive bowel surgery, despite all precautions) and began doing poorly and started going downhill (or "went sour" as commonly used medical slang would have it). Eight days after our encounter he expired from complications that may or may not have been exacerbated by his little snacks; as you may well expect, the entire episode had a rather profoundly unsettling effect on me, especially so because of my neophyte status and the fact that this was my first real clinical experience where I was intimately involved in the medical care of another human being.

CHAPTER / 9

DURING THAT same general period there was an outbreak of gang warfare between some local black and Puerto Rican groups. As a consequence of one rumble (Do they still call it that, or am I dating myself?) an eighteen-year-old Puerto Rican male was admitted through the emergency room after having been shot in the belly with a "Saturday night special." Although these guns are usually of low caliber, they can nevertheless cause extensive damage, and surgery was required.

When the patient was sufficiently stable after the operation, I attempted to elicit a past medical history as part of my routine work-up. I found that his English was quite poor—and my knowledge of Spanish borders on the nonexistent. I could then begin to really sympathize with my resident and appreciate some of the exasperating frustration in such situations. The hospital does have some employees who are bilingual and can function as interpreters, but they have other responsibilities as well, and since they are usually busy in the clinic area, they are basically unavailable on the wards, especially at night.

As I began my attempts at questioning him, I soon realized that I was falling into a pattern that was quite common to many of my colleagues in similar situations. After my first attempt to open some communication—by asking the patient how he felt— was met by a blank stare and a characteristic shrug of the shoulders, I then went into an elaborate pantomime while attempting to "Spanishize" my question.

"Mucho hurto? Where?" I said, while grimacing and pointing

to the general area of his abdomen. After further attempts to elicit information met with no success, I started to raise my voice. Rationally, I should have realized how absurd and ineffective this would be, but my instinctive reaction was to shout, as if the problem was simply that the patient could not hear me. So there I stood at the side of the bed, wildly gesticulating and shouting at the top of my lungs, "Have you ever been in the hospital before? What was your problem?" with the understandable result that both the patient and I just got more and more frustrated.

I soon saw the utter futility of this approach, and moreover, I suddenly became aware of how terribly frightening it must be to be sick and in pain and find yourself in a hospital where you cannot make yourself understood. I therefore made a real effort subsequently to learn some street Spanish, as well as some basic medical terminology in Spanish. As a matter of fact, this particular patient, Jesus, was to prove a great help in this regard over the course of the weeks he remained in the hospital. However, I was soon to find out that there is some truth in the adage that "a little knowledge is a dangerous thing," as my limited vocabulary and comprehension were to quickly lead to some unforeseen ramifications. The week after Jesus was admitted, I had another Spanish-speaking patient on my team, and I decided to test my wings. However, as soon as I uttered the first few words of greeting in Spanish, the woman was obviously so grateful she had found a doctor who could speak her language that she immediately went off on a five-minute monologue, the overwhelming majority of which was totally incomprehensible to me. I then realized that since I didn't have anything even remotely resembling competence in the language, in the future it would be much simpler and wiser to attempt to get an interpreter and not try to muddle through.

Jesus was in the hospital for approximately three and a half weeks. As he became less suspicious and hostile, I found that he knew much more English than he had let on at the beginning, and we began to establish a relationship of sorts. Visiting hours generally found his bedside crowded with family, girl friends, and fellow gang members, complete with black leather jackets, and Jesus took great delight in showing me off as his "hip Doc," to the extent that upon his discharge, he insisted that I be the one to see him in clinic for follow-up.

However, the story doesn't end there. Several weeks after Jesus's subsequent discharge, I was in a bar fairly close to the hospital, getting some sandwiches for dinner for my team. (It seems that, traditionally, one of the duties of the medical student is to go out and purchase dinner for everyone on his team, since he is the most expendable member should a major emergency arise.)

Actually, I didn't really mind this menial task, even though there was usually enough arithmetic and money involved so that you generally ended up coming out a little short. However, I looked upon it as a welcome opportunity to get away from the demands of the hospital, if only for a brief respite.

So it was that I found myself in a fairly rough area of the Central Ward after dark. This particular tavern was noted for its cold cuts, and I had a list of roast beef, corned beef, and pastrami sandwich orders from my various team members, including a corned beef on white bread with mayonnaise for my chief resident. I had grimaced when he told me what he wanted, but I figured that tastes must be different on the other side of the Suez Canal.

I was standing at the bar calling out the orders to the couner-man when I noticed about ten rough-looking characters sitting at a back table doing justice to several bottles of whiskey. They were giving me a real eyeballing. This particular bar had a good reputation for keeping trouble to a minimum, and there was the usual complement of mixed clientele, so that I felt fairly secure, especially in my hospital uniform. However, I also knew that I would have to walk a block to get to my car, and I was feeling more and more uneasy until one of the group happened to turn completely around and I caught a glimpse of the back of his leather jacket, and I gratefully realized that they were all members of Jesus's gang. Some of them were probably staring because they must have seen me when they visited the hospital, and I made a quick evaluation of the circumstances, somehow managed to calmly walk over to the table with every eye riveted on me, and said, "Where's Jesus? I took care of him at the hospital."

Everybody started to grin and talk at the same time, and I was given a seat of honor next to the leader, who proceeded to pour me a straight whiskey. Fifteen minutes and two shots later I was ceremoniously escorted to my car by three gang members, who insisted that they accompany me to make sure I didn't run into any unexpected trouble.

As soon as I was safely ensconced behind the wheel, I took several large, deep breaths, and as I started the engine and pulled out of the space, I gave a farewell wave to my three escorts still standing dutifully at the curb. However, by the time I got back to the hospital and began to relate the story to my team, feelings of bravado had taken over, and I don't think my voice cracked more than twice the entire time.

CHAPTER / 10

ANY PATIENT admitted to the hospital, to whatever service and regardless of the presenting complaint, deserves and requires a minimum mandatory amount of laboratory work-up. These function as general screening devices and often enable the doctor to not only pinpoint the acute process that may be occurring but also to pick up clues to some occult problem that may be simmering, and which has given the patient no symptomatology as yet. This includes a chest X ray, as well as certain blood, urine, and feces studies (which I will elaborate on in a moment). A cardiogram is routinely performed on all patients over the age of thirty-five (this age cutoff is somewhat arbitrary and may vary within a slight range among different hospitals), unless the patient's symptomatology deems it appropriate regardless of the age of the patient, and similarly, examination of the sputum and spinal fluid is performed if so indicated. In general, it is imperative that the results of such studies be known as quickly as possible, as the information received is often crucial in formulating a working diagnosis and treatment plan, which can then be implemented on an immediate basis.

This means that these initial studies, whenever feasible, are performed by the doctors themselves (or, most often, by the third-year medical student) in special "minilabs" set up for just such purposes on each service; this arrangement serves both in the interest of time saved (especially at night when only a skeleton lab crew is generally available) and also the training received, as a doctor may well end up practicing in some small town rural setting and have no recourse but to perform such studies himself. In any case, to begin with the blood sample obtained, a determination of the blood count itself, or hematocrit (from Greek *haimat,* blood, and *krino,* to separate) is essential; the percentage of formed elements, composed mainly of the red and white blood cells, can be determined in relation to the liquid or serum component by means of placing a small quantity of blood in a narrow tube and then centrifuging (or spinning) it down. In addition, a drop or two of blood is spread out quite thinly on a glass slide, and this "smear," as it is commonly called, is then stained in a highly specific manner, involving various solutions and carefully timed procedures, so that the end product, when viewed under the microscope, enables the examiner to determine the morphology (configuration and shape) of the individual cells, as well as other valuable information.

As a consequence of the large black population served by my hospital, and the overwhelming predominance of sickle cell disease in such a group, an additional blood study is therefore routinely performed, especially in pediatrics, where the child may never have been tested for it previously (the disease is often referred to by the children—and their parents—as "sick as hell" anemia). Sickle cell anemia is a chronic hereditary blood disorder in which the red blood cells, as a consequence of lacking a certain component, assume actual sickle, and other bizarre but mainly crescentic, shapes when deprived of oxygen. These "sickled" cells, in addition to having a lower oxygen-carrying capacity, because of their abnormal configuration can become trapped, or "hung up," in the smaller blood vessels, which being designed to handle the normally rounded, slightly indented configurations may actually become "plugged," or stopped up completely, by solid masses of these bizarrely shaped cells, to the extent that, on occasion, no blood at all can get through. When this occurs, and it often may develop quite rapidly, you have the situation referred to as a sickle cell crisis, where the cells in the region that normally would be nourished by those blocked vessels actually die from lack of oxygen. This leads to great pain in the affected area, which may be almost anywhere in the body, but most frequently occurs in the bones and in the small vessels of the abdomen. In severe cases the condition can actually be life threatening. As already mentioned, this is a genetic, inherited disorder, and varies widely in severity, as one person may inherit the full-blown disease and others may be afflicted with only the "trait," where they generally have no symptoms. In these instances their crises often are much less frequent and severe, and people so afflicted are able to tolerate what would or could precipitate a full-blown crisis, under certain stressful conditions (anything that lowers the oxygen tension of the blood, such as cigarette smoking or riding in an unpressurized plane), in someone who had the full-blown disease.

An interesting sidelight, although not very important in the overall schema of the disease process, is the influence of social factors in the black community that can determine the blood picture. Normal blood development and maturation requires the presence of specific vitamins, one being folic acid, and quite frequently the black population, as well as other poorer minority groups, is deficient in not only this but other vitamins as well. This becomes especially significant in light of the fact that the minimum-required daily amount of folic acid is normally contained in a portion of most green leafy vegetables. The situation is therefore even further complicated, since the relatively limited supply of that vitamin in the diet of the impoverished black person with sickle cell anemia is then further decreased by the traditional custom of cooking collard greens, a frequent dietary staple, for many hours, which serves to further lower the folic acid content of the food.

To return from this digression, the routine examination of the urine also includes a microscopic "look see" for cells and other elements that should or shouldn't be normally present, as well as a "dip stick" study, where various chemical information is quickly obtained, such as the presence and amount of sugar. One of the recurring images I have of myself as a student and intern is running around the hospital with a little cup of urine in one hand, an inside out examining glove containing a fresh stool sample (which is usually spread on filter paper and tested with various chemical reagents to detect the presence of any occult blood), and the tube of blood in my coat pocket, heading for the nearest lab.

Personally, I did not seem to mind the required lab work nearly so much as many of my colleagues (and not from any pathologic pleasure derived from playing with blood and excrement!), and I enjoyed it for several reasons. For one thing, I was truly fascinated with viewing the microscopic elements of the blood and urine, and as my skills improved, I looked upon it almost as a contest to get as accurate results as possible, so I could then corroborate and check out my expertise with the main lab's official findings later on. In addition, it was an opportunity to actually be completely alone for a while, to get away from the hustle and bustle of the ward and the incessant demands, so I generally looked upon it not so much as a chore but as a respite and challenge. As a matter of fact, these were some of the few moments I truly had to myself, such as when I would have to wait for the smear to dry for example, or the centrifuge to complete its spinning down processes, and I even was able, on occasion, to sneak in quick little phone calls to keep in contact with the outside world.

A part of our training in this regard was spent in the main laboratory, primarily in the microbiology section, where we were taught by the microbiologist in charge of the section how to properly prepare and interpret the growths of bacteria that were present on the selected culture media. I was once again reminded here that medicine is an art and a science practiced with all the senses, and the point was vividly brought to mind when the department head, uncovering a round glass plate streaked with growing bacteria, suddenly held it directly up to his nose and exclaimed, "Ah, hah, the characteristic bacteroides" (bacteroides are organisms that give off a rather distinctive, characteristically foul odor). If this may appear somewhat crude, offensive, or even unscientific, the utilization of the sense of smell can often yield some particularly valuable information, and the case with bacteroides is far from unique in medicine. Certain festering wounds often harbor organisms that best grow under conditions of very little or no oxygen, and they too give off particularly distinctive, albeit offensive, odors, and a good clinician can sometimes pick up a valuable clue as to the offending organism present while waiting for laboratory confirmation. Similarly, certain more general conditions, such as uncontrolled diabetes, cause the individual to have a distinctive odor on his breath, and the knowledge of such information, available through this seemingly least sensitive of all the sense organs, can be quite valuable in helping to formulate a rapid diagnosis in a crisis emergency room situation.

The use of all the senses, including smell, in the practice of medicine has a long historical perspective. For example, in early Roman times if someone was suspected of being a diabetic, their urine was actually tasted to see if it had a "sweetness," which would signify that the person was losing sugar in his urine, which is one of the hallmarks of the disease. And although it may sound obvious and silly, another extremely valuable tool available to the clinician, yet all too frequently taken for granted, is the sense of sight. Much valuable information can be garnered by simply observing the patient, the way he breathes or moves his body about, his gait or walk, in addition to employing the other more traditional senses, such as touch and ausculation (hearing), both through the stethoscope and unaided.

There is a certain danger in neglecting or playing down the importance of information so acquired, and this tendency may be fostered to a large degree by the increasing availability of sophisticated new laboratory procedures, which are being developed and perfected almost daily. For example, it is now routine at a hospital of almost any size in this country to take two tubefuls of blood and get the results of eighteen separate tests by simply running it through a computerized testing machine. Of course, this is all well and good, and it is truly progress in certain respects, especially in regard to time and trained manpower, but the individual doctor, and especially the training physician, runs a strong risk of falling into such a convenient routine that he is not forced to exercise, develop, or sharpen his clinical judgment. He may, therefore, approach any given situation in a shotgun fashion, where although an abnormal result may fortuitously show up, the doctor is basically negating his training (in which he was taught to think systematically and logically), and in addition, perhaps, he could also be saving the patient time, expense, and even pain. Naturally, the risk of this occurring is much greater at the student level, and in an attempt to keep us aware of the potential dangers inherent in slipping into the habit of permitting a machine to do our thinking and reasoning, I was always struck by the irony of how frequently a criminal was quoted in this regard. Willie Sutton, the noted bank robber, upon being asked why he robbed banks, answered simply, "Because that's where the money is." The same axiom holds true in medicine, and it is obviously good judgment to employ the simpler, more innocuous tests indicated on the basis of your clinical judgment in the areas where you believe the pathology lies rather than shotgunning, or going immediately to the more sophisticated procedures. If the patient tells you he has come because it burns when he urinates, my God, you better look at the urine first.

A more formal aspect of the educational experience, in addition to the scheduled conferences and lectures, is the venerable institution commonly referred to as attending rounds. These are specifically intended for teaching purposes, and should be distinguished from so-called work rounds, where the residents, interns, and students see each individual patient at least once a day, and usually more frequently. At that time the patient's condition is carefully reevaluated on the basis of results of the most recent diagnostic tests, and decisions then made as to which further tests and/or treatment modalities should be instituted.

Attending rounds include the presence of the attending physician (hereafter referred to as attending) assigned to the team for that particular time—he or she is a physician who has completed most, or all, of his or her postgraduate training and is either employed by the hospital as a full-time staff member or is an outside practitioner with a private practice, who then devotes a certain number of hours each week to teaching. The attending is ultimately responsible, both morally and legally, for each individual patient's well-being and care, and as such he or she is expected to be available for emergency situations when his or her expertise may be required, as well as scheduled times when he or she is expected to see problem cases and aid in the day-to-day decisions concerning patient management. This person is the highest rung on the ladder.

As a rule the attending would first be brought up to date on the status of the more seriously ill patients already being cared for by the team, and then any problem or situation that might have arisen since he or she last saw the patient would be discussed. Then the new admissions would be presented to him or her, usually by the third-year student.

These rounds are usually the type of learning experience that most people call to mind when they think of medical education, and this image is reinforced by the vast majority of novels and movies that deal with this subject. There is a strict, detailed protocol regarding the order and manner of presentation, and the student is quickly made aware of the importance of the proper presentation. This is not done simply out of dogma or mere tradition but is a highly systematized formula structured in such a way as to be both logical and inclusive. Very briefly, it begins with the presenting complaint that brought the patient to the attention of the doctor, the duration and a detailed description of the quality of the symptoms, pertinent social and family background, a comprehensive past medical history, the findings from the physical examination, the preliminary laboratory results, the working diagnoses, the proposed further diagnostic studies, and the therapeutic regime being followed at the present time.

The manner and style of the rounds conducted are as varied as the individual attendings, and unfortunately, personality is as significant a variable as expertise. This was usually hot-seat time, and how hot it got would depend on the philosophy and style of the attending. Some attendings are very low key, and their rounds reflect this, while others are of the fry 'em school, where the student is expected to squirm. You must bear in mind that it is a very public spectacle, as it involves not only the individual student and the attending but includes your fellow students, the residents and interns on the team, and often the patient. Although they constitute only a small proportion of the entire teaching experience, these sessions should ideally be a valuable complement. However, this is often not the case for several reasons, the most prominent one being when an attending lets his personality dominate and appears to take more pleasure and pride in showing up how little the student knows, and attempts to embarrass him rather than trying to educate.

There were men in each department who were notorious in this respect, and their rounds were fearful exercises in trying to blend as inconspicuously as possible into the group while at the same time assiduously attempting to avoid eye contact so that you wouldn't be singled out. This proved especially difficult for me both because of my situation (the "let's-see-what-the-movie-star-knows" mentality) and my size, as it's obviously not easy at six-feet-four to blend in inconspicuously in any small group. These rounds could last anywhere from one to two hours, and some of them were definitely the longest hours I have ever sweated out!

And as if this wasn't enough, the anxiety of the third-year clerkships was intensified even further at the completion of each rotation, when each student would generally be examined and evaluated on three separate levels. The emphasis might be somewhat different in each department, but basically there would be a written, numerically graded examination, an oral examination with anywhere from two to five doctors firing questions at an individual student for upward of thirty minutes, a practical examination, or any combination of the three.

The practical examination was often the most unsettling aspect of the testing process, and how uncomfortable it might be depended again to a large extent on the individual doing the testing. Each student would be assigned one particular patient in the hospital with whom he was supposedly not familiar, and the tester would stay unobtrusively in the background and observe as the student conducted the history taking and physical examination. Approximately ten minutes were then allotted for the student to write down the positive physical findings, list what further laboratory and other diagnostic studies he would order, and formulate a list of the most probable diagnoses; then the case would be discussed in toto with the examiner.

I had one classmate who became notorious for roaming the hospital the day before the practical exams were scheduled in an attempt to familiarize himself with all the unusual or difficult cases on the wards. He was a poor student in general, who had already been forced to repeat a year's study because of academic difficulties, and he was the object of a great deal of resentment because of his cheating. It seemed to me that if he had devoted as much time to actual study as he did to his scheming and conniving, he would have had little difficulty learning the required material, and I remember once telling him to go to hell when he asked me about several patients on my team. I further warned him that I would turn him in if I so much as caught him looking through any of my patients' charts.

A rather curious facet of the practical exam involved the

individual patients, and relates to the fact that Martland is a teaching hospital. Consequently, every patient admitted to the hospital is a teaching case, in addition to being an individual in need of medical assistance, but unfortunately, too often the human dignity of the patient seems to be secondary to his value as a "teaching specimen." This happens most frequently with a patient who has particularly interesting physical findings, and it must be quite disconcerting and annoying for a sick person to be prodded or poked scores of times each day by troops of white-coated students and doctors, the vast majority of whom he will never see again. Many patients understandably resent being treated like "house specimens," and these individuals can become quite ornery and uncooperative, and if he or she happens to be assigned to a student for his practical exam, then in all likelihood the student is in for a rough time.

However, this can sometimes work to the student's advantage. For example, I was once assigned not to an obstinate patient but to one who spoke very little English. By being patient and employing a little ingenuity, I was able to elicit some very pertinent data, and I ended up being graded quite favorably.

Occasionally, a patient will enjoy all the attention he receives, and before the student can even ask the first question, much less begin his examination, the patient will spout off his pertinent history, physical findings, lab data, and even diagnosis. This results partly, I think, from the patient's need to feel important, but just as often he probably feels that by volunteering the information he knows to be important, he is also helping out a young doctor.

CHAPTER / 11

I WAS FORTUNATE, however, in that my indoctrination into the pitfalls and trauma of successfully surviving as a clinical clerk was made a great deal pleasanter, and, more important, meaningful, *because of* the particular individual who functioned as my attending during that first clerkship in surgery. He was a full-time professor of surgery at the hospital, and a Dean of students at the college as well. He was not only an excellent teacher, who was extremely well organized, with a great ability to communicate what was truly important and not get bogged down in academic trivia, but just as important he was truly sympathetic and sensitive to the pressures and anxieties of third-year medical students on the wards for the first time. He is still extremely popular around the hospital, and has been a frequent recipient of the "Golden Apple" award for best clinical professor (as voted by the students). With a full head of pure white hair and dark olive skin, he makes a striking figure, especially as he dashes up and down the stairs of the hospital, generally followed by his team, which always seems to be at least one flight behind.

One day, as the entire team was making rounds on the ward, Dr. L. was discussing a point about a patient's progress when a nurse rushed over and informed us that a patient was experiencing a great deal of difficulty in breathing. The particular patient, it turned out, was a thirty-two-year-old Portuguese woman, under our team's care, who had undergone an exploratory operation two days before, at which time it was discovered that she had massive, widespread cancer throughout her entire abdomen. I had not been present at the beginning of the operation, but all the students had subsequently been called down to the operating room when Dr. L. saw that it was an excellent teaching case. I remember, quite vividly, seeing and touching those rock-hard little growths scattered like pebbles everywhere you looked in this woman's abdominal cavity, and it was a completely different, almost sickening feeling compared with the feelings I had when I was back in pathology and looking at a fixed preparation of a cancerous stomach under the microscope. I recall how powerless and frustrated I felt when we were told that the cancer was so widespread and far advanced that any attempt to cure her surgically would be futile, and there was absolute total silence as Dr. L. himself called for the suture material and started to close the incision.

Thus we were all too familiar with the case as we rushed to her bedside, and at the very moment we arrived, she suddenly ceased her violent thrashing about (in an attempt to get more air into her lungs), and lay perfectly still. It was obvious to all of us that her heart had stopped, and we all looked up at Dr. L. as one of the residents started to apply external cardiac massage in an attempt to get her heart beating again. Dr. L. stood there very quietly, and slowly shook his head from side to side, and everyone immediately understood that he was telling us not to make any further attempt at resuscitation. Her husband had been waiting outside in the corridor, and somehow he instinctively sensed that something was terribly wrong, and ran into the ward .and flung himself on her bed, weeping uncontrollably. Dr. L. drew the curtain tightly around the bed, and after giving the man several final minutes alone with his wife, he gently took him by the shoulders and guided him out of the ward. And as Dr. L. told him that she was finally free from the terrible pain, the husband kept sobbing over and over, "My children, my children, my children." (There were four children in the family under the age of ten, I was later to learn.)

Everyone was subdued and restrained as we continued our rounds a half hour later. It was not necessary for Dr. L. to justify his decision to us not to attempt resuscitation. We all now realized, as he knew then, that even if we had succeeded, her heart would ultimately have failed again, perhaps in five minutes or perhaps in five hours, and we also knew the harsh reality that the strongest pain medication available had not given her any appreciable relief from the constant pain she had suffered over the last twenty-four hours.

When I went home that evening, I'm sure I was not the only student who had doubts about his choice of medicine as a career, or whether he was even cut out to be a doctor at all, but I do know how very important it was for me to experience the compassion and wisdom displayed by Dr. L. during that critical time.

There was another occasion, again while on rounds, when Dr. L. revealed a different facet of his personality, and it took all of us students by surprise. A new admission was about to be formally presented by a fellow student when Dr. L. announced that he could predict whether the patient's complaints were centered on the right side of his body or the left simply by observing the male patient as he lay naked on his back. Nothing further was said, and when we arrived at the bedside, Dr. L. casually removed the top sheet, then quickly replaced it, and rather solemnly pronounced that the problem was to be found on the patient's right side. At this, the student who had worked the patient up and knew that he was a chronic alcoholic with a long history of liver disease (and keeping in mind that the bulk of the liver is located primarily in the right side of the abdomen) audibly gasped at this awesome display of diagnostic acumen. Everyone could see that he was chomping at the bit to know how Dr. L. did it, but the student knew better than to say anything in front of the patient.

When we finally left the bedside, Dr. L. stood silently for several seconds, letting the tension build. He then somberly explained that it was simply a clear-cut application of the "angle of the dangle" rule, and since the patient's penis was clearly resting on his right thigh, the pathology was therefore on the right side of the body. He somehow managed to keep a straight face throughout his explanation. As he walked away one of the other students had such a quizzical look on his face that I'm certain he wasn't 100 percent sure if Dr. L. was teasing us or not. I only wished that the patient had had an erection at the time, but crafty old Dr. L. would probably not have been fazed in the least, and said the man was obviously suffering from headaches!

If competent observers had seen the aforementioned scenario taking place in the general surgical ward, they most likely would have noted the rather peculiar fact that although the vast majority of the patients were garbed in traditional hospital gowns, there were approximately three others scattered about who were attired in identical fire engine red pajamas. Upon inquiring, they would have found out that these particular men were not, as might have been assumed, more affluent than their peers, nor on the other hand were they the fortunate selected recipients of a local charity or social service agency that could not afford to supply the entire ward population. On the contrary, they would probably have been a bit surprised to find out that those three men were all currently serving time in the Essex County Penitentiary. Their presence was a consequence of the fact that since Martland Hospital, in its capacity as a public institution wholly supported by city, state, and federal monies, is obligated not only to serve the needs of the city populace as a whole, but has the additional responsibility for the health care of anyone being held in the custody of the Newark City police or Essex County authorities, as well as any party injured during the commission of a crime.

At one time there used to be a totally separate prison hospital ward, but the number of prisoners and their respective ailments varied to such an extent that it was found to be more efficient and economical simply to have each prisoner assigned to the general ward of whatever particular service was treating him, and position a policeman or correction officer to guard the entrance. The red pajamas were thus issued to each patient-prisoner so that they would hopefully be more easily visible, and thereby facilitate the operation.

Naturally enough, especially at the outset, these patients evoked both a sense of fascination as well as uncomfortableness because you would not immediately have any way of knowing whether any particular individual was being incarcerated for making book on the horses or for committing a homicide. As you might expect, this type of situation lent itself to some rather bizarre incidents, sometimes comic and sometimes tragic.

For example, on the more bizarre side, a prisoner was brought in from the penitentiary after deliberately swallowing a single-edge razor blade. Not only that, but it turned out that this was the *third* time he had done the exact same thing in the three years he had spent behind bars, for it seems that he preferred the pain of an operation and the three weeks' recuperation in the hospital to being in jail. Since the blade had the potential to cause serious damage to his gastrointestinal tract, especially at those times when the body would attempt to spontaneously expel it by reflex peristaltic action, the blade would have to be removed surgically. After the barium X-ray studies had pinpointed the general location of the blade, I was sent down to scrub and then prep the patient right in the operating room so that the chief resident and the rest of the team could come in and rapidly perform the surgery. As I stood and shaved the man's abdomen, I was struck with the irony that the blade of the razor I was using was perhaps no more than three inches from the blade in his stomach, and I kidded the nurses that it would probably be more appropriate to use an electric shaver.

Several days later our team was again on duty, and at approximately 10 P.M. I was down in the X-ray department vainly searching for some X rays that had been taken on several of our patients that same afternoon. I spent the customary half hour of utter frustration as the clerk and I went through the ritual of looking through pile after pile of X rays, accompanied by the standard dialogue:

"You sure these X rays were taken today?"

"Positive, I brought the patients down to the X-ray department myself."

"You sure these hospital ID numbers are correct?"

"Look, I stamped every admission on a file card. These are definitely the correct numbers."

"You sure that someone else didn't take these out already?"

"Man, I'm the goddamn student. Who else would they send to do this?"

The clerk could not refute that piece of logic, and we continued our search and found two out of the four X rays I was looking for, which is about the hospital average, when suddenly I heard what sounded like thirty sirens converging on the hospital. Naturally, at a hospital, you are used to hearing sirens, but I had never heard anything quite like this before. My first thoughts were that a fire had broken out, although I didn't hear the customary hospital code being broadcast over the PA system. The public is generally unaware that hospitals employ special codes that are understood by the staff, but hopefully not by the patients or visitors, so that in case of an emergency a general panic may be avoided. For example, if a fire broke out on the seventh floor, North Ward, the PA would broadcast, "Dr. Firestone to 7N, stat," rather than, "Fire on the 7th floor, North Ward, respond immediately." "Stat" is the term employed in any hospital emergency situation, and it functions to alert the appropriate staff member to drop whatever he or she is doing at that particular time and respond immediately to the command.

However, there was no announcement to that effect, and the number of sirens seemed to be increasing, so I grabbed the two X rays I had been able to locate (I think if the roof had been falling in, I still would have grabbed those X rays after all the crap involved in getting them) and started to run up the stairs to the general surgical ward.

When I got to the first landing, four policemen rushed past me with their guns drawn, and one of them shouted to me to get the hell out of the stairwell. Looking at the shotgun he was carrying, I thought this an excellent suggestion, ducked out the nearest door, and found myself on the pediatrics floor. I rushed over to the nurses' station, where a crowd had gathered, and I joined them at the window and saw scores of Newark City patrol cars ringing the hospital. No one else had any idea what was going on, and we stood around and speculated about what might have happened (bomb threat led the list, followed closely by riot), until the PA system announced that everyone could assume his normal duties. However, there were still a great number of policemen milling around. When I finally reached the surgical floor, a nurse was excitedly relating what had transpired.

It seems that one of the prisoners on the ward (and not my razor blade swallower, since he appeared to be resting comfortably in bed, as I quickly scanned the ward) had had a female visitor that evening, and she must have somehow slipped him a gun without being detected. When visiting hours were over, the prisoner had waited until everyone had settled down, and then on the pretense of going to the bathroom, he was somehow able to surprise the policeman who was ostensibly guarding him and hit him over the head with the butt of his gun. Timing and luck must have been on his side, as he was able to drag the unconscious cop into the stairway unnoticed, where he proceeded to strip him, put on his uniform, and handcuff the cop to the banister with his own handcuffs.

I found out later that the prisoner was quite a large man, and the uniform must have looked ridiculous, but nevertheless, he proceeded to run down the eight flights and rush out the rear employees' entrance to the hospital. Here he had to pass one of the crack private security guards who was employed by the hospital, and the guard obviously must have realized that something was wrong when he saw the way this "cop" was dressed, and by the fact that he was holding a gun in one hand and had another in his holster as well. As he attempted to run after the cop/prisoner to find out what was going on, the prisoner whirled and fired a shot in his general direction. Being unarmed, and paid basically to check employees' ID cards, he quickly beat a hasty retreat.

The only information we were able to ferret out that evening was that the the escapee was last seen entering a taxicab, and we had to wait until the newspaper came out in the morning in order to find out the subsequent chain of events, as well as fill in some of the gaps. The cab, it seems, had just discharged some passengers, and the driver was concentrating on some paperwork, when the cop/prisoner burst into the back of the cab with his gun still drawn and announced that he was in the process of pursuing a dangerous suspect who had fled by car from the immediate vicinity, and he was therefore commandeering the cab in order to continue the pursuit. He instructed the startled cabbie to quickly drive off in a certain direction, and after proceeding at high speed for several miles, the escapee suddenly shouted, "There he goes, pull over," opened his door even before the cab had come to a complete halt and darted down a side street, never to be seen again.

The episode, as might be expected, was a source of much embarrassment to the Newark Police Department, and especially for one very chagrined patrolman whose wallet was hurt as well as his pride, since to add insult to injury he had to pay for a new uniform and weapon out of his own pocket. The old adage that truth is often stranger than fiction really hit home as I realized that if I had tried to submit a scenario such as this to a TV or movie producer, he probably would have thrown me right out of his office and told me not to come back until I could come up with something believable that the general public would accept.

CHAPTER / 12

A SEGMENT of my surgery rotation, as well as subsequent portions of my general medicine training, was spent at the Veterans Administration Hospital in East Orange, which is an affiliate hospital of the medical school. In essence, this means that both institutions are basically autonomous, with each maintaining its own separate staff of attending and full-time physicians, but with students and general house staff rotating through both hospitals, and each offering somewhat different educational opportunities.

The patients at a VA hospital are naturally all former servicemen and servicewomen, and except for rare emergencies, all have completed their active duty. The ages of the men range from patients in their early twenties to others who have seen active duty in the Spanish American War, so there is a dramatic cross section of ages, experiences, and backgrounds. There are generally a few female veterans being treated at any given time, but their number is quite small, and this, combined with the fact that virtually no children are represented, does restrict the educational opportunities to a great extent. All in all, the nature and structure of the VA system offers a far greater opportunity to gain experience in handling chronic long-term patient problems than does Martland, where a great deal of the emphasis is on acute care, and the two experiences complement each other well in this respect.

Being fully federally funded, the physical plant is quite impressive, especially in contrast to Martland's facilities, and includes a modern, extremely well equipped and equally maintained 1,100-bed hospital, as well as many ancillary buildings and research facilities located on the sprawling grounds. The nursing staff is large and well qualified, and there are an extensive number of sophisticated paramedical personnel as well.

Consequently, I was eagerly looking forward to this and future rotations at the VA, but I soon became quite disappointed and disillusioned. I found the overall environment to be extremely depressing, and this, combined with mounting frustration at having to deal with a massive, unyielding bureaucracy at every level, made it a very unpleasant and exasperating experience. As trite and hackneyed as it may sound, a great many of these vets were truly "forgotten men" who simply had no other place to go. A staggering number of these men were alcoholics, with many other problems as well, and since society, and all too often their own families, had apparently given up on them, they naturally had given up themselves, and all they had left to turn to was the VA system. But unfortunately, even though the medical care available is probably the best anywhere in the world, the VA system ultimately fails them as well because it is forced to function as a social agency and not just a hospital, and it does this very poorly. There are sincere efforts made through various programs within the system, as well as through volunteer organizations, but the problems are massive and extend far beyond the hospital walls; all too frequently, the VA Hospital ends up as the last stop. There are just too many men who require a great deal of help, and simply not enough money, good programs, and people who care.

Whereas at Martland the pervasive influence of the inner-city problems, such as poverty, ignorance, and fear have a profound effect on your medical education and growth as a person, the VA experience is greatly affected by the strong undercurrent of despair, bitterness, and loneliness that is felt by so many of the men. Of course, this is a generality, and there are a significant number of patients who are not alcoholics or beset with a great many social problems. To put things in perspective, then, the VA Hospital does afford an excellent exposure to many valuable facets of medicine, and I did ultimately learn much there, but it was often at the expense of a great deal of time, energy, and emotion that had to be invested in order to transcend the circumstances.

One of the first patients I had on the surgical service at the VA Hospital was a forty-five-year-old diabetic. His diabetes was quite severe and was compounded by the fact that he was also an alcoholic, and generally took very poor care of himself. His circulation was severely compromised (an all-too-common complication of the disease, especially when it is severe and poorly treated), and several toes on each foot were becoming gangrenous and would require amputation. I learned a great deal from treating this particular patient, and his situation will serve as a good illustration of my VA experience.

In physical diagnosis it was strongly emphasized that in the course of taking a patient's history, the doctor should never assume anything, either on his part or on the part of the patient. This really hit home during the course of our initial interview when I asked the patient if he drank any alcohol, and he initially answered, "A little." I then asked what he meant by "a little," and after some hesitation he confessed that he had previously drunk one quart of vodka a day for over twenty years. When I inquired whether he drank anything else, like beer or wine, he grew quite indignant, and told me most emphatically that he was not a "wino."

This was my first introduction into what I was later to see was a rather bizarre hierarchy that exists among alcoholics. I subsequently had a patient who drank an entire case of beer daily. Yet when I asked if he drank anything else, he replied, again with great indignation, "What do you think I am, some kind of alcoholic? I'm too smart. I never touch the hard stuff, it rots your gut." And I found that the wine drinkers, in general, looked down their noses at the beer drinkers, and it occurred to me that it must therefore be very important for an alcoholic to be able to rationalize that he is never quite as "bad off" as the guy next to him and that no matter how low he sinks, there is at least someone who is in worse shape.

This particular patient was actually a transfer from the medical service, where he had been admitted in a diabetic coma four and a half weeks before. The medical team worked very hard to get him through the critical period, and then had gotten his diabetes under sufficient control so that he could safely undergo the needed surgery.

However, in the three-day period before his scheduled operation, his blood sugar level steadily rose, even though he continued to receive the same amount of insulin. This in itself was not that unusual, as certain factors, such as a smoldering infection for example, can cause an increase in a patient's insulin requirement, but a thorough work-up over the course of the next few days failed to uncover any obvious reason for his poor response. When I asked him if he was adhering to his diet and not sneaking down to the canteen at night, he put on a hurt look and solemnly answered, "Gee, Doc, I wouldn't do a thing like that."

As I left the room, however, one of his fellow patients followed me out and whispered in a conspiratorial tone, "I think you should check Mr. Smith's night table," and gave me a knowing wink. I then returned to Mr. Smith's bedside on the pretense that I had forgotten an instrument, and when I casually opened the top drawer of his night table, I couldn't believe my eyes. It was a veritable candy store, filled with candy bars, cookies, and other assorted sweets. Before I even said one word, Mr. Smith coolly looked me in the eye and said, "I know what you are thinking, but that stuff's not for me, Doc. I just keep it around for company." I proceeded to empty the drawer, and told him in the future his guests would have to come to the nursing station if they wanted any refreshments, and from that moment on I made it a point to constantly be on guard for any other guest piles. This might seem like an invasion of privacy (which I guess in a certain sense it technically is), but it taught me a valuable lesson, and from then on I made it standard practice to innocently browse about when any of my patients were on restricted diets. This proved especially beneficial in some instances when the patient did not actually realize that certain foodstuffs contained ingredients that could prove to be detrimental to his condition, and this was especially true, too, for patients on salt-restricted diets, who were unaware of the large quantities of hidden salt contained in so many of the commercially processed foods, and who turned out to be sincerely appreciative when so informed.

Ironically, there was a patient in the same room who was not on my team, but who was all too familiar to everyone on the service. I don't recall what his specific ailment was, but he had a secondary problem that soon became everybody's problem, and that was that he would eat virtually anything he could get his hands on, from food on the next person's tray to Dixie cups and cigarette butts. He was eventually transferred to the psychiatric service, but not before totally disrupting the ward and causing a great deal of aggravation for the staff. He would wolf his own meal down as soon as it was served (perhaps saving a milk carton or napkin for a later snack) and then walk over to a newly admitted, and therefore unsuspecting, patient, quickly ask if the other patient wanted his meat for example, and before the poor fellow could even answer, the piece of roast beef or whatever would be in this character's mouth, and he might be able to polish off half the tray before a nurse or orderly could intervene. It was really something to watch this guy devour a Dixie cup, and I remember once rushing back to his room in a complete state of panic after forgetting my instrument bag because I didn't know if he considered leather a delicacy or not, and I wasn't about to sacrifice my bag to find out.

We were soon able to operate on Mr. Smith after again getting his diabetes (and long arms and sweet tooth) under sufficient control, and I got to perform my first amputation. My resident let me do the actual surgery, and acted as my assistant ("Nurse, will you please *raise* the table"), and I remember how excited I was when the nurse handed *me* the scalpel. Everything went smoothly, as I carefully followed my resident's directions, but I distinctly remember feeling transiently nauseated at the very beginning when I felt how easily the scalpel cut through the dead and dying tissues.

Mr. Smith did well postoperatively, and soon was able to walk unassisted. However, when I told him that he was almost ready to be discharged and could probably leave the hospital in a few days, he informed me that he had no place to go and no one to care for him upon his release. I had anticipated this and had taken the precaution of contacting the social worker assigned to the ward, and I naïvely assured him that appropriate arrangements were being made. Yet, when I left the service three weeks later, Mr. Smith was still a patient in the hospital, although his condition was easily manageable on the outside.

As I listened each day while the social worker explained why Mr. Smith was not eligible for this or that kind of aid and would I please fill out still another form (in quadruplicate, naturally, "One copy always goes to Washington"), I then knew why some patients remained weeks or even months in the hospital—at tremendous cost to the taxpayer—even though their active medical problem had long since been resolved. I quickly caught on to the system, or more appropriately the lack of a system, and followed the example of my colleagues who would start the necessary machinery rolling on the very day a potential problem-placement patient would be admitted.

A certain percentage of these men truly had no suitable place to which to return, or else they would be forced to return to a lonely one-room walk-up, and many simply were unable to care for themselves. Consequently, there was a great deal of pathos involved in the gestures and implorings employed in their attempt to remain in the hospital until they were certain they were not going to be abandoned. I was soon able to distinguish these men from another type of patient who was really quite capable not only of caring for himself but of earning his own living as well. These malingerers were always trying to beat the system, and many looked on the VA Hospital as a free hotel, where they were guaranteed a clean bed and three meals a day, all on Uncle Sam (or, more precisely, compliments of you and me, the taxpayers). It was often extremely difficult to get these men out of the hospital, and there was one legendary patient who had an excellent reason why he didn't want to leave. It seems that he was reportedly making upwards of $300 a week between taking phone bets on the horses and organizing his fellow nonsmoking patients to exercise their right to buy cigarettes at twenty-five cents a pack at the commissary, which he would buy from them at cost and then sell on the outside for a profit. This Sergeant Bilko character put up quite a struggle to remain a patient, including filing a complaint with his congressman, but he was finally booted out on his well-rested rump.

One afternoon I was sitting at a table in the cafeteria with some other students when suddenly a patient in a wheelchair at the next table started to convulse. He couldn't have been more than eighteen or nineteen years old, and as I rushed over, I noticed that his skull was badly deformed. I squatted on the floor next to him and inserted a makeshift tongue blade (a wooden coffee stirrer) so that he wouldn't bite down upon or swallow his tongue and choke. A buddy of his told me that the patient had gotten his skull blown open in Viet Nam as a result of a hand grenade explosion. He had been operated on several times, and although heavily medicated, he often had these grand mal seizures.

I cradled his head in my lap so that his violent movements would not cause any additional damage, and as I watched his contorted face and saw the urine stain spread through his bathrobe, I again had an overwhelming feeling of hopelessness and frustration, and I was afraid I was actually going to puke. Up to that point I think I was similar to many other people in this country who had not been directly affected by the American involvement in Viet Nam. I had been against the war in college, as were most of my friends, but it had been easy to be virtuous and argue in abstract, philosophic terms when protected by the safety of a college deferment, and knowing that I couldn't be drafted until after medical school.

But this youngster was not an abstract statistic in some newspaper (this was at a time when the Nixon Administration was gloriously announcing that there were only "thirty-five battlefield casualties last week"), and I only wished at that moment that President Nixon and the other policy makers could be down here on the floor of the cafeteria to see and experience what was happening. Mercifully, the seizure abated fairly quickly, and fortunately the youngster was quite drowsy and unaware of the gaping crowd of fellow patients, staff members, and visitors who looked on as I helped an orderly get the patient back into the wheelchair.

It was only after everything had finally calmed down and I had filled out the required accident form that I was aware of how close I had come to actually throwing up. It was a vivid reminder that one of the toughest adjustments to make as a medical student is the effort required not to appear outwardly revolted and repulsed by the physical deformities and conditions of any patient, no matter how grotesque. This was particularly difficult at a VA hospital at that time, when so many of the younger patients were casualties of the Viet Nam War. These men, with their fragmented, splintered bodies (and minds—but that is another story in itself) would never have survived their wounds twenty years ago, but with rapid evacuation techniques, and the sophisticated advances in surgery and medicine in general, they were truly a testament to the miracles of modern medicine. Of course, there were often severe psychological problems, and a critical factor in how well they adjusted to their situation was whether or not society would look upon them as freaks or monsters. The attitudes of the doctors and staff was extremely important in this respect.

This point was further reinforced, albeit on a much less dramatic level, when I was working up a female patient several days later. She was in for elective surgery, after having been recently discharged after five years of active duty in Southeast Asia. As I was taking her pulse, she casually mentioned that she had worked for several years in a leper colony, and despite my new awareness, I nevertheless had to fight off an overwhelming impulse to drop her arm and run out of the room, even though I knew from my reading that one had to have years of intimate contact in order to contract the disease. Although they were only relatively minor in terms of my vast overall medical experience, the two incidents nevertheless served to further reinforce my growing realization that the *art* of medicine must be experienced and absorbed firsthand by the training physician.

CHAPTER / 13

IN ADDITION to the general surgery rotation we were given a magical mystery tour through the various surgical subspecialties, with only a week, or two at the most, spent on each service—enough time to absorb only some basic principles.

For example, my most vivid recollection of the week spent on the ear, nose, and throat service was the quickness and dexterity of the attending otolaryngolist (ear, nose, and throat specialist). He displayed moves when in the process of examining the back of a patient's throat with the long examining mirror that would make Muhammed Ali envious. At the first hint that the patient was about to gag, the doctor could have the mirror out and shift his body position quicker than he could say "vomit," and he proudly bragged about never having been soiled in his twenty years of examining patients.

I was truly impressed with the adroitness and finesse of the opthalmologist during my week's rotation on the eye service. The surgery performed in this field is absolutely astounding. Because of the minute areas that are operated upon, the surgeons actually must wear magnifying lenses, in the form of eyeglasses, so that they can perform the incredibly delicate procedures.

The following two weeks were spent on the orthopedic service—the specialty dealing with the skeletal system (the bones) and related structures. Although much of the surgery performed is delicate and requires a great deal of dexterity, certain of the procedures are more reminiscent of construction work than of surgery. For example, I assisted on an ankle fusion operation where the bones of the ankle, which normally articulate and move when the ankle is bent, are manipulated in such a way that they fuse together and actually lock permanently. This naturally reduces mobility to a great extent, but it is generally done for the relief of severe, chronic pain, which might have resulted from a poorly healed fracture or some other cause, and, as such, it is often quite successful. The actual operative procedure necessitates exposing the ankle bones and filling in the spaces between them with small pieces of crushed bone, and then letting the body do the rest by the normal healing process (the bones will then "knit" together in the same fashion as would a properly set fractured arm or leg bone). Of course, this is grossly oversimplifying the procedure, but it is basically the general concept. The bone that is used as filler should come from the patient himself so that it will not be rejected as foreign, which would occur if someone else's bone were used. This donor bone is most often obtained by chipping away at a small, exposed portion of the patient's own pelvis, where the bone is plentiful; the quantity taken will not do any harm to the area, and will soon be regenerated.

An actual chisel and hammer are employed, and my specific function at one point in the operation was to strike the head of the chisel, which was being positioned and held by the resident. The bone chips were literally flying around the room.

The orthopedic operating room fascinated me because of the vast array of gleaming stainless steel instruments of incredible variety, shapes, and sizes. It was like a huge tool chest, filled with chisels and ball peen hammers, hacksaws and electric saws, manual and automatic drills with diamond-cutting bits, and one instrument that looked suspiciously like an overgrown hedge clipper.

The orthopedic ward looked like some arty movie director's vision of a grotesque playground inhabited by adults; it was filled with the ropes, bars, weights, pulleys, and sandbags used for the patients who were in traction. I quickly learned that one of the most humane acts one human being can do for another is to scratch an itch for some poor person who is so rigged or restricted by a cast that he can't even touch his own nose, much less scratch an itch anywhere else on his body. One of the orderlies told me that before the hospital food service switched to disposable plastic eating utensils, the orthopedic ward was notorious for losing silverware, especially knives. Anyone who has ever worn a cast for any appreciable length of time knows how much it itches underneath, and although it is dangerous to poke around under the edges (you could easily scratch yourself or puncture the skin, which could then become infected, or you could even distort the plaster and defeat the whole purpose of the cast), it seems that almost everyone on the ward had a bread knife stashed in the drawer of his night table for just such a purpose.

I particularly enjoyed learning how to apply a cast. After practicing on each other for a day, which in itself was a great deal of fun, we were then allowed to cast simple, uncomplicated fractures of the patients. After my first session in the cast room I quickly realized why most orthopedic residents carry a nail file around, and it became quite easy to spot someone on the orthopedic staff, because they were the ones who were invariably picking at the plaster under their fingernails or trying to scrape off the white droppings on their clothes and shoes.

As a consequence of my somewhat longer anesthesiology experience I became quite adept at administering spinal anesthesia. It was also a time when I got valuable experience in starting IV's and learning how to intubate. The latter entails placing a tube down a sedated patient's throat directly into the trachea (the main windpipe leading to the lungs). This requires some degree of skill and a great deal of practical experience, as it is very easy to misplace the tube into the esophagus, the passageway to the stomach. Intubation can often be a life-saving procedure when a patient is brought to the emergency room unable to breathe spontaneously.

There was a sign hanging in the office of the chief anesthesiologist that succinctly summed up the general experience. It read, "Anesthesiology—hours of total boredom, interspersed with moments of sheer terror." There is a great deal of truth in this, as I found out from my three weeks in the OR, as so much in this field is quite routine *except* and *until* the patient has a crisis, such as a heart attack or respiratory arrest while on the operating table, and then, often in a matter of seconds, the anesthesiologist must act appropriately in order to save the patient. It is true that you don't need the best bedside manner in the world ("Just count down from one hundred, and don't fight the drowsiness"), but you had better have strong nerves and a cool composure.

The last of the surgical subspecialties to which we were exposed for any appreciable length of time was the genitourinary service, referred to most frequently by its medical abbreviation, GU, but also facetiously nicknamed by some of us as P³, standing for prostitutes, prostates, and piss, as the field is primarily concerned with the diagnosis and treatment of diseases of both the male and female urinary tract. I found the rotation both interesting and stimulating. Although it is technically a surgical subspecialty involving considerable major and minor surgical procedures, it also relies quite heavily on an extensive working knowledge of internal medicine and radiology as well.

For example, the complaint of a great many of the patients would be fairly severe flank or abdominal pain. Quite often, it is found to be secondary to the presence of a calculi, or stone (from *calculus,* the Latin word for pebble), which could be located virtually anywhere in the urinary tract, from the inside of the kidney itself to the ureter, the bladder, or even in the urethra. These stones may result from a variety of causes, and often remain undetected, if they are small and do not cause any discomfort in the area in which they are formed, until the body attempts to expel them along the normal pathway. If this fails, either as a consequence of the size of the stone involved or because it may get lodged in any of the aforementioned areas—but most especially within the narrow conduits of the ureters or urethras—the pain may then become exquisitely severe, as the body responds to the stone's presence by attempting to push it along with intermittent and frequent muscle spasms. These spasms, actually involuntary contractions of the supporting muscles, are closely analogous to the waves of contractions that normally occur in the gastrointestinal tract, which serve as the mechanism by which the body regularly moves food through the gut. The presence of a stone or stones in the urinary tract may require immediate surgical intervention to avoid irreversible damage to the kidney. In the majority of cases, however, complete blockage does not take place, and after proper evaluation an attempt is generally made to treat the patient conservatively with a variety of medications designed to help dissolve or break up the stones and special diets low in stone-forming elements, combined with forced fluids, in an attempt to flush the stone out through the normal pathways. The treatment also requires a great deal of patience and the use of pain-killers.

Unfortunately, a great many of the stones are formed from material that is radioluscent, meaning they do not show up on routine X rays, although a certain small percentage can actually be seen. By means of a specialized X-ray technique, the intravenous pyelogram (or IVP in medical jargon), findings may be obtained that might either show the presence of the stone itself or, more likely, implicate its existence by revealing the effects of a urinary blockage. The test itself is quite simple, both in design and application, as a liquid substance that is specifically designed not only to show up on X-ray examination but which the kidney itself naturally extracts or filters out into the urine from the blood that passes through is injected into a vein, and then a series of X rays is taken at timed intervals (thirty seconds, one minute, two minutes, five minutes and so forth) after the injection. This liquid dye is easily seen on X rays, and the findings will then in most cases and in conjunction with certain other concomitant physical signs and symptoms confirm the diagnosis, as well as help formulate the best plan of treatment.

The absolute, definitive diagnosis can best be confirmed by actually documenting the physical presence of the stone itself. This is important clinically because it can then enable the pathologist to determine the exact composition of the stone, and therefore be an important factor in determining future preventive treatment. Thus, except in those selected cases where the urologist goes in and surgically removes the stone or stones, it is not an uncommon sight on the service to find many men and women carefully attempting to urinate through fine strainers.

A urologist must also be trained to intervene surgically in situations involving the male genitalia, where procedures may range from correcting defects secondary to trauma, disease, or birth defects from the testis to the very tip of the penis. The latter may involve anything from removal of foreign bodies forced up into the urethra to circumcision.

Most individuals do not realize that a great number of circumcisions are performed each year on adults, and not just on children and newborns, and for a wide variety of medical reasons, the most frequent being chronic infection under the foreskin. Thus, I actually got the opportunity to perform several circumcisions, mainly on adults and older children, and naturally under the guidance of a resident; since it is an actual surgical procedure, involving the use of local anesthetics, cutting, and suturing, it must therefore be performed under sterile conditions (in the operating room). Even though I did not particularly enjoy my exposure to general surgery, especially in light of the fact that all I got to do most of the time was to stand hunched over and hold a retractor for five hours, I did enjoy being the primary surgeon in these cases.

The particular resident I worked with was quite a character, and there was generally a good deal of verbal bantering and a general relaxed atmosphere in the operating room itself. For one thing, being the only Jewish member on the service at that particular time, and doing most if not all of the circumcisions, the resident liked to tease me by saying that they were going to set up a special "mohel" residency just for me. (A "mohel" is a pious Jew, most often a rabbi, who is trained to use a special instrument designed expressly for such a purpose in order to be able to remove ritualistically the foreskin of newborn males, as dictated by Jewish law and tradition. This is quite different, by the way, from performing a circumcision on an adult, as the newborn has not yet arrived at the stage of development where the nerve supply to that area is functioning on the level it will when the child is fully grown. As such, the technique employed is quite different, with much less danger of complications, and the ceremony is most often performed at the infant's bedside with the family members present.)

The kidding would continue even as I would complete snipping the last part of the foreskin free; then the resident would pass it to the circulating nurse in order that it could be sent for pathology examination, which is standard protocol. However, even this could not be done without a ritualistic wisecrack, as the resident would invariably say, "Here, why don't you take some of this and make it into a small change purse, because then if you needed a valise, all you would have to do is rub it!"

On one occasion I performed the procedure on a young man in his early twenties. I injected the penis with a pain-killer, removed the foreskin, and applied the sutures and protective dressing when all was completed. The next morning when I went in to change the dressing and make sure there had been no abnormal bleeding or signs of infection, I got the shock of my life. I unwrapped the bandage and found that the penis had a definite bend in the middle and was quite pronouncedly and unmistakably crooked.

Frankly, I panicked, and although I should have known better by this point, I went chasing off to find the resident to show him what had happened. I was later to find out that occasionally the local anesthetic penetrates more on one side of the penis than on the other, and it is merely a matter of time before the situation resolves itself spontaneously and the penis assumes its natural configuration. But, of course, my resident wanted to see me squirm a bit and wouldn't tell me that I hadn't permanently ruined this young man's sex life. Instead, he told me that I had better hope I hadn't injured the vital nerve supply to that side, in which case the prognosis for eventual complete recovery was poor.

I was too embarrassed and upset to report it to the head of the department or one of the attendings immediately, hoping, on the one hand, that the latter instance was not the case, and also rationalizing that if something was drastically wrong, the resident, as the senior man in the OR, even though he had not actually done the procedure, should be more concerned than he appeared and at least should initiate any appropriate treatment or intervention if it was at all possible. Nevertheless, I was still shaken up when I went back to reapply the dressing, especially since the patient was examining his now crooked penis and didn't seem very pleased with its new shape. I stammered that it was a routine side effect and everything would straighten out in a matter of a few days, and he just had to be patient.

I'll never forget the feeling of dread I had the following day when I rushed into his room first thing, and as I held my breath when I unwrapped his penis, my worst fears were realized. The bend was still there, although not quite so pronounced. Over the course of the next several days I made sure that I was the only one to change the dressing, and I even went so far as to actually massage his penis in an effort to get it to straighten out. I think the patient would probably have thought I was making some kind of play for him if he had not been as upset about the general situation as I was, even though I tried not to show it. Finally, by the fourth postoperative day, the penis had returned to its normal configuration, minus the foreskin of course. When I ultimately found out that the chances of having caused any permanent damage or disfigurement were quite slim, I was so angry at the resident for leading me on that I wanted to put a permanent bend in *him*.

CHAPTER / 14

"WHOEVER IS next up better scrub quickly. The resident's down in the ER, and I've got a lady on the table fully dilated and ready to go. He'll never make it up in time!"

As the nurse turned and hurried out, my friend Paul and I literally exploded out of the on-call room and raced over to the sink. This was only our second day on the obstetric and gynecology service, but we had already had a full day of lectures and demonstrations, and had observed five deliveries as well. It was now time for us to actually deliver our first babies, and Paul, having won the coin toss, was to be first.

As we scrubbed, Paul appeared to be pretty calm, but I could tell from his chatter that he was excited and a bit apprehensive. I'm sure he would have preferred the resident to be present, especially at his first delivery, but the situation could not be avoided. Naturally, policy dictated that a resident *should* be present at all deliveries, but Martland at that time averaged over three thousand deliveries per year, and it sometimes happened that the resident would get caught in the emergency room with another patient, or perhaps be covering an emergency on the wards, or be tied up in the operating room, and in those instances the student would be the only "doctor" available. This happened to be one of those times, and the resident could be summoned fairly quickly if any serious complications should develop, although even a very short span of time can prove to be critical. However, we had been quite well prepared—through lectures, films, and demonstrations on life-sized plastic and rubber models, as well as observation of actual deliveries—to know what to expect and how to foresee potential difficulties.

"Doctor, I think you better hurry. It's really close," the nurse shouted to us from the delivery room. "You better get in here on the double."

"Everybody remain calm. I'm on my way," Paul shouted back. I kept thinking about what our instructor had previously emphasized, which was that the good obstetrician is constantly aware of the potential complications before they become real emergencies and that if careful attention is paid to various key factors, the odds are then favorable that the ultimate delivery will be accomplished with good results for both the mother and the baby. Besides, policemen and cabbies delivered babies all the time, and women had obviously been doing it by themselves successfully for thousands of years before doctors were around, so it couldn't be all that difficult. However, despite all this, I'm sure that Paul would have preferred a resident looking over his shoulder rather than me.

We entered the delivery room itself, and Paul rushed over to the instrument table where the gloves and gown were laid out.

"I don't think there will be time for that," the nurse insisted, as the woman was now crying out in pain almost continuously, her contractions now only seconds apart.

"I'll have the gloves on in a second. Just relax," Paul said, as he fumbled with the gloves with his back to the delivery table.

"Doctor, Doctor, hurry!" the nurse persisted, as the woman's cries grew even more intense.

"Okay, ready!" Paul exclaimed as he spun around, and I wish I had had a camera at that moment so I could have recorded the look of surprise on Paul's face when the nurse calmly handed him the baby with the umbilical cord still attached.

This particular nurse had delivered more babies than she would probably have liked to admit, and the calm, efficient manner in which she handled the entire situation made me suspect that similar incidents with previous students were not uncommon. Paul quickly recovered his poise, clamped and cut the cord, gave the newborn a cursory examination and found him healthy and in no distress, and then proceeded to deliver the placenta (the afterbirth). There were no tears or lacerations of the vagina to repair (since it was the woman's seventh child, she had had no difficulty stretching to accommodate the baby), and the entire scenario could not have taken more than ten minutes at the most, but what an exciting ten minutes!

After Paul had filled out the birth certificate and other records, we went back to the on-call room. It was my turn next, and it could happen in as little as five minutes or as much as five hours. It should be explained that what happened with Paul's case was not at all unusual with a patient population in which only 50 percent of the mothers received any prenatal care; most of the others were not seen by a physician until the moment they presented themselves to the emergency room, frequently already in the late stages of labor. It became somewhat more difficult, under such circumstances, to apply what we had learned in lectures regarding the importance of evaluating whether or not the delivery would be complicated.

Paul and I were discussing what had just happened when the resident burst in and told us that he had checked the mother and child, and they were both doing well. At that point we heard the elevator door open, and upon hearing the loud moans coming from down the corridor, I realized that I was soon going to get my chance.

The woman was not yet in an advanced stage of labor, and upon first examining her, I was amazed at how young she looked. I was even more shocked when I found that she was only sixteen and that this was going to be her *second* child. When the resident told me that he had delivered girls as young as twelve years old, it was quite unsettling to realize that these mothers were really only youngsters themselves.

This time the resident was able to review the proper procedure with Paul and me in a step-by-step fashion. I started the IV, and we were shown the proper technique of administering the local anesthetic so that the delivery might be made as comfortable as possible. We went over the proper evaluation of the different stages of labor and discussed several of the other procedures, such as determining the position of the fetus, as well as monitoring the fetal heartbeat. At the appropriate time the woman (although "girl" would actually be more precise) was transferred to the delivery room, but I still hurried through the scrubbing and rushed into my gown and gloves because I didn't want my first delivery to be a "hand-off" like Paul's. Everything proceeded uneventfully until the baby's head began to "crown," or first appear, at the opening of the vagina. The resident felt that the baby was fairly large and that it would be advisable to make a small incision (an episiotomy), which I could control, rather than permit a rip or tear to occur spontaneously in the walls of the vagina. I did as he showed me, and the rest of the delivery went smoothly —relatively smoothly, that is.

Since I am right-handed, I naturally prefer to use instruments with my right hand, and the instrument tray was therefore positioned on my right side. During the course of the actual delivery I consequently attempted to grasp the emerging child with my left hand, but the newborn was so slippery that I was frightened I might actually drop it, and I rather awkwardly juggled the infant so that I could grasp the tiny feet between the fingers of my right hand, which made me feel much more secure. However, I had to pay a price for this security, and that was that I was then forced to reach across for the instruments with my left hand, which led to even more awkward maneuvering. Nevertheless, I soon had the child safely in my hands, and I yelled out, "It's a girl," since I was the only person at that point who knew the sex of the child. Even when held upside down, slimy and covered with mucous and blood, with eyes squeezed shut and her hair wet and matted, I thought she was absolutely beautiful. After I clamped and cut the cord rather awkwardly with my left hand, I brought the child around to the head of the table, and her mother thought so as well.

I suctioned out the accumulated fluids from the child's nose and mouth, and found her in good condition after a quick examination. She would shortly be examined much more thoroughly by the pediatricians.

To prevent potential complications from the possibility of the child having acquired gonorrhea as she passed through the birth canal—if the mother was so infected but was perhaps unaware of it herself—I placed silver nitrate drops in the infant's eyes, which were still squeezed tightly shut and which I had to gently pry open. Untreated gonorrhea acquired in this manner can lead to actual blindness, and this prophylactic intervention is done as a standard procedure in a population where the mother's general condition at the time of delivery is often unknown. Additional blood tests of the mother would be run immediately in order to check for the possibility of any other latent infection that she might be harboring and which could have possibly been transmitted to the child either during the period of gestation or at the time of the actual delivery. I was so totally engrossed with the infant that the resident had to remind me that the placenta still had to be delivered and that the laceration still required suturing. Half an hour later I was back in the on-call room feeling very good about obstetrics, babies, and myself in general.

CHAPTER / 15

DURING MY three weeks on the obstetrical service the women were generally young and healthy, and usually went home with their babies after three days. The newborns themselves absolutely fascinated me. Even though most of the infants weighed only six or seven pounds, they were perfectly formed in every respect, right down to their tiny fingernails.

One afternoon I was in the on-call room when I heard a great commotion coming from the direction of one of the delivery rooms. It was not the customary moans and groans of a woman in labor or delivery to which I had grown accustomed, but was actual shouts and curses. The voice grew even more shrill as I entered the room and saw that the target of this invective was a fellow student, who was standing at that moment rather sheepishly in a corner as the resident attempted to calm the woman and complete the impending delivery. The woman kept pointing her finger at the student while shouting in broken English, "I no whore. You whore," intermingled with long strings of Spanish phrases, and I didn't have to be fluent in Spanish to sense they weren't complimentary, to put it mildly.

The resident motioned for both of us to leave the delivery room, and as we headed back to the on-call room, I found out what had caused this commotion. It seems that my fellow student knew even less Spanish than I, and he had previously overheard other students and doctors giving instructions in Spanish to their Spanish-speaking patients in regard to such key items as when to breathe deeply and when to bear down and push. Unfortunately, he had confused the Spanish word for "push" so that instead of saying it properly as *puha* he said instead *puta,* which is Spanish for "whore." Under the circumstances I thought the woman's response was quite understandable.

As I said, a great many of the women who presented themselves to the emergency room in a state of imminent delivery had not seen a doctor previously in regard to their pregnancy. Whatever the reasons, it was an unfortunate situation in that the mother, and especially the child, would have benefited greatly from proper prenatal care and counseling. In addition to the crucial situation of the presence of maternal disease, such as gonorrhea or syphilis, and the transmission to the unborn child, there are instances that can make it even more critical that the expectant mother be examined and evaluated by a physician early in her pregnancy, as well as continue to be followed at regular intervals. It can literally be a matter of life or death, not only for the yet unborn child, but for the mother as well. This is clearly demonstrated in the situation where the mother and the fetus have a serious blood incompatibility (most commonly involving the Rh factor) or, as is far too common an occurrence in Newark, when the expectant mother is addicted to heroin. This latter instance involves the tragic implication that the child has also become addicted to the narcotic while still a fetus, and, as such, will consequently suffer symptoms of acute withdrawal soon after the delivery. Unless this situation is known beforehand or is recognized early and properly treated by actually administering morphine or some other synthetic equivalent of the narcotic in gradually diminishing doses over the course of those first critical days, the struggling newborn may not survive.

In addition to the circumstances already mentioned, by not placing herself under the care of a physician, an expectant mother is also often unaware of the significance of certain danger signs for which to be on the alert during the course of the pregnancy, which should serve to warn her when to seek immediate treatment, and, perhaps, be able to avoid a miscarriage. Finally, if the woman has not been properly informed as to the right time to come to the hospital for the actual delivery, this, too, can not only have a considerable effect on the ease and eventual outcome of the labor and delivery but, again, might play a significant role in the actual survival of the child and mother should there be any complications.

An important part of our training, then, naturally involved the methods for the proper evaluation of whether or not a woman was truly in labor and whether she therefore warranted admission at that precise moment or could safely be sent home and instructed as to what to look for to indicate the appropriate time to return. When a resident was satisfied that the student was competent to make that decision, the student was often sent down to the emergency room alone to make such an evaluation. However, there were safeguards in that the student had the authority to admit a patient by himself, whereas the resident had to see the patient if the student thought that she should be sent home.

The second night on duty of my obstetrical rotation, the resident was busy in the operating room when a call came to the floor that a pregnant woman was in the ER complaining of severe pain in her lower abdomen. I hurried down and proceeded to examine her as I had been taught, and as I inserted my gloved hand, I noted what appeared to be bloodstains on her panties. However, she denied any bleeding. As I proceeded, I suddenly felt something quite sharp and metallic, which I knew immediately should not have been there. I recalled instances where women had gotten pregnant with intrauterine devices (IUD's) actually in place in the uterus, and I knew that in those cases, the devices could be safely left in the womb and generally would come out when the baby was delivered, usually with no complications. There have been documented instances of babies that have been delivered actually clutching the IUD in one hand.

In any case I figured it was time to get the resident down to see what was actually going on, and I attempted to extricate my hand as gently as possible. However, the glove seemed to be caught on the object, and the more I struggled to pull my hand out, the more the glove snapped back inside her vagina. Thankfully, the nurse was in the next cubicle preparing another patient, and my own patient was so concerned by her pain that she didn't appear to notice my difficulties, but I was still getting more than a bit panicky and embarrassed. After struggling for what seemed like an eternity but was probably no more than thirty seconds, I very quietly, and as inconspicuously as possible, took my hand out of the glove, and left it protruding from her vagina, while I got on the phone and told the resident that I needed help in the ER and that someone should get down as quickly as possible.

When he arrived and entered the cubicle and saw the glove dangling between the woman's legs, he began to laugh. But the cries of the woman alarmed him, and he immediately called to the nurse for a speculum—an instrument that is inserted into the vagina so that the doctor can see inside. As I peered in over his shoulder, I couldn't believe what I saw. There was a broken off piece of wire coat hanger lodged securely in the cervix, onto which the finger of my glove had obviously gotten caught, in addition to a fair amount of clotted blood and debris.

The woman had been simply too frightened to tell me or the nurse that she had previously attempted to abort herself with the wire coat hanger, and the resident later explained that this sort of thing happened all too frequently in Newark. This was long before the Supreme Court had made its ruling on the right of a woman to have an abortion on demand, and even before New York State had adopted its liberal state abortion law. On the way to the operating room the resident told me some real horror stories concerning attempts at abortion involving rulers, pipe cleaners, letter openers, and even Clorox douches.

It was necessary to call in the attending surgeon, who was fortunately able to save the woman's uterus, and it required some skillful surgery. Besides repairing the damage caused by the hanger, it was necessary to remove all the products of conception from inside the uterus itself as well, because if any of it was retained, it could cause continued hemorrhaging and could easily lead to severe infection as well. This is generally accomplished by literally scraping out the superfluous tissue so that the uterus can then contract, as it would do under normal circumstances. You have to take some normal healthy tissue with it as well, but this is no problem because a certain portion of the uterus is designed to regenerate itself, which it must normally do every month after menstruation. This scraping procedure is called curettage, and can be accomplished by passing an instrument, the curette, through the vagina and cervix; it must be done with great care and delicacy, because the walls of the uterus are fragile and easily punctured by a sharp instrument.

I became all too familiar with the procedure when I moved on to the gynecology portion of the rotation. Here I was no longer responsible for deliveries but was concerned with learning about, and treating, the varied disorders of the female genital tract, which included all the varied complications of pregnancies, abortions being just one.

Every evening I was on duty it was not uncommon to admit anywhere from three to five women who were actively hemorrhaging, and the vast majority were a direct consequence of criminal abortions. Some of these women were in serious condition, due to massive blood loss, and others had delayed coming in for treatment for as long as several days out of fear of criminal prosecution. The women in this latter group were often infected, and these septic abortions, as they are called, had a nauseating, putrid odor unlike anything I had been exposed to previously.

All these were true emergencies that demanded immediate treatment. Fluids had to be given intravenously to begin to replace the lost blood volume, and blood samples taken for testing purposes for those cases where actual transfusions of blood were found to be necessary. Curettage was then performed via the vaginal route, and it was not usually necessary to give any drugs to widen or dilate the cervix so that the instrument could be passed into the uterus itself. As already stated, scrupulous attention must be paid to insure that nothing is left behind to cause further bleeding or infection. The wire loop of the curette, grating and tearing at the tissue, makes a distinctive, unpleasant sound that I'll never forget. The visual aspects are best left undescribed, especially when the fetus had begun to take form, and the entire experience was quite upsetting. It was compounded by the fact that most of the girls were so very young and extremely frightened.

It was even more unsettling because the women would come in at all hours, and we were expected to grab whatever sleep we could when time allowed. I found it totally impossible to be involved with a patient under these circumstances and then calmly fall off to sleep.

One afternoon I was on the wards changing dressings and doing various other chores that fall to the medical student when suddenly I heard a woman scream out, "Holy shit, that's my doctor!" I rushed over with several patients to see what the commotion was all about when, much to my chagrin, I saw myself on the TV, getting ready to go down to still another defeat on the *Dating Game*. I had forgotten completely that it was scheduled to be aired, and surely wouldn't have been there if I had remembered, but the women were getting a big kick out of the whole thing. There I was in the gynecology ward of the Newark City Hospital, surrounded by wildly enthusiastic and quite vocal rooters, who couldn't believe that the dumb girl didn't pick their "celebrity doctor." I was quite the talk of the ward for the last week I had remaining on the service, and soon afterward I overheard some of my patients explaining to a new admission that she would have a celebrity for her doctor. Well, it seems that the only famous doctor this new patient was familiar with was Dr. Joyce Brothers, and when I came over to introduce myself, you should have seen the disappointment on her face when I didn't turn out to be blonde and female.

I learned quite a bit about the patients and their general situations from listening to them talk among themselves. For example, one time a patient had been admitted several days before for an incomplete abortion, and after undergoing a dilation and curettage she must have heard the doctor and staff refer to the procedure as a D and C, which they quite commonly do. I had to suppress a laugh when she began to tell her companions what it was like to get a "dusting and cleaning." This naturally led to a general discussion about their collective medical experiences, and at one point in the conversation I had absolutely no idea that one woman was referring to her menstrual cycle when she said she was currently "falling off the roof" until another patient remarked that she, too, was experiencing her "monthly friend."

One of my patients in this group had been admitted for a gynecologic condition that occurs fairly commonly among black women, in which the uterus is infiltrated by excessive growths of muscle and connective tissue—the general condition being referred to as fibroids of the uterus. When it was her turn to explain her reason for being in the hospital, it came out instead that she was suffering from "fireballs of the useless."

There were to be numerous other instances of malapropisms that I would run across as my experience widened, but there were two other examples on the ob-gyn service that particularly stand

120

out. One involved a woman who repeatedly referred to her vagina as her "virginia" ("Doc, you got to do something about this discharge from my virginia"). The other involved one of the younger patients, who asked a nurse if she was required to drink a lot of milk in order to give a proper "pasteurized" sample of urine, after she had obviously overheard a discussion between me and my resident regarding the fact that our results would be much more accurate if we obtained a catheterized specimen, which carried with it much less risk of contamination.

CHAPTER / 16

IN ADDITION to the time spent on the wards, part of the obstetrics and gynecology rotation included several weeks' attendance in the various outpatient clinics that were conducted by the department. These included the birth control clinic, where the various contraceptive methods and devices were discussed and prescribed; the infertility clinic, where couples who were apparently unable to conceive were evaluated and treated if possible; and the prenatal clinic.

You could usually tell when the particular clinic was being held because, as you walked through the waiting room, you would invariably see many of the women nervously clutching the brown paper bags that contained the early morning urine samples. The clinic might be best summed up as "vitamins, iron pills, and a pat on the belly." Here the junior medical student had a great deal of responsibility and functioned to a large extent as the primary physician. Although a resident was assigned to the clinic area as well as a staff attending physician, the student basically saw each patient alone, with a female nurse or aide in attendance in the examining room. The resident was called upon to see only those patients the student felt had significant complications or underlying problems that were beyond his scope.

After a pregnancy had been confirmed, a complete history was obtained, and a physical examination performed. It involved a digital examination of the woman's pelvis in order to determine if she is large enough to permit a normal, spontaneous delivery without complications. A Pap test for cancer was routinely done at the same time. A regime of vitamins and iron supplements was prescribed, and there was dietary counseling. Follow-up examinations were then scheduled at regular intervals so that the course of the pregnancy could be monitored. These examinations ultimately included listening for the heartbeat of the unborn child (generally audible by the fifth month) and checking on the position and size of the growing fetus. There was also the moment of truth when the patient stepped on the scale. This generally led to a discussion on the importance of not gaining too much weight for the safety and well-being of the mother, as well as the child.

There was one particular patient who had gained almost ten pounds in less than eight weeks, which was obviously far, far too much. When I questioned her about her dietary habits, I received more than I bargained for. It seems that the woman was a starch eater, and I don't mean that she simply liked starchy food, like potatoes and bread, but that she literally ate handfuls of pure starch, much as you or I might nibble on some popcorn or fruit. I later found out that this was fairly common in the general community; it was a long-standing custom that had been brought up from the South. The woman went on to explain that she had been eating starch since she was a little girl and that she quite liked the taste.

Even after hearing this, I was still unprepared when she proceeded to tell me that she also ate quite a bit of clay (yes, clay, as in mud). This again turned out to be another cultural heritage, and she said that the clay was actually sent up to her family by relatives still living in the South because the particular clay her family was accustomed to was unavailable in the North. She described it as reddish in color and best eaten moist, and again, it seemed to involve a matter of taste and upbringing. I did some subsequent research and found that there is a certain type of anemia that is often associated with chronic clay ingestion. I made certain to explain this when I later told her it would certainly be in her and her baby's best interests if she would refrain from ingesting any starch or clay while she was pregnant.

A staggering number of the patients I saw were teen-agers, and many were in their early teens, as young as fourteen or fifteen. Most of them were understandably frightened and upset, especially during the initial examination, and the overwhelming majority had never before had a pelvic examination. Many times the examining instruments were simply too large, and at times, I actually had to use pediatric equipment. Sometimes, the girls would come in with their mothers or, more often, an older sister or cousin, and as I would stand outside the cubicle while the nurse would call out the patient's name, I would be shocked when the patient almost invariably turned out to be the youngster.

Since we were only assigned to the clinic for three weeks or so, there was no continuity of patient care, and we usually saw an individual patient only once during our rotation, except in some isolated cases. The patient was then next seen by whomever was assigned to the clinic at the time of her next appointment. This situation existed on most other services as well, and it is unfortunate, not only in terms of medical education but, more importantly, for the patient. There is no opportunity to develop any sort of rapport between doctor and patient—imagine how difficult it would be for a frightened, often uneducated youngster to have to ask embarrassing, highly personal questions of a new person each time. Obviously, many important questions were therefore far too often left unasked, and it became a bit more understandable then why so many women in the community came to the emergency room with impending deliveries, without having any prenatal care whatsoever.

There was one young woman in her early twenties who was quite upset when I informed her that she was indeed pregnant. It seems that she had been to the birth control clinic six months before and had been fitted for a diaphragm. She insisted that she understood how to insert it and how to check to make sure it was properly in place, and she was emphatic in stating that she never failed to use the spermicidal jelly. She went on to say that she had followed the doctor's instructions explicitly, especially regarding the importance of inserting it before retiring at night and then not removing it until the next morning.

She had brought her diaphragm with her, and after seeing that it appeared intact, I had her insert it and had the resident double-check to see that it was in the proper position. It was, and I was ready to assume that the woman was either not as conscientious as she had claimed or that this was truly one of the small percentages of cases where the device had failed, until she casually happened to mention that with three other children already in the household, the new addition would impose such a financial burden that her husband was going to have to work nights during the week in addition to the weekend night job he already had.

It then dawned on me that with her husband working a night job on weekends, he must come home on Saturday and Sunday mornings and naturally go off to bed. At those times she, in turn, must have inserted the diaphragm at night before retiring and removed it on awakening as instructed, and then proceeded to have intercourse when her husband came home later in the morning.

It was an unfortunate case where the patient had taken the doctor literally, and there obviously had been poor communication and understanding. I was never quite sure, even after checking around, if the doctor in the birth control clinic had merely been too lazy to sit down and explain to the woman how the diaphragm functioned, while making sure that she understood the principle involved, or that he simply assumed that the woman had enough common sense and innate intelligence to comprehend. Thankfully, here the error in judgment did not result in a real tragedy, but the unplanned-for child was going to cause some definite hardships, and it served as another lesson to me about how dangerous it is to take anything for granted when dealing with any patient.

When I got to the birth control clinic portion of my rotation, I rather naïvely felt that I was quite competent to cope with the emotionally charged area of human sexuality. My bubble was quickly burst when I was in the process of counseling a twenty-seven-year-old black woman who had recently given birth to her eighth child. It seems she had tried several different means of birth control, but none were satisfactory, and she was having difficulty caring for her family. The oldest child was only eleven years old, and she was experiencing other difficulties in her personal life as well. She was desperately in need of help and guidance. She certainly fulfilled the criteria that the state of New Jersey required for an elective tubal ligation, wherein the Fallopian tubes that normally carry the ripe eggs from the ovaries to the womb are tied off so that the woman is unable to conceive, but her hormonal functions would remain intact and appropriate for her age. Because of her relatively young age, I was reluctant to suggest such a procedure, since it would mean that if her present husband died or if she became divorced, she would then be unable to have any children with her new mate if they so desired.

I discussed the general situation with both her and her husband, and during the course of the conversation, I mentioned a possible alternative. There was a brand-new procedure that could be performed on the husband where his spermatic cords would be tied off, and while he would still be able to achieve an erection, have intercourse and experience orgasm, he would be unable to impregnate a woman. I carefully explained what the operation entailed, and although early reports had been somewhat contradictory, I told him quite truthfully that he couldn't count on being able to have the operation successfully reversed, as some people were claiming was possible in most, if not all, cases.

The husband sat across from me and didn't say anything for almost thirty seconds, and then, with controlled fury, he spat out: "You've treated me, all you white people, like a piece of crap all my life. I'm living in a hole. I work two lousy jobs to feed my children, and now I got to sit here and be told by some whitey doctor that he wants to cut my balls off. That's the only thing I got left, do you understand? That's the only thing I got left!" He then grabbed his wife by the arm and stormed out of room. I think that the experience affected me as profoundly as any other I was to have as a student or an intern, and it gave me a little more insight into the situation as it really existed for the people of the community.

It made an interesting juxtaposition to go in one week's time from the birth control clinic to the infertility clinic, where the situations were completely reversed. There are many reasons for a woman's failure to conceive, and before embarking on the much more elaborate and detailed investigation of the female, it makes sense to first rule out any difficulty with the male. It is logical then to begin with an examination of a sperm sample, which is evaluated from both a quantitative and a qualitative standpoint in order to assure that not only is there an adequate number of sperm present but that they are well formed and function properly. Obviously, the fresher the sperm, the more valid the examination, but it can often be very uncomfortable for everyone concerned to simply hand a man a small glass bottle and tell him to go into the bathroom and masturbate.

A much more considerate and fruitful approach is to give the man the bottle the night before and instruct him to deliver the sample to the lab the following morning, hopefully no more than one-half hour after the specimen is obtained. One young man laughingly told me, when I presented him with the bottle, that I had better go get a wide-mouthed mayonnaise jar for him because not only was he going to have no difficulty filling the little bottle up but he also wanted to make damn sure that he didn't get stuck.

There is a widely circulated story (again most likely apocryphal, but as time went on, I began to believe that anything could happen at Martland) concerning a young man who misunderstood the instructions and thought he was supposed to bring in a *full* bottle. They say that when he arrived that morning, he almost had to be carried into the clinic.

CHAPTER / 17

IT WAS 9:30 P.M., and I was alone in the newborn nursery, except for the twenty or so infants who were scattered about in bassinets, most of them sleeping soundly after just having been fed. I was now a fledgling pediatrician, currently assigned to the newborn nursery, where I would spend a total of two weeks, and then be on the general pediatrics ward for an additional eight weeks. My primary responsibility in the nursery would be to conduct the first thorough and complete physical exams on the newborns as they came directly from the delivery room, monitor their progress for several days, and then do another complete follow-up exam in three days, when they would normally be ready for discharge.

At first glance this may appear quite mundane and routine, and it often seemed so, but this is actually a very important responsibility. Quite frequently, a student will pick up a defect or abnormality, which can then be corrected fairly easily because it was detected at such an early time. This can run the gamut, from a congenitally dislocated hip, to respiratory difficulties that can be potentially life-threatening, to the detection of evidence of blood incompatibilities, in which instance it may be found necessary to transfuse and replace the baby's entire blood volume or else the infant may not survive. Hematologic disease of the newborn is quite dramatic, and it is often largely misunderstood by the general public. It may be the consequence of several different factors, but the most common causes are the result of either an AB incompatibility or Rh sensitization.

Every person carries certain identifying markers on his red blood cells that determine that person's particular blood type. Blood type is genetically predetermined, meaning it is inherited from the parents, like the color of the eyes. For example, a person may have an A marker on all his red blood cells, which would mean that his blood type is A, a B marker, meaning obvious B typing, both A and B, which is type AB, or that person may carry no marker on his red blood cells and thus be referred to as type O.

The significance of this becomes clear if you consider a hypothetical case in which someone requires a blood transfusion. Let us assume that a person whose blood type is A receives blood from the only available donor, whose blood turns out to be type B. Patient A will suddenly have a quantity of blood circulating that is different from his own, and his body will then respond in a specific manner. This occurs as a consequence of the existence within the body of a mechanism referred to as the immune system, enabling the body to protect itself from outside infections, be it a virus, a bacteria, a fungus, or whatever. The body is able to recognize something introduced into itself as "foreign" and, therefore, as potentially harmful. The body responds by manufacturing substances specifically directed against the invader, and through various mechanisms the foreign substance is destroyed.

In the case of blood incompatibility, however, the invader is not an infectious agent, such as a germ, but simply a red blood corpuscle that is different, albeit in only one small respect. The body, unfortunately, is unable to make a differentiation; the immune system responds appropriately; and substances are consequently manufactured against the B-type blood cells. These anti-B substances, called antibodies, attack the newly transfused cells and destroy them. A virtual war is then in progress, and furthermore, if you take into consideration the fact that the breakdown products of the attack cells are damaging to the body in themselves and superimpose this on a situation wherein the recipient's status is already being compromised, since he is being denied survivable red blood corpuscles that he may desperately need, it becomes obvious why blood typing is so vitally important.

This is the reason why people with type O are referred to as universal donors, because their red blood corpuscles carry no marker and, therefore, should not evoke any negative immune response in a potential recipient. Conversely, people who are type AB are referred to as universal recipients. They can receive blood of any type and not react to it as if it is foreign. Of course, this explanation is somewhat oversimplified, and there are many other markers on the red blood corpuscles as well, which may or may not come into play, but roughly, this is the basic principle involved.

Similarly, there is another major marker present on the red blood corpuscles called the Rh factor, and here it is simply a question of a person having that particular marker or not. Approximately 15 percent of all Caucasian women are Rh negative. This can become an important factor in childbirth because it is possible for a developing fetus to be Rh positive, if he inherits that trait from his father, even though the mother may be Rh negative. Although there is not a direct crossing over of the respective blood circulations of the mother and the fetus, there is some intermingling, and it may be enough so that the mother becomes sensitized to the presence of these Rh-positive red blood corpuscles, which her body then "recognizes" as foreign, and begins to make antibodies that are directed against all Rh-positive cells. Because of the limited cross circulation the sensitization does not normally occur to any great extent during the first pregnancy, but the mother becomes "primed" to respond to any further similar invaders, so that most difficulties begin with the second child. If this does happen, the maternal antibodies can then cross the placental barrier between the two circulations and actually attack the unborn child's red blood corpuscles; another dramatic conflict takes place wherein the child struggles to grow and develop normally inside the mother's womb while she, at the same time, is making antibodies capable of destroying the baby's limited and much-needed supply of blood. Conditions are such that the baby can generally survive this before birth, but soon after delivery, the difficulty really begins, because then the baby is unable to make new cells rapidly enough to replace the ones destroyed. The breakdown products of the dead cells rapidly accumulate, which, as previously noted, are potentially lethal in themselves. The only way to save these children is to replace their blood totally with new blood, which, of course, doesn't contain any offending antibodies.

There are new means available for preventing such situations, but in order to accomplish this, it is imperative that both parents have their blood tested so that the doctor can be forewarned of the risk of potential complications. However, as previously explained, a great many of the women delivering at Martland had not previously been seen by a physician. Some were not sure of, or were unwilling to identity, the father. It is still a large problem in the inner-city hospitals, and one major reason it is so very important that each newborn be examined and monitored as early as possible.

"My, you're going to be a pretty young lady when you grow up," I cooed to the hours-old infant as I prepared to unpin the diaper. I did not foresee any of the aforementioned difficulties for this particular youngster, as I had taken a quick glance at the chart and had seen that the mother had been followed in clinic, and the father had been tested as well. However, after I removed the diaper, I found I was in for a few small surprises. To begin with, not only had the "pretty young lady" turned out to be a little boy, but he had also determined that now seemed as good a time as any to test out his apparatus, and he proceeded to urinate straight into the air and hit me literally between the eyes. As I grabbed the diaper with one hand and used it to shield myself, I had to marvel at how much pressure these little guys were able to build up in their bladders after drinking only a few ounces of sugar water. After he finished, I bent over to wipe him dry and smelled the presence of the third surprise before I even saw it. The little guy must have figured that he should check *everything* to make sure it was all in good working order, and the results were quite obvious.

The first several bowel movements of a newborn are actually quite interesting and informative as the child progresses through the early stages of its postpartum development. Observations of the character and quantity of each movement are carefully recorded, and this information can prove valuable in the early diagnosis of certain abnormal conditions. The earliest stool is composed mainly of amniotic fluid, which the child has previously ingested while still in the womb, as well as tissue debris and other elements, and this so-called meconium stool is normally greenish in color, slimy, and often very foul smelling. These "meconium surprises" are therefore quite messy, and the student is usually the one who has to clean it up, but the presence of a bowel movement is important to note for still another reason, in that it indicates that superficially, at least, the child's gastrointestinal tract is not grossly obstructed.

As I went to the sink to wash my hands before proceeding with the actual examination itself, I heard some giggles emanating from the general area of the nursing station. Since the newborns are susceptible to infection, it was constantly emphasized that we should wash our hands not only before examining each child but each time we went from one infant to another as well, in order to lessen the likelihood of spreading any infection. Although strict sterile technique was not in effect, we were required to wear a sterile gown over our hospital whites whenever in the nursery. At that time I sported a full red beard and a healthy head of hair, so I suppose I did make an incongruous sight for the two Philippine nurses, who were giggling like schoolgirls as I headed toward the sink, dressed in a three-quarters-length pink gown that fit me about as well as the OR greens, daintily holding the soiled diaper at arm's length.

The examination of a newborn infant, and a young child as well, is conducted in a different manner than that of an adult. Whereas in the adult the examination proceeds in a systematic fashion so that nothing is inadvertently overlooked, in the infant the examination begins in the areas that will hopefully disturb the baby least. Knowing that the child will most likely react poorly to an instrument in his ears or to someone squeezing and probing his abdomen, those areas are examined last. The child is first carefully weighed again, although a birth weight had been previously recorded in the delivery room, and in addition the child's length, chest circumference, and head circumference are also carefully measured and recorded.

The size of the head is extremely important, as it may be the earliest indicator of the development of a serious condition known as hydrocephalus, which is basically an accumulation of fluid in the brain. Normally, the spinal fluid, which also bathes the brain, is manufactured in a specific region of the brain and then exits through special passageways to the spinal column, where it continues to circulate. It is a dynamic system, with fluid being continuously formed, circulating, and then being reabsorbed. However, occasionally, the passageways out of the brain may be blocked, usually as a consequence of a developmental failure, and although the fluid continues to be formed, it has no place to go and, therefore, accumulates inside the brain. This has serious consequences, for even though the human body is designed so that the skull of a growing infant and child can expand to accommodate the growing brain, if there is hydrocephalus, the system quickly becomes overloaded, and since the skull is bony hard to protect the fragile brain, there is no longer sufficient space into which the swelling brain can expand. This is a life-threatening situation in the more severe cases, and it demands quick intervention, not only from the point of view of immediate survival but because even if it is only slightly or moderately severe, if left untreated, there will generally be some degree of retardation, since the swelling compromises the actual brain cells themselves, and this has a profound effect on the chances for normal development and maturation.

It is therefore imperative to become aware of such a situation as early as possible, for the sooner it is diagnosed and treated, the better the chances for the child, and the lesser the risk of ultimate brain damage. The prognosis for this condition used to be quite poor until the development of a new technique, which actually creates an artificial passageway from a cavity in the brain where the fluid is accumulating to one of the large vessels of the body that leads directly to the heart, thereby allowing the fluid to harmlessly drain off into the general circulation. However, there are still problems involved with the technique, such as a high risk of infection, clotting of the shunt, as the passageway or tubing is called, and the rather paradoxical fact that if it is successful, the child may actually "outgrow" the shunt as he or she develops. Despite the drawbacks, great strides have been taken in the treatment of this disorder, although much work remains to be done. It is therefore extremely important that the head size of every newborn be constantly and scrupulously monitored.

There is a further consideration as to why careful attention is paid to the general configuration of the head—a direct consequence of the actual delivery process. It has previously been noted how the child's head is frequently molded to fit the contour of the mother's pelvis as it traverses the birth canal. This is not at all abnormal, but even when it is carefully explained to the parents, it still often leads to a great deal of worry, especially in the first several hours immediately after birth when the parents' major concern is that the child will be deformed permanently. Sometimes, it takes only a matter of hours, but occasionally, it may take up to several days before the disfigurement is resolved through natural processes. Until the parents see this happen with their own eyes, the doctor can talk himself blue in the face and the parents just won't be reassured.

CHAPTER / 18

THE ONLY Saturday I was scheduled to be on duty in the new-born nursery also happened to be the day when the first rugby game of the year was to be played against another medical school. As an active member of the team I was naturally anxious to participate. Fortunately, I was able to strike a bargain with the fellow student who was also assigned to work that day. It was agreed that I would come in early and do all the follow-up physical exams on the babies ready to go home and then go over to the nearby park for the game. I would be gone for only a couple of hours, and then would return to the hospital to help him catch up with the new deliveries. It was quite a strange transition to go from wearing a pink gown to cleats, and from gently examining a 7-pound newborn to tackling a 240-pound fullback.

There had been few opportunities for any organized extra-curricular activities throughout medical school, and most of those available were directly or indirectly related to medicine, such as medical fraternities or professional associations, like the student branch of the American Medical Society. However, in the fall of my first year of medical school a rugby club was formed, of which I was subsequently to become a member.

Rugby itself is a rather violent contact sport that is a sort of cross between soccer and football, but with no time-outs permitted, no padding or equipment, and no substitutions allowed for anyone injured on the field during the course of the game. It originated in England and has always enjoyed great popularity over there, and it is now rapidly gaining favor in this country because of the fast, exciting quality of the play, the physicalness of the tackling, and the bruising, open-field running contrasted with the finesse involved in passing and kicking. An additional plus is the economic factor, since all you really need to play the game is a ball and a field, and the high overhead involved in the purchase of protective equipment, such as helmets and shoulder pads, is thereby eliminated.

The impetus for the formation of the team had come—during my first year at medical school—from one of our instructors in gross anatomy. He was a young surgeon who had spent a year abroad studying in England and had come back quite enthused about starting a rugby team, which could then play other schools and clubs in the area. Naturally, some of the former college jocks, especially the football players, needed very little coaxing, but there were many more of us who were hesitant to participate because, quite frankly, we were afraid of getting hurt, and we also wondered what implications our involvement might have academically. Yet here was a surgeon, whose skill and livelihood depended on the use of his hands, who was rhapsodically extolling the joys of the game while emphasizing repeatedly that rugby was not *necessarily* a violent sport. And at least for the first few days we all believed him, because practice at that point consisted mainly of calisthenics and conditioning exercises. The game involves a tremendous amount of running, and in order to play effectively, you have to be in good shape or else all you can do during a game is to desperately try to catch your breath. However, around the fourth day of practice, our surgeon-coach was preparing to demonstrate a particular drill wherein we were to run downfield at full speed, pounce on a loose ball, gain possession, and learn how to protect it. He carefully explained the proper technique, then sprinted about thirty yards, dived on the ball, and came up howling and holding instead a badly dislocated finger. And we hadn't even started to tackle yet.

That first year we were still located in Jersey City, where the basic science building was approximately fourteen stories high. Our still enthusiastic, though now somewhat chagrined, coach had a brainstorm, and he ordered all the team members to run up and down the stairways rather than use the elevators as a painless means to help facilitate conditioning. It made quite a comic scene after lunch, in the ninth-floor lecture room, to see ten or twelve heavily perspiring guys scattered about, desperately trying to take notes and catch their breath at the same time while struggling not to sweat all over their notebooks.

The majority of the games were played against other medical school teams, with the remainder of the opponents being various colleges and athletic clubs in the metropolitan area. Our first season was anything but a success, as we were heavily penalized for our lack of experience and ignorance of the often complicated rules. We counted more broken bones than victories in our first eight games, and we quickly came to see that a dislocated finger was a minor nuisance compared with broken ankles, broken legs, busted noses, and the all-too-frequent crippling knee injuries, which unfortunately were to follow over the course of the next several seasons. It seemed that at least once during a game, someone would have to be taken to the hospital in order to get a busted lip, chin, or other laceration sewn up.

Whenever an injury did occur, there was surely no dearth of readily available medical opinions. This was especially appreciated by the players on the nonmedical school teams that we played, who did not often have the dubious distinction of having the same guy whose elbow accidentally split his lip be the one to sew it up after the game. This actually happened on more than one occasion, and it was also not uncommon, just before game time, to see one or more players, still garbed in their surgical greens, rush straight over to the park from the hospital, where we would then huddle around them so they could change into their rugby uniforms (some uniforms—cleats, shorts, and a shirt). They would then go out and bang heads for an hour and a half, maybe have time for a quick beer, and rush back to relieve the guys covering for them in the emergency room. They would then proceed to start treating injured patients, one of whom might be a former opponent but who more likely would turn out to be some poor soul who unluckily happened to get bashed over the head in downtown Newark.

As we learned the game, and picked up some of the finer points, we became a team to be reckoned with—to the extent that one season we actually were undefeated. Part of our success had to do with the fact that several of the players had grown up in the Newark area and, as such, weren't averse to throwing a few fists when deemed necessary. (And sometimes when *not* so necessary. "Tell me, he didn't just really hit the referee?" "Oh yes he did.") One of my classmates wore a big American flag sewn on the back of his rugby shirt, and "Captain America," as he came to be known, was a vital part of this police force. And through all this the poor wives and girl friends could only sit huddled together on the sidelines, wondering if and when we would ever outgrow these kid games and hoping that some part of a husband's or boyfriend's anatomy was not going to be permanently rearranged.

It always seemed paradoxical to me that so-called healers and men of science, supposedly dedicated to the well-being of their fellow men, should take such pleasure and enjoyment each week in going out and knocking themselves and others senseless. However, it really proved to be an excellent way to blow off steam. Not only that but it also served as a discipline to force us to stay in good physical condition, and there was also a great deal of cameraderie that I know I would have missed had I not participated.

In actuality, we found that we would work off some of the pressures that built up during the week at the hospital and in the classroom. It was like a throwback to high school and college days, when winning the big game was so important. Rugby supposedly evolved as a gentlemen's sport, and strong vestiges of this remain, such as in the respect expected to be shown the referee, who is always addressed as "sir," and even in the traditional rugby shirt, which still retains its starched white collar and usually gets quite filthy during the course of the game. Therefore, no matter how violent and frenzied the contest, the winning team will always clap or applaud their opponents as they leave the playing field. Then both teams immediately retire to the nearest pub, where the spirit of competition generally continues on a more social level in the form of drinking bouts and singing contests—end results, not unpredictably, being some very drunk people singing some very ribald and lascivious songs.

Our team's clubhouse was the back room of a bar in downtown Newark that was located fairly close to the hospital. The drinking games would soon begin, some beer would inevitably get thrown around, and the singing (or some reasonable facsimile) soon followed.

Needless to say, I wasn't always in the greatest condition when I managed to return to the hospital after a game, but at least I was still in one piece, albeit bruised and battered. I was usually smart enough to drink only just enough beer so I couldn't feel the aches and pains (but oh wait until the next morning), and only a couple of hours after being hit, tackled, and mauled, I was once again wiping away a meconium surprise in the warmth of the newborn nursery.

CHAPTER / 19

SOME OF the greatest moments of joy and exhilaration I would experience as a medical student occurred during my eight-week rotation on the general pediatrics ward. I don't think any feelings could surpass the ones I had when I was part of a team that helped save the life of a tiny, helpless infant. It was the highest of highs to be able to share with a mother those moments when she knew that her baby was going to survive, when she knew that her child had passed the crisis and would live. It is undoubtedly one of the most satisfying times in all of medicine when you feel that you've saved a life, but the feelings are so much more intensified when it is a young child's life.

But to be involved and helplessly watch as a child dies is one of the most upsetting and frustrating experiences imaginable. And in those brief eight weeks on the wards five youngsters being cared for by my team expired, with the youngest being only six weeks old and the oldest a child of twelve. My reactions to each death were as different as each child and set of circumstances was different, but needless to say, each affected me profoundly.

The six-week-old infant became my patient when she was just two weeks of age, after she had been transferred from another hospital for a work-up and evaluation of a feeding problem and a persistent, unexplained fever. I expended a great deal of time and energy, along with my resident and attending, in an attempt to formulate a diagnosis and a cure, but we were totally frustrated. After an exhaustive set of tests we could still only classify her condition as a fever of unknown origin. Her parents lived more than an hour's drive from the hospital, and for a number of complex reasons, they could not bear to see the child and visited the hospital very sporadically. However, they were very concerned and upset, and I spoke to the mother on the phone every day. I soon began to dread these daily calls because there was very little new information I could give her, and as time progressed, it became more and more difficult to sound comforting or reassuring.

As a consequence of her intolerance to normal feeding, it became necessary to feed the infant by means of a feeding tube, which was passed through her nose, down her esophagus, and into her stomach. Naturally, this was quite distressing to the child (and to the parents as well, which was a significant factor in their being unable to visit her). Despite our best efforts, she would fairly regularly dislodge the tube, and I would be the one most often called to reinsert it. It really upset me when I got to the point where I had no other recourse than to wrap her tiny arms securely with gauze and pin them to the mattress so she couldn't pull on the tube. I also spent a great deal of time and energy making sure that the child was fed slowly and properly, which involved actually feeding her myself at the times when the nurses were overwhelmed, and this entailed "squirting" the special formula through the tube by means of a large syringe.

Although a six-week-old infant does not have a true personality as such, as a consequence of the countless hours spent at her bassinet, I was soon able to acutely discern when the child was comfortable and when she was irritable and in distress. She responded to me and my touch, and I in turn responded to her. All in all, I had contact with her for less than thirty days, yet despite her age and the relatively short amount of time involved, I felt almost as emotionally involved as her parents. Yet, when she did ultimately expire, I nevertheless felt that somehow her death was easier to handle than if she had been older.

It was, then, a great deal more difficult to deal with the death of a twelve-year-old black boy, especially since I had known him slightly even before he actually became my patient on pediatrics. I had previously met Melvin, and become somewhat familiar with his situation, while I had been on the urology service several months before as part of my surgical subspecialty rotation. As I learned at that time, it seems that the youngster had initially had problems when he was about two years old due to a congenital malformation of his urethra. Due to the presence of so-called valves, which should not normally have been there, the urine had backed up all the way to his kidneys, and before the condition was properly diagnosed and surgically treated, it was already too late. The kidneys themselves had been insidiously and irreversibly damaged.

This all meant that by the time I met Melvin, his kidney function had deteriorated to such an extent that he was in a condition known as chronic renal failure. His damaged kidneys could no longer maintain the proper chemistry of the body fluids under the conditions of normal living. Not only were there biochemical disturbances resulting directly from the impaired kidney function but there were also significant secondary changes resulting from the body's attempts to compensate for these primary disturbances. Consequently, there were disruptions in the functioning of other organs and tissues remote from the kidneys, and the complications were therefore varied and widespread.

Yet, surprisingly, despite repeated and often prolonged hospitalizations over the previous ten-year period, Melvin was in his proper grade level in school and was obviously quite an intelligent youngster. He was so bright, in fact, that I found I really had to watch my step when I was around him because Melvin took great delight in putting me on and teasing me, especially in front of other people.

One afternoon I spent four hours at Melvin's bedside, performing an exchange transfusion. Another consequence of chronic renal failure is anemia, where due to both a decreased production and an increased destruction, there are too few red blood cells. It then becomes necessary to make up the deficit periodically, but due to the damaged kidneys, there is also a fluid imbalance. The patient thus has a tendency to retain too much fluid, and the heart must naturally work harder to push all that liquid around. For these reasons you don't want to overload the body with fluid, and the only alternative in a case like this, where the patient urgently needs blood, is to perform a modified "exchange" transfusion. This is where an equal amount of the patient's cell-poor blood is exchanged for an equivalent amount of fresh blood *cells,* which the patient so desperately needs, while leaving out the serum, or fluid part, of the blood, which he not only doesn't need but which may actually do him harm.

The so-called packed cells that are given are prepared in the laboratory, where the donor blood is spun down in a centrifuge and the liquid, or serum, part is skimmed off, leaving only the solid-formed elements, the blood cells. The procedure is analogous to that performed on an infant suffering from hemolytic disease of the newborn, and it is a tedious, time-consuming process because you must carefully withdraw a measured amount of the patient's blood, wait a specified period of time, and then inject an equal volume of the packed cells.

During those hours Melvin and I talked about everything and anything. He was fascinated by automobiles and wanted to know what kind of car I drove, what model I would choose if I had my pick, and related his own dreams and desires. We spoke about our families, and even exchanged hospital gossip.

At one point my attending, who was a pediatric kidney specialist and who had known Melvin for several years, came by to see how things were progressing. At the time my resident, who was sort of keeping an eye on things, was off doing other chores. Melvin grew very quiet as my attending watched me withdraw ten cc of blood from one arm, wait several moments, and then inject ten cc of cells into Melvin's other arm. The needles were kept in place in the veins, and attached to appropriate tubing, so at least Melvin didn't have to be stuck each time. But occasionally, the needles would become dislodged or clotted, and the overall procedure was rather uncomfortable and did involve some degree of pain. I should have suspected that Melvin was up to something because I had never seen him so quiet for such an extended length of time, and sure enough, just as the attending was saying goodbye and starting to leave, Melvin finally spoke up. "Hey," he said, "don't you think I've been in the place enough times to rate a real doctor doing this and not some student?" The attending, even though he knew both Melvin and his antics quite well, nevertheless gave a somewhat quizzical laugh, looked at me for a moment, and walked away.

The second he was out of the room, Melvin started to laugh uproariously, and I asked him what was so funny because I knew that he was well aware of the fact that the attending graded me and made recommendations based on my performance. Melvin quickly grew quiet, took my hand, and gently stroked it, and said, "Aw, come on, don't sweat. He knows when I'm just kidding around."

Melvin would often hold on to my hands and arms and stroke them, and I noticed how much he liked to touch and fondle many of the staff, both male and female. Melvin's own skin was extremely dry because of the loss of protein through his damaged kidneys and his generally disarranged body fluid composition. As a further consequence of his situation, he also suffered from intense itching. I'm sure this all played a part in his actions, but I noticed that there was a great desire, or perhaps it was more of a need, to touch, to cling, and to be held among many of the other children on the ward, and not only those suffering from renal failure or other conditions similar to Melvin's. I think this might partly have been a consequence of the largeness and diffuseness of the average family in the inner city, where there are usually so many siblings—and only the mother present most of the time—that there can be only just so much fondling and caressing to go around. It therefore appeared that the children almost had to reach out and hold on to someone responsible out of fear that the person might desert them.

Because of the tendency in children with chronic renal failure to retain fluids, they often get a very distorted body picture, with a pendulous, bloated abdomen and skinny, narrow limbs. They are also generally stunted in height, which might be an attempt by the body to prolong life because it gives the already stressed kidneys less "body" to have to care for. As a result of all this, Melvin was very self-conscious about his appearance, and it was very upsetting to see this small youngster looking, for all practical purposes, like some wizened old man gone to pot.

I remember how excited Melvin was on the Wednesday before Thanksgiving because his mother was picking him up after work to take him home so that he could spend the holiday with his family. He described to me what he was going to eat (although he was on a somewhat restricted diet, it was not so severe that he couldn't indulge in a regular meal on occasion), and he had a big orange and black crepe paper turkey fastened over his bed, which had instigated him to refer to me as a "big turkey" for the previous few days. As a matter of fact, that was the last thing I remember Melvin saying to me as I left the hospital that day. "Good-bye, you big turkey. Have a good time."

As a student, I was off for the Thanksgiving holiday, and I was not there when Melvin was forced to return to the hospital the following day because of increasing drowsiness. When I came in early on Monday morning, expecting to hear a detailed report of his holiday, I was told instead that Melvin had died on Saturday. Somehow, I had to know exactly what had happened, and I quickly sought out and questioned the resident whose team had been on duty over the weekend. It seems that Melvin had become progressively more and more drowsy on Thursday and Friday, and had slept a great deal of the time, and when he was able to be aroused, he was quite irritable. Initially, he had suffered muscle twitching and, finally, convulsions, and even though I was told he had been totally out of touch with his surroundings for his last twenty-four hours, I still felt I had somehow betrayed him by not being present. Yet I also knew I had extremely mixed emotions. In addition to the grief and guilt I had a feeling of relief in not having had to confront the reality of the actual event and of being able to remember "So long, you big turkey" and not the agonizing picture of a dead child.

I was informed by my attending that the results of the autopsy were to be presented in the morgue, and as the student on the team, I knew I was expected to go down and present the case history, as was the usual procedure. I was kind of numb, but somehow managed to follow my team downstairs and recite the clinical history, with which almost everyone was already familiar because of the long nature of the illness. However, when the pathologist took a big knife and started slicing through the organs, laid out before him like so much meat, and began to describe the findings in the brusque, impersonal way in which an autopsy is, by necessity, presented, I found myself unable to take it any longer, and I quickly ran from the morgue. It was just too painful to realize that this was not merely some isolated liver or kidney that the pathologist took from a jar for demonstration purposes but that they were Melvin's kidney and liver. As I ran out into the hallway, I was finally alone, and I let out the great sobs and tears I had been holding in since 8 A.M.

For the next several days I could not even enter the room where Melvin had been because I couldn't bear to see the empty bed. To further compound the situation there was also another youngster in the hospital at the same time who was about the same age as Melvin and also suffering from a form of renal disease. He had known Melvin for several years because they attended the renal clinic together. The youngster became so agitated and upset at Melvin's death that he had to be sent home because he was so unmanageable. As for me, it helped somewhat to know that I was expected to carry on with my duties and studies, and I had other patients who were getting better and going home to their families. Even after a week or two, when the memories were not quite so raw, there were still difficult periods because Melvin's case kept being regularly discussed and dissected at numerous subsequent conferences. I would be the one who had to make the opening presentation each time. All in all, as upsetting and unsettling as the experience was at the time, I can now look back and realize not only what an important part it actually played in my education and personal growth but also how fortunate I was to have known Melvin for even as short a time as I did.

CHAPTER / 20

THE PEDIATRIC house staff was extremely capable and enthusiastic. Of all the different services I worked with in the hospital, it seemed to be the one where almost every individual appeared truly and deeply concerned about the individual patient, his problems, and the quality of care received. There was a higher percentage of women on the staff than in any other department, and the majority were foreign. Only about one half of the male staff members were foreign born and trained. The department had strong, firm leadership, with duties, practices, and performance levels expected of the staff very well delinated. There was an overall sense of genuine camaraderie and shared concern, and this was constantly reinforced in the frequent coffee klatches.

When an infant or small youngster needed blood on an emergency basis, the residents would donate the required amount themselves, with the family of the patient frequently being totally unaware of the contribution. This usually happened either when the lab did not have the exact blood type required or when it would have been necessary to release a whole unit, which would have meant that a portion would have gone unused and might thus have been wasted.

As I've already said, a great deal of skill and patience are required for the proper examination of an infant or a small child. Many of the residents developed their own little tricks and stratagems in an attempt to make the task as painless as possible for both the patient and the doctor. However, as enviable a goal as this may seem, it can sometimes backfire. For example, one resident gave each youngster a syringe with the safety top on to hold during the examination, explaining to the child that since he was holding the needle, the doctor or nurse couldn't sneak up and give him a shot. This worked out fairly well for several weeks, until one day when the resident was in the process of examining a rather precocious five-year-old boy. He went through his preliminary explanation and handed the child the syringe, and everything went smoothly until the resident turned to get an instrument off the nearby examining table. At that moment the youngster must have decided it was now his turn to play doctor, and he proceeded to take the safety top off and plunge the syringe squarely into the resident's backside right up to the hilt. Needless to say, the resident quickly abandoned the strategy.

Several weeks into the rotation I admitted a two-year-old black girl for a work-up and treatment of suspected pneumonia. When I sat down with the mother for my initial interview and inquired as to the child's full name, she replied, "Femalee Tanya Jones." I did not give it much thought at that moment and merely assumed that the woman had married someone with an Hispanic background, which was a fairly common practice in the community. When her husband subsequently joined us, however, he turned out to be a black man who spoke with no trace of an accent and gave no other indication that he was Spanish or Puerto Rican. I had heard the name Femalee before around the hospital, and my curiosity was definitely aroused, so I casually asked the mother if this was a common name for girls in this area. She responded that she knew of several other youngsters with the same name in her own housing development, although some spelled it differently. Neither she nor her husband had given the child that particular first name. The child, she said, had been named by the hospital when she was born, and it suddenly dawned on me what must have happened. As part of the standard procedure each newborn child is given a wristband that reads either "Male Jones" or "Female Jones." That is also how the child is listed on the chart. Obviously, the parents had never had much experience with hospital deliveries. When they saw "Female Jones" on the chart and the release forms they were required to sign, and then saw it repeated on the child's wristband, they must have simply assumed that it was the usual practice for the hospital to name each newborn child. Being too unsure to ask or question, they believed the child was henceforth and forevermore to be legally known as Femalee. They did go on to say that they almost always called her Tanya, which was the name they would have selected, but they truly thought it could only be used legally as the middle name.

The child, as it turned out, did not have pneumonia but a rather severe case of the croup, a viral infection that often resembles pneumonia, especially in her age bracket. Although it was moderately severe, the child had a fairly typical case, with the usual symptomatology of a great deal of difficulty in getting air in and out through her congested airways. The disease is most often viral in origin, and there is no medication available per se, such as an antibiotic, to eradicate the offending organism. The child was therefore placed in a croupette, similar in appearance to an oxygen tent, in which the oxygen the child inhales is mixed with a fine aerosol mist. The child is also forced to take fluids, either by mouth or intravenously, and may be given aspirin for fever. The disease generally runs its course in a matter of several days to a week if there are not added complications, and the child can then be discharged from the hospital.

Over the course of the next few days Femalee was not markedly improved, which was not cause for any great alarm on our part at that time, but the parents were getting quite impatient over her seeming lack of progress. The father kept demanding that the child be given penicillin. I carefully explained the disease and its accepted treatment and further pointed out that the indiscriminate use of antibiotics could possibly make things worse by allowing a superinfection to take place. Briefly, this can occur because the penicillin or other antibiotics kill certain bacteria that are normally present in the mouth, throat, and lungs and which don't ordinarily lead to infection. These so-called normal flora are quite important, however, because their presence usually does not permit a different, potentially more harmful, bug from invading the body and gaining a foothold. This becomes a distinct possibility if an antibiotic is used persistently when it is not indicated.

Femalee's father kept insisting that his daughter was not receiving the best medical care because she was not receiving any antibiotics. He said he had seen a television program where a doctor wouldn't give a child patient a certain medication. The child had survived only because Marcus Welby had stepped in and administered the particular drug in question. I again explained the situation as clearly and carefully as I could, but the father would not accept my explanation. On the fourth day of hospitalization he signed the child out of the hospital AMA (against medical advice), which was most certainly his right (this is done in such a manner that the doctor and the institution are protected from potential lawsuits), and had her transferred to another hospital "where she can get her penicillin and get better."

This was not an isolated example of this type of thinking, for there were many other instances when parents, as well as adult patients on other services, would demand a specific treatment similar to that received by characters on the various medically oriented TV shows. In addition, many of the patients, especially the women, would read something in a popular magazine, and inspired by a headline or a cursory reading of an article, they would make specific demands on their doctors regarding treatment.

I would like to emphasize that I am not talking here about folk remedies or cultural traditions; I stopped scoffing at these when I once treated an adult patient who had a severe case of hiccups that we were unable to break for over a week, no matter what we tried. The poor man would probably still be hiccuping away today if I hadn't listened to a nurse's aide, who suggested giving the patient a tablespoon of nongranulated sugar, which stopped the hiccups almost immediately. It turned out to be a remedy that her grandmother used fifty years ago in the South, and it obviously worked.

What I am referring to are the wild, basically unsubstantiated claims that abound in the popular literature, such as the new cures for cancer or even for the common cold. These magazine articles instigate the public to make unreasonable demands on their doctors and actually attempt to dictate their own treatment. I don't mean to imply that the patient should not be as well informed as possible, but the danger in most cases is that the patient, or reader, all too often receives a distorted, one-sided

150

picture from a lay magazine writer who is out to make a point, often as spectacularly as possible, and who is not bound by the caution and restraint the medical profession must exercise.

The whole question of doctor shows and their glamourization of the medical profession has fairly widespread repercussions in the real day-today practice of medicine. The father of my young croup patient was incredibly indignant one evening when he came to visit his daughter and found that I was not at the hospital. Even a subsequent explanation that I was not scheduled to be on duty that night and the reassurance that other doctors had been present did not stop him from actually threatening to report my absence to the head of the department. I'm sure that good old Marcus Welby would probably have stayed up every night with the child until she was out of the hospital, but the general public does not want to accept the fact that the vast majority of practicing physicians are simply not the supermen they see portrayed on TV. Of course it would be best for the patient if his doctor could spend most of his time tending to his individual physical and emotional needs, but that is impossible both from the practical viewpoint of economics and the fact that each doctor has his own family and emotional needs to consider.

It would be unfair not to note that it is also quite true that often it is the doctor who helps contribute to fostering these unrealistic expectations by falling prey to the illusion that he is more than just a human being and is truly the healer who is going to perform the miracles and make everything better. This attitude on the part of either the patient or the doctor often leads to ill feelings. It establishes unreachable standards and goals that cannot be achieved in the present structure of our society. When the public do not receive the type of service and miraculous results to which they feel they are entitled, they then feel that they are being cheated. Doctors are merely ripoffs, who aren't interested in the patient except as a dollar sign.

As early as my first year of medical school I began to realize what the concept of a doctor means to the general public. It didn't seem to matter one bit to most people that I was only a first- or second-year student. The fact that I was going to be a doctor was enough for them. At first, it was flattering when someone would ask me for medical advice, but more often than not I had no more idea at that point what was going on than did the other person. Even though I carefully explained to these people that I hadn't even been on the wards yet and had had no practical experience, this usually did not deter them from continuing with question after question. They seemed to have an insatiable need for an opinion or advice and for someone, almost anyone, to tell them what to do. I'm sure that this also is strongly related to the fact that they thought they were getting something for nothing. To show how truly absurd the situation can get, I once told a woman in California who kept badgering me about her arthritis that there was a new treatment for the disease. It involved the taking of two aspirins at the exact moment the patient was jumping off a bridge into a calm body of water. The woman stood there and didn't bat an eye. She asked me in all earnestness what would happen if the person couldn't swim.

Yet despite all of this, it is ironic how many doctors and medical students continue to watch the medical programs. It is quite common to hear conversations such as, "Well, I got the diagnosis by the first commercial," or "It took me a half an hour because I got thrown off by the rash!" On the one hand, there is a spirit of competition to see who can get the correct diagnosis first, while on the other, there is a fair amount of ridicule of the dramatic license taken and the impracticality of a doctor spending so much time with a patient. Nevertheless, many doctors and medical students continue to watch such programs as regularly as their schedule will allow.

CHAPTER / 21

AT ANY given time there might be one or two children on the floor who were admitted because they were either neglected or abandoned or else were suspected battered children. On Thursdays or Fridays, and especially before a holiday period, there would invariably be several youngsters brought in by the police, who had found them either totally abandoned or with no one who would admit responsibility for them. The city did not have adequate facilities for the very young infants to be cared for properly, and it generally took several days and much aggravation and paper work to get the older children accepted at the city shelter. Even if there was nothing obviously wrong, the children still routinely got full physical examinations and minimal base-line lab studies, which necessitated a full write-up. These admissions generally stayed in the hospital over the weekend at least, and then, most were somehow miraculously found by their parents as soon as the weekend or holiday period was over. Many didn't even bother to come up with a plausible explanation, but simply came and claimed the child as if he were some sort of lost wallet or key case.

The situations involving suspected battered children are even more disturbing and complex. Unfortunately, they are far from rare in an inner-city hospital. I would like to point out, however, that they are also found in other communities as well; child abuse is definitely not just a disease of the poor and ignorant, as some would have it. Bruises, broken bones, cigarette burns, hot water immersion ("You do what Mommy says, or I'll dunk you in the scalding tub again!"), chainings, isolation, beatings, even death, are not uncommon. Most tragically, they are inflicted on children by the adults, who are actually the sick ones.

I have seen a six-week-old baby girl brought in with a broken arm and two broken legs, and I have also seen a severely beaten five-year-old who was so obviously terrified of saying anything that might anger his father, or might get him into any sort of trouble, that he chose to remain completely mute rather than say what really happened.

In these instances the children were not allowed to return to the same environment, but incredible as it may seem, there was a time in the not-so-distant past when those children might easily have been allowed to return to the same home. This was partly a consequence of a still-prevalent attitude, which holds that children are basically property and the parents thus have almost an inalienable right to do with their children whatever they please. Furthermore, not too long ago, in the state of New Jersey, a doctor could be sued by the child's parents for filing a suspected battered child report. Yet despite those constrictions, many doctors still stuck their necks out and risked the consequences of a long drawn-out court battle, with all its unpleasant implications. But all too often, the horse was already out of the barn, and the damage, perhaps permanent, had already been done to the child.

That particular aspect of the law has subsequently been changed so that the doctor need now only testify as to the physical findings—and cannot be held libelous—and the judiciary and social work and law enforcement agencies are beginning to take on a much greater active role. It is still the frontline doctor who most often must make that initial decision, which can then have such a profound effect on both the parents and the child.

For the doctor and society in general, in those clear-cut cases where there is not any reasonable doubt that the child has been beaten or abused, satisfactory legal avenues are generally available. The state can quickly intervene for the sake of the child's safety. The great danger, however, lies in that large gray area where the facts are not so obvious, and the consideration of the parents' rights must be taken into account. For example (and this is hardly hypothetical), a child might be brought into the hospital for a legitimate medical complaint, and both parents (or perhaps just one) will obviously be drunk, and the child will be dirty, disheveled, and apparently not well cared after. Does this then classify them as unfit parents who deserve to have their children taken away from them? If so, why not the banker's wife who drinks like a fish but who can afford to have servants to keep the children clean?

On a personal level I tried to approach each situation with an open mind and take advantage of the services and agencies that were available. If I suspected anything out of the ordinary, I would immediately notify one of the social workers assigned to the ward. (The social workers deserve enormous credit for the fantastic job they do on many, many levels, especially in light of the limited resources available.) They would then set the wheels in progress so that the judiciary and social services could determine, after a thorough investigation, whether the child was actually abused or not and what course the community should take. I'm sure that nothing was done in many instances, and in most of the situations probably no action should have been taken, but I felt that at least I was facing up to my responsibility.

I admitted one child who was suffering from a rather severe, generalized skin condition, which could have been kept under good control if the child had received conscientious home care. The youngster was a three-year-old boy who was the product of a union between a black woman and a Puerto Rican man, who had abandoned them both. The mother was a frequent patient on the psychiatric service, with a diagnosis of schizophrenia, but who was generally under fairly good control and could be maintained as an out-patient if she took her medication. Periodically, she would have psychotic episodes and wouldn't, or perhaps more fairly couldn't, medicate herself. During those periods the child's skin problem was left untreated, and as a consequence of this neglect, it would become so exacerbated and flare up to such an extent that the child would require hospitalization. The mother would also require hospitalization, and this revolving door policy for both mother and child had been going on for almost two years at the time Ricki became my patient. Although he was three years of age, because of the skin rash on his legs and a general lack of sustained maternal stimulation, he could neither walk nor talk and was quite slow in responding to any outside stimulation.

The child made remarkable progress in the few weeks he was on the floor, learning to walk and open up and displaying a warm, affectionate nature. I spent quite a bit of my time paying attention to him and stimulating him with toys and play; a young student nurse assigned to Ricki deserves a great deal of credit, as well, for his remarkable progress.

I conferred with the psychiatrist treating the mother around the time she was scheduled to be discharged from the hospital. He told me it would be in the best interest of the mother to continue to have the child at home, but he thought her past history made it almost certain that if Ricki did remain in her care, he would invariably suffer greatly in his physical, mental, and emotional development.

It was thought by many familiar with the circumstances that a court battle to force the mother to surrender custody of the child would be quite destructive for the mother in her condition. It would, therefore, be in the best interest of everyone involved if she would voluntarily give up the child and, at the least, permit him to be placed in a foster home. I worked closely with the social worker, who knew the family well from previous contacts and in whom the mother had a great deal of trust. We finally convinced her, after much time and discussion, that it would be best for Ricki to be placed in a foster home, where he could get better care and treatment and where she would still have the right to see him.

During my stay on the general pediatrics floor I was struck by the relatively large number of accidental poisoning cases that I saw, and particularly by the fact that such a large number were the direct result of negligence and poor judgment on the part of parents, guardians, and older siblings. These incidents ranged from drinking lye, which occurred with a frightening frequency, to the ingestion of kerosene and aspirin. Lye ingestion is particularly grave, since even if one succeeds in getting the youngster through the initial crises, as a consequence of the caustic, acidlike property of the chemicals involved, the long-term prognosis is quite poor. One of the most pathetic accidental poison cases involved a two-and-a-half-year-old girl who was brought in unconscious and breathing at a rate of only six to eight times per minute. It seems that she had gone to the refrigerator and had drunk some orange juice that contained her father's weekend dose of methadone. Thankfully, the father realized what must have happened and rushed the child to the emergency room, where she was treated in time to save her life. But she was quite ill for several days and had to be subjected to a tracheotomy in order to pull through.

Similarly, I became aware at that time of the insidious, often-times lethal, disease of plumbism, or lead poisoning, which was rampant in Newark at that time, and which still accounts for a tremendous amount of morbidity and mortality in the general pediatric population. I saw a number of children in the emergency room or clinic each week who were otherwise healthy, but who exhibited such symptoms as vomiting, lethargy, hyperirritability, muscular incoordination, joint pains, convulsions (and even death) as a direct result of ingesting lead, most usually in the form of lead-based paints.

Thankfully (and not unexpectedly) the pediatrics department had an effective, fairly wide-reaching lead-screening program, and every child seen in the clinic or the hospital was routinely tested, even if there was no complaint or any other indication. This was done partly because of the wide variety of symptoms a child can manifest when suffering from plumbism. In addition to the blood and urine studies employed, X rays were also taken, as they can actually show the presence of lead that has already been deposited in the bone, and sometimes, you can literally see the actual chips of lead in the intestine itself.

Investigations have shown that in some instances, the paint peels off the walls and ceiling and drops right into the infant's crib. Often, the child is actually fed the paint chips by an older sibling, who simply doesn't know any better. In any case the condition is treatable, but there is always the possibility of perma-nent damage. The injections required for treatment are quite painful and require a three- to four-day stay in the hospital as well. Despite all the publicity and empty rhetoric, the problem is still severe and widespread in the impoverished inner cities. I lay much of the blame directly on the various city governments, which appear unable or unwilling to take any effective positive action against the landlords. I venture to say if thousands and thousands of affluent suburban youngsters were stricken with this almost totally preventable disease each year, the problem would have been eradicated or at least brought under control long ago.

CHAPTER / 22

THE PEDIATRICS floor was divided into an infectious and non-infectious side on the premise that this would lessen the risk of an infectious youngster spreading a contagious disease to the rest of the patients. This was especially true in the case of a child suffering from diarrhea resulting from an infection. It is quite easy for such an infection to spread with incredible speed and soon run rampant through the entire pediatric population. Therefore, all patients with diarrhea were kept in a special isolation room, even though many times the cause of the diarrhea would ultimately be found to be noninfectious (such as milk intolerance, allergy, or poor feeding technique by the mother), and in 50 percent of the cases, no specific cause could ever be determined. Since there was no way of determining initially who was infectious and who was not, semisterile procedure was always in effect in the diarrhea room, and children were handled only by gowned staff members who were required to wash their hands meticulously not only when entering and leaving but in between touching the individual children as well. Unfortunately, this rule was not strictly adhered to, and many recent studies have confirmed a fact that most nurses have known for a long time. The biggest offender for the intrahospital spread of infection is the doctor himself.

One of the greatest dangers in an infant with diarrhea is that of dehydration, and therefore, the body chemistry must be frequently monitored. Quite often, many of the youngsters must be placed on intravenous therapy to guarantee the proper fluid balance. These children are naturally watched very closely, but even

159

then, since many of the IV's are kept in place for several days, it is not uncommon for them to clot or become dislodged, and somehow it always seems to happen at 4 A.M. I am always struck by the irony that the most difficult patients to start and maintain IV's on are either the elderly and debilitated or the tiny infants, and some of the longest, most unpleasant times I recall on pediatrics were spent attempting to restart an IV at 4 A.M. on a tiny, irritable, restless infant in a room full of diarrhea.

At one point during my rotation in pediatrics I came down with a cold and a sore throat approximately two weeks after admitting a fourteen-year-old girl for a work-up of a persistent fever, skin rash, and sore throat. This was a fairly common occurrence among the students rotating through pediatrics. We were constantly being exposed, often for the first time, to a wide variety of infectious agents to which we never had had the opportunity to develop any resistance. Many students consequently spent a large portion of their pediatric rotation with a constant case of sniffles and a chronically running nose. However, there have been occasions where more serious infections have been acquired, so when this particular youngster was subsequently diagnosed as having a moderately severe case of mononucleosis, I began to read up on the disease with somewhat more than just academic curiosity. Certain thoughts entered my mind as I reviewed some of the major clinical manifestations: (a) malaise ("Well, I have been tired and fatigued a lot lately"); (b) sore throat ("definitely!") (c) fever ("None at the moment, but I don't generally run a high fever when I get sick"); (d) rash ("None apparent, but it probably is just late in developing") and so forth. I thoroughly convinced myself that I had a case of mononucleosis. Despite the fact that three separate doctors after reviewing three different blood tests all told me they felt I didn't have the disease, I still wasn't convinced—to the extent that I insisted that my girl friend, who is now my wife, go to her own private physician for a checkup, even though she insisted she felt perfectly well. Her lab report also proved to be negative, but it really wasn't until the patient was discharged from the hospital and my throat cleared up that I felt reassured.

This was not the first time something similar to this had occurred—many of my classmates had related almost identical experiences—so even though my girl friend and her doctor thought I was turning into a hypochondriac, I tried to deny it by claiming that it was an occupational hazard of being a medical student. I remember the phenomenon starting as early as my sophomore pathology course, when all I would have to do would be to read about a certain disease and its clinical manifestations, and then, almost on an unconscious level, I would filter through the listed symptoms and determine if I met enough of the criteria to consider myself afflicted. Naturally, the situation was exacerbated when I got on the wards and began to have actual patient contact. Throughout the rather short course of my medical career to date, I have variously been convinced that I have somehow contracted tuberculosis, mononucleosis, hepatitis, diabetes (not an infectious disease, but I rationalized that my case had just been of the latent variety and had not been previously detected), and even cancer.

It got to the point where my poor girl friend would simply walk into her doctor's office, and he would say immediately, "Okay, what does he think he's got now?" I anticipated that the situation would get even worse when I got to the psychiatry service. For at least in the realm of physical medicine there are concrete parameters, such as lab tests, X rays, and physical findings, which can prove conclusive and rule out the presence of an organic disease. If you think you may be just a wee bit crazy however, it becomes somewhat more difficult to convince yourself that you are not. Just to set the record straight in this regard, I can report that I was stable and secure enough not to think I was schizophrenic, but I will admit that I did agonize a bit at times over a suspected neurosis or two.

As it turned out, I really didn't have mononucleosis, and I was particularly happy that it proved to be only an ordinary, run-of-the-mill upper respiratory infection because I had just recently been informed by my agent that another of the cigar commercials was scheduled to be filmed. The advertising agency was well aware of my extremely limited availability, and the kicker turned out to be that this particular commercial was to be filmed in Tijuana, Mexico. I had informed the agency the date of the weekend I was not scheduled to be on duty, and arrangements were then concluded, wherein the remainder of the cast and crew were to fly down and film during the week and I would join them over the weekend.

That particular Friday turned out to be typically hectic, but fortunately, I only had some minor sniffling lingering on. I was able to complete my tasks so that I could leave the hospital a little earlier than usual. I had my suitcase packed and in the trunk of the car, which included my extensive wardrobe for these particular commercials—sneakers, a pair of shorts, and an Ohio State sweatshirt. I drove directly from the hospital to Newark Airport. After a Superman-style quick change from my hospital whites, I hopped a helicopter and arrived at Kennedy Airport just in time to make the last available evening flight to San Diego.

As I sat there in the first-class section sipping champagne, I realized the futility of trying to read any pediatrics, as I had planned. I just relaxed, got pleasantly intoxicated, and enjoyed the pampering of the stewardess. There were going to be no meconium surprises or urine between the eyes for me this weekend.

When I landed in San Diego, I found out that there had been some sort of foul-up and that my luggage was probably still on the helicopter somewhere between Newark and Kennedy airports. The earliest I could hope for its arrival was the next day around noon. I called the motel in Tijuana where everyone was staying, and they told me to get a room near the airport, wait for the luggage (and that all-important Ohio State sweatshirt), and meet them as quickly as I could. They still had some other scenes left to shoot. So I spent a lousy night by myself walking the streets of scenic downtown San Diego, where I almost got a ticket for jaywalking, and wound up being propositioned four separate times. Two of them turned out to be sailors. Needless to say I was quite happy when my luggage finally arrived the next day, and I rented a car and drove to the motel, which turned out not to be in the most luxurious section of Tijuana. I was later told this was done by design so that the camera could capture more local flavor. As I drove carefully through the dirty streets, concentrating on avoiding the omnipresent packs of dogs, roosters, chickens, and little children, I was amazed by how much the town reminded me of Newark—the major differences being the unpaved streets and the highly visible livestock on the loose.

The director of the commercial had a thing about wanting to shoot my jogging sequence at dawn in order to achieve a certain lighting effect, so I actually didn't film until sunrise on Sunday morning. I proceeded to get up with the roosters, and spent a grand total of twenty minutes in some nearby rolling Mexican hills, darting out from behind some palm trees in the middle of nowhere, punching our cigar-smoking hero on the arm, and then jogging off again in the early morning mist, leaving him, and I'm sure many subsequent viewers, with a look of shocked surprise. ("Where the hell did *he* come from?")

Several miscellaneous scenes were shot, including an encounter with a bona fide cape-carrying matador at the local bullring, before we could return to San Diego in the late afternoon. The only available flight back to New York that evening, which I took, involved switching planes in Chicago. As it turned out I was in my apartment by 2 A.M. Returning to the hospital at 7:30 that same morning, I had to keep reminding myself that I had truly left the pediatrics ward only sixty hours before. I was really there in Newark, in the pediatric treatment room of Martland Hospital, preparing two injections of cryoprecipitate that I would soon administer to two hemophilic brothers, who desperately needed the clotting factor their own bodies were unable to manufacture. Talk about getting away for the weekend!

One of the youngsters was seven years old, the other nine. Actually they were half-brothers. When the first son had been born and was subsequently found to be a hemophiliac, the mother had refused to accept the fact that it was she who carried the gene that determined that her male offspring would have the dread bleeding disease. She proceeded to divorce her first husband, to whom she had shifted the blame, remarried, and bore another son. When he, too, was found to have the disease, the mother was finally convinced, and subsequently underwent voluntary sterilization. The two brothers were constantly in and out of the hospital, and the oldest had a permanently deformed ankle as a result of frequent injuries that had resulted in bleeding in the ankle joint. They were both hyperactive youngsters, who were always running about, crashing into things, and fighting and wrestling, and then had to pay the consequences by having to be hospitalized for several days in order to receive the clotting factor they needed, as even the smallest injury carried the potential to become life threatening if their blood would not clot.

There were other hemophiliac children who were also treated at my hospital on a fairly regular basis, and it appeared that they, too, were often hyperactive on the ward, running up and down the hallway and throwing toys and objects around. As I observed the behavior of the parents toward these youngsters during visiting hours, it became much more understandable why these children so often acted the way they did. From only the brief interactions that transpired, it was clearly obvious that at home, and probably in school as well, these youngsters were forced to lead a sedate, very unspontaneous type of life-style, which must have been extremely difficult and frustrating for a growing, otherwise normal youngster. Regardless of the understanding of the reasons behind it, their presence on the floor invariably seemed to lead to even more confusion and chaos than was normally present. Yet somehow, the turmoil seemed quite appropriate after my whirlwind weekend, and I suspect that if it had been lacking, it just wouldn't have seemed like the Martland I knew.

CHAPTER / 23

ONE EVENING about 11 P.M. we were in the process of checking on the more seriously ill patients on the wards when suddenly a nurse burst in and shouted that a youngster in the next room had suddenly stopped breathing just as she was about to take her temperature. We all rushed to her bedside, and although she was not one of our team's patients, it was obvious from her physical appearance that she was a mongoloid child and had most probably suffered a cardiac arrest. This is not at all uncommon in youngsters afflicted with Down's syndrome, the current medical terminology for this condition, which occurs as a tragic consequence of a genetic abnormality. Unfortunately, its victims are far more likely to have also inherited other genetically determined defects and deficits, such as a damaged heart, than would a normal child without any chromosomal abnormalities. My friend Paul immediately pinched off her nostrils and began to administer mouth-to-mouth resuscitation while I applied external cardiac massage. It took several minutes before the cardiopulmonary resuscitation cart could be wheeled over, and Paul and I switched places until an ambu-bag could be located.

An ambu-bag is a football-like device with a mouthpiece attachment which can be fitted over the patient's nose and mouth and can then be alternately squeezed and relaxed, thereby forcing freshly oxygenated air into the lungs. A surgeon was quickly summoned to perform a bedside tracheotomy, but after half an hour all attempts at resuscitation failed, and the child was pronounced dead.

Over the next several days a great many comments were made regarding the fact that Paul and I had risked exposure to any possible communicable disease the child may have been harboring. I was somewhat surprised to learn that most of the house staff, and many of my fellow students, would have waited for the ambu-bag to arrive and would not have placed their own mouth on the youngster's, even though it might have proved to have been a life-saving maneuver.

The incident stimulated a great deal of general discussion, which became even more intensified soon after when all the students on pediatrics spent an afternoon at an institution for the severely mentally and physically handicapped in central New Jersey. The overwhelming majority of the youngsters were so severely handicapped that they would require institutionalization for their entire lives, and most of them had quite a short life expectancy due to their general condition. A large proportion of the children would not even have been alive as little as twenty or twenty-five years ago, and many laymen would look upon this, as did several of my fellow students, as something of a mixed blessing. For even though the staff of the institution appeared extremely well motivated and genuinely concerned for the well-being of the children, many of the children were in such poor condition that the most the staff could do for them was to try to keep them from doing any further harm to themselves or to others.

The visit to the institution was an extremely unsettling and moving experience. Feelings of resentment were expressed over the high price to the taxpayer for "the nothing more than custodial care" that was being given to the large number of youngsters, the vast majority of whom would either be dead in a relatively short period of time or else had absolutely no hope of ever leading meaningful lives. One classmate, who had a younger brother who was moderately retarded and in an institution, strongly felt that both he, and especially his parents, would have lost a great deal if the child was not alive and well cared for. But he also said that his brother was able to relate to him and his parents at certain times, which was a lot more than could ever be expected from most of the severely handicapped youngsters we observed.

One student posed a hypothetical situation and asked what each of us would do if we were obstetricians and delivered a grossly deformed baby. Would we take any action at all to resuscitate the child if he was stillborn, or keep him alive, if possible, by heroic measures, or would we simply permit him to die naturally without any positive intervention, or perhaps even go so far as to take steps to *ensure* that he would not survive? These extremely provocative and difficult questions naturally evoked a spirited debate among us, which quite logically expanded to include the broader topic of the medical aspects of mercy killing, or euthanasia (from Greek *eu,* meaning well, plus *thanatos,* meaning death). The majority of students, myself included, expressed the feeling that they probably would not go beyond any heroic measures in an attempt to keep the infant alive (so-called negative euthanasia) but would also not take any direct action to hasten or ensure the infant's death (so-called positive euthanasia).

Even more significant about what came out of the discussion was a rather strong, shared feeling of resentment that it was the doctor alone who was the one forced to make this split-second decision and that, almost regardless of whatever course of action was taken or not taken, such a decision involved a great moral dilemma that went beyond the deeply personal consequences that must be confronted by individual soul searching. It also included substantial risk on the broader level of society and its laws. If there was anything resembling a consensus, it was that such decisions should never be solely in the province of the physician but should include representatives of the legal system, the clergy perhaps, and, most important, the parents or the individual himself, if at all appropriate. The hope was expressed that society would ultimately face up to its responsibility and as satisfactory an agreement as possible under the complex circumstances would be worked out.

That time is unfortunately not yet with us even today, and there is a strong possibility that this may prove to be such an emotionally charged area that it can never be concluded to everyone's satisfaction (very much like the issue of abortion); consequently, I'm quite sure the discussions and individual soul searching continue unabated on the student level. I feel secure about making such a statement because even after experiencing all that I subsequently have in the course of my training, including, as you shall see, being placed in certain analogous situations as an intern, I still find myself extremely ambivalent about many aspects and ramifications of this terribly complex and sensitive area.

CHAPTER / 24

THAT THIRD year of medical school was undoubtedly the most stimulating, challenging, stressful, and frustrating of experiences. Yet all in all, it was one of the most productive and personally gratifying periods in my life. The time seemed to fly by. The scheduling was such that I had six weeks off before the beginning of my fourth year, and I really felt the need for a change of environment. Southern California again beckoned invitingly.

Despite the one or two commercials I had been able to squeeze in during the year, I still had college loan payments to meet, and there would be tuition and expenses to cover for the upcoming year, so there was a definite need to earn additional money during my vacation. I explained the situation to my agent. I told him I would be willing to gamble on finding some work on the Coast but that I couldn't shell out any money for the plane fare. He not only found a way to get me free transportation but also to earn some money on the way out. He accomplished this by booking me on a syndicated cable TV cooking show, which originated from Cincinnati, and which paid the guest's plane fare from New York to Cincinnati, and then on to California, as an incentive for getting the guests to go to Cincinnati in the first place.

The title of the show was *Parsley, Sage, Janie and Love,* and it was a half-hour program where the hostess chatted with each guest for fifteen minutes in a little breakfast nook. Then, the remainder of the program was spent with the guest preparing his or her favorite dish in the kitchen. I spoke with the producer by phone regarding my culinary expertise, and he seemed quite upset when I told him that I made a pretty good cream cheese omelette.

It seems that a great many of the guests who came on the show attempted to prepare egg dishes, and they usually turned out to be a disaster, so he asked me to come up with something else and to call him back with a list of whatever ingredients I would need. I proceeded to whip through my mother's trusty *New York Times Cookbook* and somehow came up with gazpacho—Spanish raw vegetable soup—which not only sounded exotic as hell but looked like a snap to prepare, since it only seemed to require the ability to throw some vegetables into a blender.

Arrangements were completed, and I flew to the Cincinnati airport early one morning, where I was met and taken directly to the studio. I was dressed in jeans and a workshirt, expecting to change my clothing when I arrived, but instead I was rushed immediately into makeup, introduced to the hostess (the Janie of the show's title), and soon found myself seated in a corner of the studio at a kitchen table, all of which combined to look so vaguely familiar that I half-expected Robert Young to come strolling in and tell me why father knows best.

The producer had explained previously that the chatter was to be light and informal, with no reference to "heavy topics" (his exact words) like Viet Nam or whatever. So after a rather flattering introduction, I was really taken aback when old Janie really zinged it to me right between the eyes when she asked what I thought about a recent *McCall's* article entitled "Doctors Make the Worst Lovers—Doctors' Wives and Mistresses Tell It All." I sat there dumbfounded for several seconds as I thought to myself that all I wanted to do was make my gazpacho, grab the money, and get the hell out of there. I most certainly had not anticipated being placed in the position of being anyone's straight man, much less become engaged in a defense of my manhood on nationwide TV, but since my feathers had already been ruffled, I decided to hang in there. I finally managed to blurt out some lame retort about how the article didn't mention anything about medical students, and the interview was off to a roaring start. From that point on I did a good impression of a hostile witness. I was never sure what was going to come next, and I think Janie was as relieved as I when she finally announced that the talk portion of the program was over and we went off to the kitchen.

I had actually made the gazpacho a grand total of once, at my parents' home two days before the show, with some coaching from my mother and a friend who is a gourmet cook. It had seemed so straightforward at the time that I figured it would be a snap if I just set everything up in a straight line and simply kept adding the ingredients one by one until everything was gone. I therefore began by placing two cucumbers in the blender, and while Janie kibbitzed over my shoulder, I did my best to ignore her. (Doctors make the worst lovers, my ass!) However, for some unknown reason, I noticed that the cucumbers were not blending the way they did when I had practiced it at home, but I didn't panic, and nonchalantly picked up a rubber spatula, which I had previously noticed in an open drawer full of kitchen utensils. I then calmly proceeded to push the reluctant cucumbers down into the blades but I inadvertently pushed down too hard, and suddenly there was this horrible tearing and mashing noise, and the blender soon contained a very unappetizing mishmash of cucumber, rubber, and wood.

The director started hysterically shouting, "Cut, cut!" When the tape stopped rolling, he took me on the side and rather patronizingly explained that nothing other than foodstuffs should ever be put in a blender. This time, when the cameras started rolling again, the cucumbers were safely preblended by a staff member, and Janie faked it by announcing to the viewers that I had blended the cucumbers in advance in order to save time.

The recipe now called for the addition of a clove of garlic, so I unhesitatingly picked up the rather large hunk of garlic lying on the counter and proceeded to throw the whole thing into the blender. I was told later that there were something like twelve to fourteen cloves in that one piece. I surely didn't know that at the time, so when Janie started to mutter something like "Isn't that an awful lot of garlic?" I snapped back that it was my recipe, and besides, I liked my food highly spiced (which I don't by the way). Well, the instant all that garlic hit the blades, everybody's eyes immediately began to water profusely. Everyone was trying desperately not to cough. Janie kept dabbing at her eyes, which were quite bloodshot by this time, and in the midst of all this confusion, I became aware that the blender was rapidly filling up and would soon overflow and that I still had over half the ingredients left to add!

Only then did I realize that the recipe was calculated to serve eight people, and the blender capacity was obviously not going to be adequate. Unless I transferred some of the contents, I would never be able to add all the called-for ingredients. While still making small talk with the hostess, in an attempt to stall, I looked around for a pitcher or any type of container so that I could transfer at least some of the glop that was already threatening to spill over. The only thing I could find was a small pot on the top of the stove. Suffice it to say that I proceeded to make a horrible mess on the counter as I struggled and juggled with the blender. Somehow, I managed to get everything mixed in together in roughly the right proportions, and I even succeeded in getting some finished gazpacho into a bowl so we could all taste some.

By this time the studio was getting chilly because all the doors and windows had been opened wide in an attempt to get the smell of garlic out of the room. As I cut up the parsley that was to be used as a garnish, I mentioned to Janie that I was suddenly reminded of a poem about parsley that I had written in college. I explained that I had been a waiter at school during my four years as an undergraduate, and with a straight face, I went on to say that we poets often get our truest inspirations from the commonplace things about us. I asked her if she would like to hear the poem, and of course by this time she had absolutely no idea of what to expect next. At that moment I'm sure she must have been wishing that they had stuck with the policy of having safe guests, like Mike Douglas, or Totie Fields, or someone else of that genre. It was certainly too late to do anything about that now as the director shrugged his shoulders and made a face like, What do we have to lose at this point?, and I got the go-ahead.

Turning completely away from Janie at that point, I looked directly into the camera and announced in my best deadpan, Henry Gibson-like drawl, " 'Pity the Poor Parsley,' by Michael Meyers."

Pity the poor parsley,
Picked, pampered, but rarely palated.
He's always pushed about,
And generally finds himself, either in the ash tray;
Or under a plate,
Until a later date,

When, he can then,
Be more propitiously thrown away,
With the lobster shell,
Or whatever the hell,
Else is not for eating.
Some life!

I then turned slowly back and asked her, still with a straight face, if she would like a copy for her personal collection, and all she could do was shake her head and shrug her shoulders. (They seemed to be very big on shoulder shrugging in Cincinnati.) The director yelled "Cut!" and the entire crew cracked up; after viewing a sort of instant replay (one of the bonuses of tape over film), everyone concerned was quite pleased (even Janie) with the funny way everything worked out, and my only regret was that I never got to see the show on the air.

However, I did subsequently get to see one show on the air, which was a T.V. dramatic show that I guested on that summer. After finally getting to Los Angeles, I played the part of a young Viet Nam war veteran undergoing psychiatric treatment. Rehearsals were held on an old deserted sound stage at Universal Studios, where the original sound version of the horror classic *The Phantom of the Opera* had been filmed. We spent two days reading through the script and trying to get some insight into our characters. Then we went on to involve ourselves in experiencing actual group techniques under the guidance of a trained psychiatrist. One exercise involved blindly selecting a picture of an animal and then behaving as that animal would, especially in relating to the other animals in the group. One time I was supposed to be an eagle, and I remember wondering how my patients would have reacted if they could have seen their doctor perched high on a balcony, preparing to swoop down onto the stage where the phantom of the opera used to lurk.

It was the first real dramatic part I had undertaken in which I wasn't simply a dumb jock type, and I quickly realized that I wouldn't be able to get by with gum chewing, backslapping, or grinning sillily into the camera. I had several tense scenes involving confrontations with other group members, and I had some anxiety about whether I could bring it off or not. Fortunately, I have a good friend who was living in Los Angeles at the time.

He is not only an excellent actor but, more importantly, has the ability and patience to effectively teach others what he has learned. He spent a great deal of time working with me and coaching me in some fundamentals. Without his help I'm sure the filming would not have gone nearly so well as it did. I learned a little something about acting. I also learned a few things about myself in the process, including, quite importantly, some of my limitations. When the show was eventually aired and the credits started to roll, I almost half-expected them to read, "The Part of Joe Shmoe was played by Michael Meyers, as interpreted by Kenneth Sylk."

All in all, the summer was quite enjoyable, and remunerative as well. For not only did I do the cooking show and appear as a guest on the dramatic series but I managed to lose one last time on the *Dating Game* and spent four hours one morning getting conked on the head with 300 empty soda cans for a soft drink commercial.

I was safely back in my element, so to speak, in this particular commercial, because in it I portrayed a basketball player who has just completed a game and is swaggering into a locker room sucking the last bit of soda from a can. I proceeded to open a specially rigged locker, which was triggered to release instantaneously 300 empty soda cans, and the force of the ensuing avalanche was more than sufficient to knock me on my backside. In a matter of only seconds I was completely submerged. As the camera zoomed in for a final close-up, I was lying prostrate in the aisle between the lockers, buried under a mountain of cans, and only my head was visible.

It turned out that it was much easier for the commercial people to use regular cans of soda and pour out the contents rather than attempt to locate new, unfilled cans. There was still some residual soda left in each can that cascaded out of the locker. It took about ten or twelve takes to get it just the way they wanted, and each time several cans would invariably hit me on the side of my nose or forehead and actually cause a little cut or bruise. As I lay in the aisle between the lockers after each take, with a curious mixture of blood and soda dripping from my face and nose, waiting to be rescued by the crew, I couldn't help but think about all the people who were constantly asking me if show business was really as glamourous as it was cracked up to be.

After the movie's lengthy run, and subsequently as a consequence of my varied TV appearances on the dramatic shows, cooking shows, game shows, commercials, and especially the interview programs, I began to realize some of the problems in store for someone who is regarded by our society as a quasi-celebrity. To add to my credibility in this regard I'll make a full breast of things and admit publicly that I once helped open a new shopping center. I really got a laugh when the publicity pictures appeared in the local papers and I found myself wedged in between a third-string Yankee shortstop and, you guessed it, Dr. Joyce Brothers. Actually, all it entailed was riding around in an open car, festooned with signs, balloons, and other publicity giveaway gimmicks, and stopping and chatting occasionally with the shoppers.

Any possibility of my getting a swelled head from all this attention was quickly squelched when the public relations man stopped one woman shopper, who was loaded down with packages and rushing toward the parking lot, and asked her if she would like to meet Michael Meyers from *Goodbye, Columbus*. The harried shopper took a quick glance at the new car and all the decorations, looked squarely at me, and said, "No, I'm sorry, I just can't buy any more raffles. Besides, I already have a car," and proceeded to walk right on by.

At first most of my encounters with the general public were quite enjoyable, and I usually got a big kick when someone recognized me and asked for an autograph. However, I quickly got tuned in to a particular type of individual who would simply be content to stare and gawk, even to the extent of alerting his companions or even unknown passersby ("Hey, guess who that is?") but who would never approach me directly.

Then there would be another type who would invariably come directly forward and, without any introduction whatsoever, point an accusing finger in my face and proclaim in a loud voice, "You're him, aren't you?" There is absolutely no way to answer anything like that intelligently, and furthermore, it usually turned out that it really didn't matter what I went on to say anyhow. If I answered that I was in *Goodbye, Columbus,* the person would often say, "Go on, you're lying. What would a movie star be doing in a place like this?" and often they would actually demand proof of my identity. Or else, if I wasn't in the mood, or just didn't have the time to stand there making small talk, and attempted to slip quietly away by saying they were mistaken, the questioner would often persist; there have been occasions when I have actually been hounded to the point of being called a liar.

The situation was exacerbated and threatened to get completely out of hand after I started to make fairly regular appearances on the late-night talk shows. By appearing on people's TV screens, especially if it is late at night and they are watching in the privacy of their bedroom, some people feel they then have unlimited claims on you and your time. As a direct corollary, this further entails some kind of inherent right to treat you as public property. For example, I was once shopping in a supermarket several days after appearing on the *Merv Griffin Show*, when a large, rather fat middle-aged man spied me in an aisle and exclaimed in a loud voice, "Well, look who we've got here!" as if I were some kind of unexpected catch at the end of his fishing line. Before I knew what was happening, he threw his arm around my shoulder and literally dragged me to the next aisle, where he didn't even have the courtesy to introduce himself or his family but proceeded to display me to them like some sort of captured prize animal. As I stood there in disbelief that this was actually happening, the man ranted on to his son (I am assuming it was his son, but then again, I wouldn't have been surprised if he turned out to be a stock boy who, unfortunately, just had the bad luck to be working in that particular aisle) about my being in the movie and studying to be a doctor. Finally, I could take it no longer, and simply took the man's arm off my shoulder and walked away without having said one word the entire time, leaving the man still rambling on among the cabbages and heads of lettuce.

Oftentimes, a situation will develop where someone chances to recognize me but can't quite remember how he knows me. I was astounded when I realized that this could even happen in the brief seconds that it takes to pass someone on the sidewalk. I quickly discovered, in the interest of time and my own sanity, the best way to handle such instances. Even today, I'll see someone approach, give me a curious look, hesitate as if they were going to stop, and then walk on by. What then usually happens is that I'll wait a few seconds and then look back over my shoulder, and almost invariably, I'll catch him standing there looking back at me with a quizzical look on his face. At other times the person may actually stop me, thinking I'm an old friend or a passing acquaintance that he should remember but just can't seem to place. Invariably, such people usually are too embarrassed to ask me outright why I look so familiar, and the conversation usually goes something like this:

STRANGER— Well, how the hell are you?

ME— Fine, and yourself? How have you been?

STRANGER— Good. How's the family? (Maybe I'm a relative.)

ME— Everybody's fine. How's your family?

STRANGER— They're all fine.

ME— That's good. Regards to everyone, and take care of yourself.

STRANGER— You too.

This is usually the critical point, when it is incumbent upon me to terminate the conversation as quickly as possible because if I don't, the stranger, more often than not, will then awkwardly continue to stand there with a confused look as he attempts to formulate some way in which to satisfy his curiousity. I'll therefore smile sociably and firmly take my leave, with the end result that the person is generally even more mystified than he was before our brief encounter but, hopefully, at least not offended.

CHAPTER / 25

MY FOURTH year as a medical student was spent primarily on electives, such as hematology and radiology, where I was able to get additional exposure to some of the medical subspecialties, and I spent several additional months as a so-called "acting intern." As such, I functioned in the capacity of an intern, with much of the attendant responsibility, but was still technically a fourth-year student. In other words, I still paid a tuition fee and they didn't pay me anything.

The year went by very quickly, with everyone in the class looking forward eagerly to that day in June when we would receive our medical degrees and begin our internships as true doctors of medicine. For several reasons in the middle of that fourth year I made a decision to remain at Martland for my internship. During my clinical experience the overall situation at the hospital had been improving, and there was no reason to believe the trend would not continue. It was not only becoming possible to get a medical question addressed to a specialist answered quickly but to get it answered by someone who was knowledgeable and anxious to teach as well. There was a "hard sell" campaign by the various departments to get the fourth-year students to stay on and do their internships at Martland, and promises (unkept) of pay increases, to bring salaries if not on par with New York City hospitals, at least in the same range. There were additional promises (some kept, the majority not) of improved cafeteria services, a habitable doctors' lounge and on-call rooms, a medical intensive care unit, and improved clinic procedures, among other assurances.

My plans at the time were to take a rotating internship, which would be similar to my medical school experience in that I would again rotate through the various services and subspecialities. I hoped to receive credit for the year's work toward a family practice residency, and I wanted the crisis atmosphere of a city hospital, with its concomitant responsibility and pressure. I felt I could then switch to a community hospital for the next two years, where I would have much more out-patient responsibility and receive much-needed guidance in the area of the private practice of medicine, and more polish in general.

In retrospect I see that my decision was also one of convenience. By choosing to remain at Martland, I would not have to compete for a more desirable position. I would not have to make explanations as to why I had done poorly in certain courses in the first year. Frankly, I guess I was selling myself short and was afraid of being rejected.

But be that as it may, I made my decision to remain at Martland for one additional year as a rotating intern. As graduation approached and I reflected back on the four years of medical school, it seemed appropriate to codify some thoughts I had regarding medicine and my medical education up to that point.

Someone was once quoted as saying that the practice of medicine is 90 percent art and 10 percent science, and even with my limited experience, I would heartily agree. The successful practice necessitates the ability to establish a unique, highly personal, one-to-one relationship with each patient. This requires a great deal of skill and talent that is difficult, if not impossible, to acquire from a textbook.

It is not simply a computer print out of blood chemistry, or an interpretation of a chest X ray, the arriving at the most probable diagnosis, and then, hopefully, effecting a cure. Of course, this is an integral part of medicine, and it appeals to my intellectual and scientific curiosity, but I think there is a huge difference between being a skilled diagnostician and a true physician. For medicine to work, the doctor and the patient must be able to relate to each other as people. There must be a trust, a giving and a taking, and, most importantly, a caring. "The true physician has a Shakespearian breadth of interest in the weak and foolish, the proud and the humble, the stoic hero and the whining rogue. He cares for people."

But this is not easily achieved. It is extremely satisfying to be in a position to be able to help someone in need, but it is also extremely difficult and threatening. It is not easy to deal with sick people, people who are in pain, frightened and insecure, and obviously not at their best. Sickness is disturbing, not only to the patient and his family but to the doctor and medical student as well. Unfortunately, this is a consideration that is usually overlooked. It is obviously impossible not to react to a sick patient in a personal way, and I feel strongly that my training as a medical student did not include sufficient instruction as to how to deal most effectively with a sick person.

As a medical student you are constantly exposed to fear, distrust, suspicion, and death. You are expected to be able to accept as commonplace the grotesque and the deformed. People, circumstances, and events that were previously considered repulsive must evoke no demonstrable effect, not only in front of the patient but, as importantly, in front of your peer group as well. And at the very same time you are also asked to go against one of the most basic tenets of civilized society: to inflict pain on someone else is wrong. You are taught how to hurt people with your hands, your instruments, and sometimes with the truth. Of course, rationally and intellectually, you are expected to understand that it is all for the good of the patient, but this is often very difficult to accept emotionally.

Therefore, in order to be able to function effectively, a medical student learns very early that it is necessary to disassociate as much as possible his thoughts and intellectual processes from his emotions and feelings. This emotional detachment is expected when he first cuts into his cadaver, and it is a factor, I suspect, as long as he is a doctor practicing medicine. It is what enables him to perform many extremely upsetting and difficult procedures, such as slicing off a mangled limb or a cancerous breast, or sending shocks of electricity through a person's body, or even tying down an alcoholic patient with impending dt's and forcing a rubber tube up his penis. Disassociation enables him to perform these acts and function on an effective level. However, there is a real danger that a medical student can become so good at protecting himself emotionally that he and his patient suffer.

As my medical training progressed, I realized I began to dread the vague cry of "Doctor, please" that seemed to emanate from every corner of the ward. Of course, I could never ignore a legitimate cry for help, and the gut reaction to a true emergency was always present, but it seemed to take progressively more and more conscious energy to be able to respond to each patient's needs and demands, some of which appeared never ending. I have come to realize that this hard felt need for protection and insulation does not come cheaply, and I have a certain sense of loss in knowing there is a definite qualitative difference in my spontaneous reactions to people and their needs. I have come to understand that it is imperative that there be an effective compromise between boundless concern, and detached aloofness in order for me to practice medicine effectively and compassionately.

This attitude of self-survival seemed to be pervasive among the house staff I worked with. Furthermore, it exists almost as a sort of legacy that the intern and resident leave behind so that the student may likewise survive his medical training. To illustrate how easy it can be to carry this to an extreme, I once had a resident in surgery who went so far as to dress in such a way that it was not obvious he was a doctor. In that way, when he was on duty at the hospital, he could avoid any but the most unavoidable confrontations between himself and the patient, and the patient's family.

In addition, there are other factors also operating to reinforce this house staff legacy of learned dissociation. One of these is the tendency of medical educators to segregate or sectionalize the body into systems so that they can then be studied more effectively. This process, as well, begins very early in your preclinical experience.

The liver, for example, is a unique and very important organ, and several classroom and laboratory sessions in histology are devoted to discussing and viewing its microscopic functions. The liver is again singled out in gross anatomy for dissection, and then in physiology and biochemistry the organ is again examined in detail in respect to form and function. By the second year in pathology a week or more may be spent viewing and discussing all the possible disease entities to which the liver may fall prone, and it is quite possible that sometime during the course of your clinical years, one of your attendings in medicine may very well turn out to be a hepatologist (a liver specialist).

In all fairness that individual must first be trained as a general internist with a broad medical background, who then goes on to pursue a particular subspecialty, where the major thrust of study and experience is directed to that specified area. Consequently, certain of these attendings are simply unable to keep up with all the latest developments outside their speciality and all too often are really of little or no academic benefit to the student or house staff officer if the particular patient being discussed does not fall under his ken of knowledge. It can sometimes be quite humorous to see an attending hem and haw in an attempt to finagle a patient and his problems in such a way that he can then explain and expound upon his own field of expertise. I had one attending in particular who, although not really grossly guilty of the above, for he was a very brilliant all-around physician, nevertheless was frequently quoted as saying that the main function of the heart was to pump blood to the liver. He still enjoys a worldwide reputation as a leader in research and clinical expertise regarding the liver, and was obviously being somewhat facetious, but I suspect that each subspecialist must harbor similar grandiose feelings about his own field to which he has devoted so much of his time and energy.

Yet the increasing emphasis on specialization and subspecialization, with its built-in tendency to sectionalize, is a necessary evil in today's world, where no one can possibly be as competent in all fields as he can be if he limits his studies and experiences to one particular area. However, the inherent danger here is that the specialist may then lose sight of the total picture and not view the patient as an entire, whole human being. It also becomes somewhat more understandable why many an intern or resident begins to refer to his patients not as Mr. Smith or Mrs. Jones but rather as bed number one—cirrhosis, bed number three—pancreatitis, or bed number seven—diabetic, and so forth.

There is an added protection of sorts in the institution of bedside rounds, already mentioned, where the doctors and students travel in large groups from bed to bed discussing each patient.

A patient may easily become intimidated by the presence of perhaps as many as ten or more doctors surrounding his bed, and if you compound this by the fact that they are probably talking specifically about one or two individual organs and in terms that are most probably incomprehensible, it is equally understandable why the patient may hesitate to ask a question or even express his fears and doubts to his doctor. And to really add insult to injury, at an institution such as Martland, with its large foreign house staff and large number of outside attendings, many patients don't even know who their own primary doctor really is!

If questioned specifically in this regard, most patients would probably name the third-year student as the doctor in charge. This is not really surprising when you consider that the student is the person with whom the patient deals most often and, more importantly, is probably the person on the team with the least-effective armor at this point, and is, therefore, most approachable and willing to interact on a more personal level.

Contributing to this phenomenon of separation and isolation of thought and emotion even further is the widespread use of medical terminology and, perhaps more significantly, the medical slang that is so prevalent among not only the doctors but nurses and other paramedical personnel. It is difficult to determine whether this is actually a cause or an effect, but regardless, it is intimately related to the aforementioned habit or custom of referring to an individual patient as a disease process rather than as a particular *person* who just happens to be ill. (To wit: it's 3 A.M., and the resident is awakened by a phone call from the nurse and curses as he pulls on his pants, "Aw shit, another pneumonia.")

To illustrate further a chronically ill, debilitated patient is almost universally referred to as either a turkey or a crock. The expression "PPP" (piss poor protoplasm) is all too commonly used to refer to the aged and debilitated on the geriatric wards, and a frightened girl of sixteen who is hemorrhaging from a botched up abortion is simply and coldly referred to as an incomplete ab.

Obviously, it would be very easy to pass judgment on this apparent insensitivity, but again there *are* reasons why it exists, and it, too, may also be seen as something of a necessary evil, since it does put some emotional distance between the doctor and his patient. For it would be just as disadvantageous for a doctor to become totally immersed in each patient and his numerous problems as it would be if he were to regard him solely as an object or a disease process. A medical doctor simply cannot function as a social worker, psychiatrist, confidante, and sociologist and still have sufficient time to serve the medical needs of all his patients. Again, there is obviously a compromise point, but it is as difficult in each situation as each patient is different, and the understanding of this and the ability to remain flexible is something that I have come to realize is not easily achieved.

CHAPTER / 26

"MICHAEL MEYERS, M.D."—as I glanced downward that was what I saw printed on the name tag pinned proudly to my freshly starched white coat, and it gave me quite a thrill. It was July 1, the traditional starting time for interns and residents in almost every hospital in the United States, and as I sat in a conference room at the Veterans Administration Hospital in East Orange, New Jersey, where I was scheduled to begin my internship with a two-month rotation in internal medicine, the feelings of pride and accomplishment were reinforced as I thumbed through the mountains of correspondence and regulations contained in my "orientation packet," addressed specifically to one Dr. Michael Meyers.

Yet it would be unfair if I didn't also talk about the high level of anxiety and uncertainty I felt at the same time. Intellectually, it seemed to be of only minor consolation that the particular resident with whom I was to work, our chief resident, and finally the attending physician and the hospital administration itself would be ultimately responsible for the patient's care and well-being in the strictest medico-legal sense. For I also knew full well that as an intern, I would be faced almost daily with making instantaneous and, oftentimes, critical and crucial decisions in taking appropriate action with regard to the innumerable medical emergencies that would inevitably crop up in an 1,100-bed hospital.

I couldn't stand back and wait for the doctor to come, because now *I was* the doctor, and I would soon be directly confronted with all the implications that are inherent as a consequence of the added duties and responsibilities that go hand in hand with arriving at this next rung in the medical hierarchy.

On a strictly rational level, I knew that most of the time my resident would be readily available, so that I would have the benefit of someone with more knowledge and experience whom I could call upon if a situation should develop that I couldn't handle. However, I *also* knew that this would not *always* be the case, especially at night when the intern was the first to be called for any emergency; it therefore might take critical minutes before the resident could be roused from sleep or rushed over from another location, and a crisis situation could quite easily develop that demanded immediate intervention. In those instances, the buck truly did stop with the intern, and I'm sure most of my fellow interns who were similarly busily engaged in getting fingerprinted, signing loyalty oaths, and swearing on their mother's Bible that they had never cohabitated with a Communist were also experiencing similar ambivalent feelings.

The lay public is generally not aware that a turnover of house staff officers takes place at this time each year. The transitional swing months of June and July are therefore quite chaotic in most hospitals, both with people attempting to finish up their previous year's responsibilities while projecting ahead to perhaps having to relocate themselves and their families to whatever new locale their internship or residency will bring them and with the new crew coming on duty on July 1 who simply will not have had a great deal of experience and knowledge. Just as someone on an executive level in the automobile industry, knowing that production is generally poorer in quality on Mondays and Fridays compared with the rest of the week, will therefore attempt to be certain that a car ordered for his own family or personal friends will come off the assembly line in the middle of the week, analogously, anyone truly familiar with hospital protocol would similarly think twice about entering a hospital for an elective procedure (in other words, anything that is not considered an emergency) during these transition months. Of course, this is not to say that the facilities and medical care available are not adequate during these times, but since experience is still basically the best teacher, it obviously makes sense that the more time the new crew has under its belt, the better should be the overall performance. July 1 happened to fall on a Saturday that year, and fortunately, I was not scheduled to be on duty that weekend (although not so fortunately I *was* scheduled to work on the Fourth of July holiday). I could therefore leave the hospital after our orientation, whereas several of my colleagues had to roll up their sleeves and get right down to work, while I at least had the luxury of several days in which to orient myself to my resident, our newly inherited patients, my own responsibilities, and my "beeper," or page device.

All the doctors (as well as most essential nonmedical personnel) are required to wear their page devices, referred to as beepers, while on duty so they can theoretically be located quickly anywhere in the hospital when and if they should be needed. Therefore, they are not dependent on hearing their names paged over the general PA system (with its obvious limitations). The beepers themselves are actually one-way receiving units tied in with the telephone system; as it worked in my hospital, you first dialed an appropriate digit on any house phone, which activated the system, and then the specific numerals of the beeper of the party you desired to contact. This triggered that one particular beeper, which quite appropriately would then proceed to beep incessantly until the party responded by pressing the receiver button on his unit. This permitted the person who desired to make contact to verbally inform the doctor, or whomever, of the location where his attention or attendance was requested or else to relay information as to what particular telephone extension they were calling from if direct two-way contact needed to be established.

At the very beginning you find that you wear your beeper displayed proudly—either hooked on to your belt or, perhaps, in a shirt or jacket pocket—almost as a symbolic badge of honor that says to everyone you meet, "Hey, look at me. I'm a doctor!" However, that badge seems to turn all too quickly into an albatross as a consequence of the incessant demands that are continuously being made of an intern, the majority of which are mediated through the beeper. And naturally, the beeper has absolutely no regard for whatever you happen to be doing at the exact moment, be it anything from involvement in a true crisis emergency situation, to being in midsentence in a discussion with a colleague or a professor at a conference or a lecture, or, as it seemed to most inevitably occur, to being in the awkward position of sitting on the john.

It often seemed like the old story of washing your car and then sitting back and waiting for the inevitable raindrops to begin falling, only here it appeared that the surest means to trigger your beeper going off was to unzip your trousers. Things could be relatively quiet for upwards of an hour or more where you wouldn't get beeped at all, but as soon as you unbuckled that belt to go to sleep or sit down on the pot, the room would invariably echo with the incessant, all-intrusive beep, beep, beep.

Despite all this it was still possible to have some fun with the beeper, and even use it to your own advantage on selected occasions. For example, most people kept the volume control at a moderate level so that only those people in their immediate vicinity would be disturbed by an incoming message. However, some doctors, especially the older ones, had hearing difficulties and would therefore keep the volume on their receivers turned up to a fairly high level so as not to risk missing an incoming call. It just so happened that one of the attendings, who was not very popular with the students or house staff to begin with, and was also slightly hard of hearing, had a habit of dozing off at conferences and lectures. One afternoon a student positioned himself outside the auditorium while a lecture was being held so that he could see precisely when Dr. S. started to doze off. He then quickly darted to the nearest house phone and dialed the proper beeper numbers, and the instant the loud beep startled Dr. S. and he groggily pressed the button in to receive what he thought was going to be a legitimate message, the student shouted at the top of his lungs, "Wake up, Dr. S. Wake up!" Needless to say this brought on quite a reaction not only from Dr. S. but from the rest of the people in attendance at the conference as well.

I soon discovered that the beeper could serve still another purpose and that was to function as a convenient escape mechanism from any particularly boring conference or lecture. A sympathetic nurse or fellow colleague who did not have to attend that particular lecture could wait about ten minutes after a conference was scheduled to begin and then beep you to inform you that your presence was required elsewhere immediately. If the lecture turned out to be interesting and worthwhile, you always had the option to simply disregard your cohort's message, but if it looked like it was going to be a boring and nonproductive session, you could then unobtrusively slip out without having to go into any detailed excuse. Consequently, it always seemed that when certain doctors were scheduled to lecture on particularly boring topics, you could invariably count upon a certain number of "emergency" beeps over and above the number usually expected.

CHAPTER / 27

SINCE MY first night on duty as an intern happened to fall on the Fourth of July, my resident and I were responsible not only for covering new admissions but for any problems that might arise on all the other medical wards from 8 A.M. that morning until 8 A.M. the following morning, when the remainder of the medical staff would return to duty. From that point on we would be responsible only for those patients assigned to our particular team, until we had accomplished all that needed to be done and could then leave the hospital, usually anywhere from 6 P.M. to 7 P.M., leaving the care of our patients to another team scheduled to be "on call."

A large majority of the holiday or weekend coverage deals with rather mundane matters, such as rewriting IV orders or, more annoyingly, drawing blood from certain patients so that specific lab results would then be available to their doctors early the next day and thereby enable them to better monitor and evaluate their patient's current condition. This task alone took up a great deal of time and was particularly frustrating because the job was routinely performed during the week by specially trained lab technicians. However, for some reason for which I was never able to receive a satisfactory explanation (meaning it most likely involved financial consideration—the VA being too cheap to pay someone time and a half or double time to work on a holiday, and since we had to be there anyway, why not "use us"?), the chore, not unexpectedly, fell to the intern on call.

As I recall, nothing very exciting or out of the ordinary occurred for most of that first on-call day, even though my duties included coverage of the ICU. (The ICU is where the most seriously and critically ill patients were kept in order that they could be monitored most closely and given the best possible "intensive" care by a specially trained crew of nurses, assisted by the most sophisticated monitoring systems available.) I did not have any of my particular patients in the unit at the time, but I thought it would be a good idea if I briefly went over each patient's chart (there being only five) so that should any complications arise through the remainder of the day or night, I would at least be somewhat familiar with their individual problems.

One of the patients was a twenty-one-year-old white male who was suffering from acute fulminating hepatitis, which he had acquired while stationed in Viet Nam as a consequence of intravenous heroin abuse. He had been in the hospital for only three days, but his condition had deteriorated so rapidly that he was already in a deep coma when I first saw him. This particularly virulent form of hepatitis is fairly rare and should not be confused with the vast majority of cases where the disease is self-limiting and generally runs its course without leaving any permanent damage. However, this young man was not so fortunate, and as a further complication of the disease, he was currently in acute renal failure (meaning his kidneys were not functioning properly, if at all), and was bleeding quite severely into his gastrointestinal tract as well.

Emblazoned on the front of his chart so that it couldn't possibly be missed was an order from the particular doctor managing the case, which bluntly stated that in light of the severity of the disease and the permanent damage already inflicted, the cardiac pacemaker team was not to be called if the patient suffered a cardiac arrest (in other words, if his heart stopped beating spontaneously). Now this is basically tantamount to acknowledging that the patient's condition has deteriorated to such an extent that there is no reasonable hope of any eventual recovery, and a medical judgment had therefore been made that any heroic or extraordinary measures to prolong his life would only prove futile in the long run and thereby prolong the agony for the family, who were at that very moment maintaining a constant vigil just outside the unit.

I sat there for approximately one hour that evening in that sparkling clean ICU, with its full complement of highly trained nurses, surrounded by almost all the life-support systems that modern technology had yet devised, and watched this young man die. When the cardiac monitor started its high, piercing shrill, indicating that the patient's heart had stopped beating, I walked over to the bedside and shut the machine off. I realized that as the doctor covering the unit, it would be my responsibility to legally declare the patient dead, and it would be an understatement to say that at that particular moment, I wished I could have been anywhere else rather than having to confront the task which now faced me. Fortuitously, a resident from another team was in the unit at the time checking on a different patient, and he took the time to go through the standard protocol with me, which entailed noting what to specifically look for and check in order to satisfy myself that the patient had truly expired. This included absence of an audible heartbeat and palpable pulse, cessation of spontaneous respiration, and loss of the corneal (or blink) reflex, supported by a flat or erratic EKG tracing, among others.

As I sat there filling out the appropriate forms, the youngster's mother must have instinctively sensed what had just happened because she suddenly burst into the room, raced over to her son's bedside, and began to sob uncontrollably and pummel her chest with her fists. I attempted to comfort her as best I could, but finally it became necessary to sedate her, as she was becoming more and more hysterical; thankfully, there were other family members present who were finally able to get her to leave his bedside. As extremely upsetting and unsettling as the incident was, at least I was spared the additional agony of having to directly confront a mother with the fact that her child had just died. It was certainly a quick indoctrination into, and introduction to, some of the more unpleasant aspects of medicine. And at the same time I also had tremendous feelings of anger, sorrow, and impotence at not being able to alter the course of events, and it crossed my mind that this death was as much a direct result of our involvement in Viet Nam as if this young man had been shot or stepped on a land mine three months before. My rage was massive and overflowing, and it encompassed the current administration in our country and all governments in general. I distinctly recall that an antiwar song sung by Mick Jagger of the English rock group The Rolling Stones kept running through my mind, where the line, "While the old men do the talking, the young men do the dying," seemed all too relevant and appropriate.

Beginning from practically the first day on the clinical level as students, and subsequently reemphasized repeatedly to us as house officers, was how extremely important and crucial it was in regard to a hospital's accreditation that a certain minimum number of autopsies be performed each year. In addition to the impetus of using the postmortem as a teaching and learning experience, and hopefully of gaining a better understanding of the true pathology as to *why* the patient died (which appeared somewhat academic in this particular case, but I subsequently saw that even in the most clear-cut of cases, there are often findings at a postmortem which indicate that a particular process had been going on that might have been misinterpreted, or even overlooked, when the patient had been alive or something else may be found that might have complicated the doctor's perception of the course of events, so that even sometimes "simple" clear-cut cases occasionally turn out to have been not nearly so simple in retrospect), there was the added pressure from the hospital administration to get permission for as many autopsies as possible.

In certain instances, and these vary somewhat from state to state, such as when a patient dies within twenty-four hours of being admitted to the hospital, for example, or in the case of anyone suspected of having been a victim of foul play, the disposition automatically comes under the jurisdiction of the state medical examiner, who then must decide if a postmortem should be done or not, and legally he has the authority to schedule an autopsy in such instances without permission of the next of kin. (In all other cases permission must be obtained from the next of kin in order for a postmortem to be conducted.)

However, this was not a special instance, and I was therefore confronted with the extremely difficult and emotionally upsetting task of being forced to intrude upon the acute grief of a bereaved next of kin to ask for written permission so that an autopsy could be performed. (The situation becomes even more difficult when you find yourself in the position of having to call a family on the phone in the middle of the night to inform them of a death, and then, in the midst of their anguish and tears, and without even having the benefit of being able to see the family in person, having to proceed to ask permission for an autopsy.) An additional factor contributing to the strain of such situations is that for the majority of people, an autopsy has a definite stigma and carries with it certain negative connotations, half-truths, and even superstitions, most especially surrounding the charged areas of mutilation and desecration of the dead. However, despite the already described rather unpleasant physical aspects involved in the actual performance of an autopsy, when the procedure is done properly, the deceased can be prepared by any competent funeral home so that the body can be viewed without anyone being aware that an autopsy has been performed.

In this particular instance I was again saved from further discomfort in that the family informed me that they wanted an autopsy to be performed (perhaps in anticipation of a law suit against the federal government or something of that nature).

However, despite the emotional impact both on the family and, to a lesser extent, the doctor, it is very important that permission be gotten, and I soon discovered a method employed by previous house officers to expedite such situations and thereby ensure a higher rate of success. Although on the surface (and underneath as well), it might not seem entirely ethical, it is usually quite effective. It is accomplished by telling the next of kin that although you are fairly sure of the ultimate cause of death, you can never be absolutely certain unless an autopsy is performed, and that since there are many diseases that are familial in nature (in the sense that if one family member is so afflicted, the odds may go up dramatically that another family member may also be so afflicted), it would be in the best interest of the rest of the family if the exact cause of death was determined at an autopsy. This too, however, is somewhat of a distortion of the facts, as there is no absolute guarantee that the exact cause of death can be determined in every instance. This all may sound rather cold, calculating, and even misleading because it basically *is,* but naturally you never push if a family is firmly against it on moral or religious grounds. Here again, it seems that we have another example of how far the practice of medicine is from being a precise art that deals solely with absolute truths; thus each individual physician must decide for himself what is proper and in the best interest for all those involved. Speaking only for myself, it seems that in this one specific area the end did often justify the means, at least within certain bounds.

I got very little sleep the remainder of that first night, and most subsequent nights I was to be "on" at the VA, for it seemed that my beeper was primed to go off almost every fifteen or twenty minutes. Most annoyingly, at least half the calls were not for any true emergencies but for busy work, like writing an order for a sleeping pill that a patient's own doctor had forgotten to reorder or where a night nurse might be checking through a patient's chart and notice that he had been running a slight fever for the previous two or three days, and then suddenly decide at 11 P.M. or midnight that the patient should be seen by the doctor on call, even if there had been absolutely no change in the patient's condition.

The situation was made even worse by the fact that in addition to the active medical wards, there were also several so-called intermediate care floors, which housed the more chronically ill and debilitated patients; these functioned almost in the capacity of a nursing home. These floors were attended to by doctors on staff especially employed for just that purpose, but at the time of my internship they were not required to cover at night or on weekends or holidays. This additional task naturally fell to the intern on call, and although I have learned that the situation has subsequently been changed, I nevertheless found myself responsible for perhaps anywhere from 250-300 chronically and seriously ill patients, in addition to covering my own ward and any new admissions to my team as well. Naturally, in a population that large and with such a variety of ages, diseases, and degrees of illness, there invariably seemed to be some task or another that would require my attention with almost regular frequency. These could also run the gamut from simply having to order a laxative for a patient who suddenly decided that 1 A.M. was the proper time to get his bowels moving after not telling anyone he had been constipated for the previous four days, to a full-fledged cardiac arrest, and more often than not, to having to declare someone dead.

This last circumstance most frequently occurred around two or three in the morning—as I was to quickly learn that first night I was on call—when the night nurse would be making her regular rounds and discover that a patient had expired in his sleep in the interim hours between nursing checks. These were not generally pacemaker calls, especially since the patient may have been dead for several hours before being discovered, but nevertheless, a doctor was still required by law to come as soon as possible after a death had been discovered in order to formally declare the patient dead and fill out the appropriate forms.

I was called to the intermediate care floors twice that first night (actually, early the next morning), to perform just such a task, and despite the upsetting incident earlier that evening in the ICU, I nevertheless sensed that I was already becoming able to disassociate myself from much of the emotional impact which might have been present under more "normal" situations.

Of course there was still a great deal of feeling and emotion involved, but as the weeks went by I found that I was able to rather quickly and efficiently go through the mechanics involved in examining any given patient, leaf rapidly through the chart to ascertain what the primary problem had been, and then almost perfunctorily fill out the required forms.

This was the result of a combination of several factors, but the most significant clearly related to the fact that I generally didn't have to notify the family (since, for one thing, many simply had no next of kin) and that I had not had any previous contact with the deceased. There was also the circumstance of being so involved in performing my various other duties that I generally had little time for reflection and introspection. In fact, as callous as this might appear on the surface, this "defense mechanism" was to soon operate so effectively in this one particular regard that after the first month or so I would have found myself hard pressed to actually recall the exact number of patients I had declared dead in any previous twenty-four-hour shift on duty.

CHAPTER / 28

"ALL RIGHT, sir. You're going to be all right. This is going to be a bit uncomfortable, but it's very important and has to be done. Just try and relax, breathe as normally as possible through your mouth, and when I tell you to, please swallow."

As I held up one end of the clear plastic tubing and squeezed the lubricating jelly into a clean gauze pad, I thought to myself that this guy really didn't look in too bad shape for someone who had supposedly been vomiting up blood for the previous five days. He was fully conscious, and although it was obvious that he had been drinking and was quite agitated, I wouldn't have described him as drunk by any means. Without warning, he suddenly grabbed the nearby basin on the stretcher and vomited a fair amount of coffee-ground-like material tinged with large streaks of bright red blood.

The presence of the coffee-ground material was significant, since it strongly corroborated the patient's history. For whenever blood is present in the stomach, it is acted upon by normally occurring enzymes and acids, and the subsequent breakdown product, mixed with any residual food present at the same time, strongly resembles coffee grounds. Furthermore, the man also stated that he had had black, tarry bowel movements for at least one week, which again goes along with chronic bleeding into the gastrointestinal (GI) tract, because the longer the blood stays in the gut, the longer the enzymes and other chemicals have in which to interact. One of the interactions involves the large quantity of iron normally present in the blood, and the result is the formation of very black, almost tar-colored feces. The bright red streaks of blood, on the other hand, significantly indicated that the man was still actively bleeding at that very moment.

It was around midnight, roughly one month into my internship, and I was down in the emergency room, having been alerted by the admitting officer that a GI bleeder was about to be admitted to our team. The standard protocol when someone is brought to the emergency room in serious condition or has the potential to become critical at any moment is for the team that is to be responsible for the patient's care on the floor to actually come down to the emergency room, assist in whatever emergency procedures are appropriate, and then accompany the patient either to X ray or directly to the ICU, depending upon an evaluation of the seriousness of the patient's condition.

I had previously started an IV to begin fluid replacement and had drawn blood samples, which were already on their way to the lab so that the patient's general status could be better evaluated and his blood typed and cross matched for compatability in case it became necessary to transfuse. My resident was on his way down, and all that was left to be done now was to pass the nose-gastric tube so I could then begin to pump in iced water. This is accomplished by filling a large syringe with approximately five ounces of chilled water and then introducing the iced solution into the stomach by means of the tubing. This is then repeated three times, and after permitting it all to remain in the stomach for perhaps fifteen to twenty seconds, it is removed by reversing the process. The rationale behind this so-called ice water lavage is that the coldness of the water will cause the blood vessels that are bleeding to constrict, or narrow, to such an extent that the bleeding process will hopefully slow down or stop completely.

The principle involved is a logical extension of the body's natural response to exposure to cold, where in an attempt to maintain a constant internal temperature, much of the blood that would normally circulate through a region that is so exposed is instead "shunted," or diverted, to internal organs and other areas that are not so exposed. The risk is thereby lessened that the blood itself will be chilled to the point where it could then have the potential to adversely affect other more sensitive areas through which it might then circulate. This is the same reason why our lips, ears, and fingers, all of which have significant blood flow relatively close to their surface, become "blue" when we stay outside in the cold weather.

I was all too familiar with this procedure, having performed it many times as a student at both the VA and Martland with varying degrees of success. My familiarity was due to a large extent to the relatively high frequency of alcoholism in the patient populations. This is because one of the major consequences of long-term alcohol abuse (generally in combination with poor nutrition) is the development of significant changes in the structure and functional ability of the liver, a condition referred to medically as cirrhosis, or as I have heard it quite often referred to by many patients, "roaches of the liver."

These changes that occur have serious implications and widespread consequences, since the liver is a vital organ in many respects and is involved in an incredibly complex number of bodily functions. For one, most of the blood supply that goes to the intestine, and which has therefore absorbed the nutrients that are dietarily ingested, normally then passes through the liver on its way back to the heart. The liver is thus able to select out a large quantity of these nutrients and other vital materials that the body requires, and either stores them in one form or another to a limited extent or changes them to various other forms that can then be more effectively stored and utilized elsewhere in the body.

However, if the normal architecture of the liver is interfered with, as in cirrhosis, the blood from the gut must find a new pathway back to the heart. The body in such situations then attempts to compensate for the circulatory complications by opening up new "collateral" circulations. The blood is subsequently rerouted around the liver in the attempt to establish new pathways through which to return to the heart, and one of these new routes includes the hemorrhoidal complex of veins (one of the primary reasons many alcoholics suffer from hemorrhoids), as well as veins in the region of the esophagus and upper part of the stomach. Thus, not only does this shunting in itself lead to widespread complications in regard to the general circulation but the body as whole is even further compromised as a consequence of being deprived of the literally scores of other functions that the liver normally performs as the largest gland in the body.

The pressure in these veins naturally increases greatly, as they simply are not designed to handle the increased load, and they then become quite enlarged and tortuous, to the point where these so-called varices may actually rupture and bleed. This can often lead to a true emergency situation because there is no rapid, practical means to apply external pressure to stop the bleeding of these veins in the esophagus and upper part of the stomach, and combined with the increased pressure, the bleeding can therefore become quite massive and uncontrollable. There is a certain emergency procedure, too complicated and involved to explain precisely, but briefly it involves a balloon-type apparatus that is passed in much the same manner as a standard nose-gastric tube. Also included is additional tubing, which allows for both drainage and suction, as well as permitting air to enter the lungs; after the balloon is inflated, it can be positioned in such a way that pressure can be applied by means of traction to force the balloon up against the bleeding veins. However, the procedure involves a great deal of skill and training for it to be successful, and carries as well a fair degree of risk in unskilled hands. Consequently, the first emergency treatment of choice, at least until the specialist arrives, is the ice water lavage.

There are numerous other causes for a GI bleed, ranging from a bleeding ulcer to chronic aspirin ingestion, but from this patient's prior medical history and present inebriated condition, enlarged veins in his esophagus seemed the most likely tentative cause, as these frequently may ooze and bleed at a fairly low rate, as well as sometimes massively rupture. My resident arrived just as I was wheeling the patient onto the elevator, and as I continued to lavage even on the way up to the floor, my resident and I became increasingly concerned as the returning water in the syringe became pinker and pinker.

Nevertheless, the patient was still fully conscious and quite agitated, protesting adamantly about the tube and the chilling effect of the ice water that invariably got splashed about. We were in the process of transferring him from the stretcher to the bed when suddenly and without any warning whatsoever, he heaved up such an enormous quantity of blood that the entire top of the bed literally turned bright red. He then proceeded to vomit up nothing but volumes and volumes of pure blood, and actually bled to death right before our horrified eyes in less than sixty seconds.

My entire pants' legs, shoes, and white coat were completely soaked through with his blood, and my resident and a nurse and an aide who were also present all stood completely dumbfounded, while all I could do was sit there with the man's head cradled in my arms. It had all happened with such incredible quickness, and although there was absolutely nothing that we, or *anyone* else for that matter, could have done to forestall the catastrophic event, I was just sick to my stomach with feelings of utter helplessness and an acutely concomitant sense of my own mortality. It was undoubtedly one of the most absolutely frightening, and upsetting situations I would ever experience.

Yet as difficult and unsettling as this incident was, it was somewhat tempered, at least to a certain degree, by a series of events that transpired soon after, and which perhaps lend further credence to the existence of some grand scheme of natural order that somehow operates to enable a doctor to continue to function as effectively as possible under even the most troubling of circumstances.

The particular episode began routinely enough on the general medical ward one early evening several days later when a nurse rushed over to inform me that a patient she had just been attending had suddenly stopped breathing and she subsequently could detect no pulse or heartbeat. It sounded as if the man had most probably suffered a cardiac arrest, and as I rushed to his bedside with the bedboard and ambu-bag kept in each ward for just such emergencies, I rather brusquely shouted to the nurse to quit standing around and call for the pacemaker team on the double (Stat!).

My annoyance at any delay in initiating treatment was predicated on the fact that a cardiac arrest is truly the most dramatic and potentially lethal of all the medical emergencies since the heart itself has actually stopped beating spontaneously or is otherwise "beating" so erratically as to become nonfunctional, and spontaneous respiration often ceases as well. Unless immediate resuscitative intervention is initiated, the body will become deprived of vitally needed freshly oxygenated blood, and consequently, permanent, irreversible damage can occur to the brain and other vital organs in as little as five to seven minutes. Thus for all practical purposes the patient is "dead" for those crucial minutes when an arrest occurs, but in many instances, with prompt and proper intervention, it is often possible to "restart" the heart; oftentimes, the patient can recover completely, with no permanent, residual defects.

In large institutions, such as Martland and the VA Hospital, with their large complement of seriously ill and older patients as well, cardiac arrests are fairly common occurrences, and at each institution there exists a specific multidisciplined cardiac arrest team. It is generally composed of a cardiologist, a surgeon, an anesthesiologist and specifically trained nurses and other paramedical personnel, and is supposedly "on the alert" to be able to respond within minutes to any pacemaker call. However, the team and its "crash cart," which is a mobile unit containing vital drugs and other equipment commonly required in such emergencies, are at the mercy of the elevators and the large physical size of the hospital, so that many times the first person to respond is a random member of the house staff, or even a medical student who just happens to be in the immediate vicinity at the time of the arrest.

This often proves to be quite crucial, as there are maneuvers and techniques that can be initiated with very little equipment on a short-term interim basis that are extremely vital and which can often mean the difference between whether the resuscitation will or will not be ultimately successful. These include the use of the ambu-bag to force oxygen into the lungs and external cardiac massage. The latter entails applying pressure by means of placing one's hands on the patient's sternum, or breastbone, and literally "squeezing" the heart between the sternum and the patient's back (under which a flat board is immediately placed to facilitate the procedure), which thus serves to force the oxygenated blood through the system. As soon as the arrest team arrives, more sophisticated monitoring and resuscitative measures are then initiated, which may include injection of adrenalin directly into the heart itself, or possibly direct electrical stimulation if indicated and intubation and subsequent initiation of purer oxygen flow. Nevertheless, the chances for the ultimate outcome to be successful are a direct correlation of the speed of delivery and effectiveness of the prior emergency care delivered. So I was therefore thankful on this occasion to have the assistance of a medical student who fortuitously happened to be present on the ward at that particular moment.

I began the external massage while he "bagged" the patient, in the standardized ratio of three pushes, or squeezes, on the chest, then a brief pause while the ambu-bag is squeezed, and so on. This procedure is followed so that in a situation where someone is attempting to force air into the chest while the other is applying pressure in the opposite direction, the two won't work at cross-purposes. We continued this routine for several minutes as the pacemaker team had still not arrived, and since I was becoming fatigued from the physical exertion involved and because the bed itself was in its lowest position, I found it necessary to literally station myself on the bed itself in order that I could continue the proper positioning of my hands and apply the needed force. Suddenly, I could actually feel the heart beginning to beat again spontaneously, and it was quite a feeling to put it mildly. I continued the massage, and the patient coughed several times as he began to revive; he then began to stir about, and his eyeballs slowly became visible as he gradually regained consciousness. As I perched there, straddling the patient with my hands still on his chest, he glanced up, and with a glazed look in his eyes, shouted at me, "What the hell are you doing on my bed? Get off my chest!"

I was somewhat taken aback, and I instinctively removed my hands, and the instant I did so, his eyeballs again rolled upwards, spontaneous respiration ceased, and the student and I immediately began the procedure anew.

Another two minutes or so had passed and the arrest team had finally arrived, and I was just about to relinquish the job of massaging and get out of the way when lo and behold, the exact sequence of events occurred, and the patient's heart again began to beat on its own. He soon struggled to focus his glazed eyes upon me as I continued to squat directly over him with my hands still resting on his breastbone, when suddenly he shouted at me, "Didn't I just tell you to get off my chest? Can't you see I'm a sick man?" exactly as if the intervening two-minute period had never occurred!

I was to find out later from his chart that the patient was suffering from cancer of the lung, which had already spread to such an extent that it was impossible to cure him operatively. However, he was still very much alive several weeks later when I eventually left the service, and every time I passed his room, I couldn't help but smile and recall the incident. Not only that but to compound the irony of it all, one afternoon I happened to see him up and out of bed in the lounge watching TV. As I went over to inquire how he was doing, I almost got trampled by a herd of vets, led by the patient himself, who were all responding to a little bell that signaled the arrival of the traveling sundries cart. Their enthusiasm was undoubtedly sparked by the fact that, among other items, they could purchase cigarettes for only twenty-six cents a pack, "thoughtfully" and cheaply provided at such an attractively reduced rate by the same federal government that had forced the tobacco companies to put a health warning on those same cigarette packs!

CHAPTER / 29

ALTHOUGH THE expression "Experience is the best teacher" is an overworked cliché, it nevertheless quite succinctly sums up an extremely important aspect of my medical education to which I have already alluded. Textbooks, lectures, attending physicians and rounds notwithstanding, I nonetheless must gratefully and respectfully acknowledge the large and significant contribution made by both the widely varied cross section of my fellow hospital employees with whom I was in daily contact, ranging from the paraprofessional level of the nurses, technicians, and dieticians to the attendants, aides, and orderlies, as well as on a somewhat more abstract level, the patients themselves. It did not take me long to realize (although it surely *did* take considerably longer to *accept*), that simply because someone was not an M.D. did not automatically mean that they did not have anything of value to contribute, particularly in light of their previous experiences, their judgment, and even their good old common sense. A growing realization of the seemingly endless amount of knowledge and expertise required to be a good doctor made me look more and more to my coworkers as allies, who could help make the job of getting someone better both easier and sometimes even more efficient. As in the instance of the suggestion by the nurse's aide, which had proved so successful in relieving a severe case of hiccups, as well as in what follows, I began to understand how foolish it would be to summarily dismiss without consideration, or perhaps even a trial on occasion, any hint or suggestion regarding a difficult patient's management no matter what the source.

However, I had not yet fully arrived at such a thorough understanding or acceptance of the value of this aspect of my experiences when I was called to the detoxification unit one late afternoon to work up a new admission. His wife was present, and she informed me that her husband had a long history of alcoholism and apparently had been doing well until two weeks before, when he had gone on a real bender and did nothing but drink copious amounts of beer and whiskey. He had not had any alcohol for the last twenty-four hours, and upon examination he was quite tremulous and sweating profusely. Although not actively hallucinating, I felt he was a prime candidate to go into frank dt's anytime in the next twenty-four hours. I therefore prescribed what I felt to be the proper amount of medication to "cover him" for this possible eventuality, as well as making him as comfortable as possible. At that particular time I didn't feel the patient needed to be "restrained," although the male attendant who had worked with such patients for many years and had a real feel for this sort of thing gently suggested that I leave an order if it should become necessary to do so. I thanked him and said I would be back in an hour to reevaluate him after the medication had a chance to work and would place him in restraints if I then felt it was indicated.

At this, the attendant, who had probably gone through numerous similar scenarios with a great number of young, relatively inexperienced doctors, simply gave me a knowing little smile and, sure enough, in less than forty-five minutes, I was summoned back to the unit stat. Upon entering, I found my new admission actively engaged in struggling with the nurse, who was attempting to extricate a full urinal from his hands, while, he, at the same time, was loudly and vigorously leading the rest of the ward, consisting of six alcoholics in varying stages of recovery, through chorus after chorus of German drinking songs. And as if that wasn't enough, just as I got to the foot of the bed, he slipped free, raised his "stein," and proceeded to drink heartily while spraying urine over half the unit. With the aid of an orderly I succeeded in getting the now almost empty urinal out of his hands, and after a brief struggle, we managed to successfully restrain him.

The gentleman, as it turned out, was quite personable and

engaging (as many alcoholic people are), and I began to look forward to seeing him on rounds because he was also quite intelligent and perceptive as well and always seemed to have a little comment, story or joke to relate. For example, at one point in his hospitalization he had complained to me of being constipated, and I just happened to be in the room the next day, when a nurse walked in, smiled cheerfully, and stated to the patient, "We're going to have an enema this morning, just like the doctor ordered." At which the patient, immediately picking up on this terribly overused (or at the least inappropriately overused) hospital expression (which I like to refer to as "the medical collective we" that so many nurses and to a lesser extent doctors are so prone to use) quickly snapped back, "Oh, that's nice. I didn't know you were going to have one also," and proceeded to laugh heartily when he saw the look on the nurse's face.

Of course, the patient was "right on" in observing and commenting on the absurdity of the use of the "we" in this context, but there is some sound reasoning behind its widespread usage in medicine. It most appropriately should be reserved for those situations wherein a patient is stricken with a serious disease, and therefore needs support and reassurance that the doctors and rest of the staff are not only concerned for his well-being but are also commiserating and at least trying to understand what he is experiencing. Thus, the intent is sound and humane in that the patient will hopefully get the feeling that others around him, most especially those responsible for his care, are concerned and involved. This should ideally be additionally conveyed in other verbal and nonverbal ways, but when the term is used so frequently and singularly as a mere figure of speech, as it had become with that particular nurse and so many others, the desired effect is almost certainly diluted, if not lost completely.

One morning, shortly before his scheduled discharge, he proceeded to tell me the following joke. It seems that when Pope Paul had died and gone to Heaven, he found quite a long line of people waiting to get in through the pearly gates. Spying St. Peter, the Pope implored him, saying, "I'm an old man who has served the Church, God, and my people well, and I'm very tired and wonder if I might go right in?"

To which St. Peter replied, "I'm sorry, Pope, but since everyone is equal in God's eyes, you'll just have to stand in line with the rest of the good men and women waiting to get in."

The Pope graciously accepted this, shrugged his shoulders, and was on his way back to the line, when someone wearing a stethoscope and a white coat suddenly appeared and proceeded to go directly to the head of the line, where he was immediately and quite ceremoniously ushered in by St. Peter. This naturally incensed the Pope, who proceeded to challenge St. Peter's hypothesis that if everyone was an equal in Heaven, as he had just explained, then why was this particular person treated so specially?

St. Peter replied, "Well, because He is special. That was God Himself who just passed by—He simply likes to play doctor sometimes."

CHAPTER / 30

THAT TURNED-AROUND punch line, wherein God supposedly enjoys playing doctor, began to take on a very ironic quality as I realized there were certain times and circumstances when I found it increasingly difficult not to view myself as "playing God." This was especially so at the beginning of my internship, when I had to really come to grips with taking responsibility for making the very type of decision that I had hoped would not be mine alone to make—or that of any other singular person for that matter, be he doctor, lawyer, politician, or clergyman. Nothing had really changed in either the legalistic or moralistic sense during the time that had passed since that discussion which took place on pediatrics when I was a third-year student. I still believed that it is not only extremely unfair but unwise for society to tacitly continue to expect a doctor to make certain decisions regarding the right of another individual to choose to continue to live or, just as importantly, to die. Morality and ethics are much more properly the realm for the discussion of philosophic and extremely complex concepts such as the question of who, in society, if not simply each individual alone, *should* be involved in "passing on" such judgments, as well as many other nebulous and ill-defined areas that certainly go far beyond the bounds of any straightforward medical judgment. Yet, by the mere continued acceptance of the status quo while at the very same time being quick to condemn and censure a physician *for* taking on the burden of responsibility, our society not only cops out but then has the audacity to make the medical profession its scapegoat, such as in the question of abortion for an all too obvious example. A step which therefore must be taken before anything can even begin to change is that society (or culture, or civilization, or whatever other label you would like to give to the collection of individual leaders, thinkers, and doers who are "society") must begin to come to grips with defining the proper role for a doctor in today's complex world, both in respect to what is expected and, just as importantly, what is not expected.

This little intellectualized digression is all well and good, but as a neophyte doctor early in my internship, it would all prove to be of little comfort, as I very quickly found myself confronted with all the ramifications involved with the realities of life and death on its most basic human level. For it was during only the second week of my internship when I admitted a fifty-year-old man who had come in with the chief complaint of shortness of breath and fluid retention in his lower extremities, which along with certain other criteria made it appear most likely that he was suffering with congestive heart failure. This is really a descriptive term and not a diagnosis because the etiology or cause must then be established as to the reason *why* the heart itself is failing. The differential, or probable, causes are varied and extensive, and most commonly include such entities as long-standing hypertension, or high blood pressure, where the heart is stressed from its continuous efforts to force the blood through narrowed or hardened blood vessels. If these blood vessels are the particular ones that nourish the heart itself (the heart does not simply absorb the blood that passes through its chambers but has its own specific arteries to nourish the heart muscle itself), then the situation may be such that the muscle itself is not getting the sufficient blood supply required to be able to function normally. Such a condition may eventually progress to the point where a complete shutting down of one or more of these all important vessels occurs, thereby totally preventing freshly oxygenated blood from reaching a portion of the heart muscle, with the resultant death of that segment. This is what actually occurs in the vast majority of heart attacks, or more technically myocardial infarctions, a term originating from the Greek *mys,* meaning muscle, and *kardia,* meaning heart, with infarction being the more general term for the death of any category of cell whose blood supply has been cut off.

A valvular defect in any of the several valves found in the heart may also cause stress on the heart muscle, leading to failure, as well might any substance that is a toxin (poison) to the heart muscle itself, of which one of the more common ones is alcohol. There are other well-documented reasons as to why a heart can fail (some instances of which might be sudden and catastrophic, such as a myocardial infarction, whereas others may take a long, progressively degenerating course), but in a certain percentage of cases, no matter how extensive the work-up, no specific cause or condition can be ascertained as to the exact reason *why* that particular heart is failing or has failed.

In this particular case, my resident and I worked hand in hand with the cardiologists, but no one could arrive at a definitive conclusion as to the etiology. As the physicians in charge, we were therefore in a real bind in that we could only treat the patient symptomatically (meaning the administration of medications to mobilize the fluid and stimulate the heart, and by thereby relieving some of the stress and strain, hope to allow the condition to resolve by itself). Nevertheless, despite standardly accepted management techniques, his heart continued to fail, and his general condition deteriorated gravely over the course of the next several weeks.

It subsequently became necessary to transfer the patient to the ICU, and as the weeks went by, other problems began to develop secondarily as a consequence of his continuously failing heart. One of the most significant and serious complications was the development of renal failure, since in order to function properly the kidneys require a certain minimum amount of blood flow, which they were not receiving, and by six weeks or so after his initial admission, Mr. R. was lapsing in and out of coma, and his situation was critical.

Mr. R. had an attentive and concerned wife, with whom I established a good rapport over the course of weeks, and who understandably was quite distraught over the chain of events. As the weeks went by and Mr. R. became more and more debilitated, nourished only by IV fluids and being able to breathe properly only by the aid of a tracheosotomy and mechanical respirator, Mrs. R. found it increasingly difficult to even visit her husband's bedside, although in his comatose state he certainly was in no position to be able to respond to, much less acknowledge, her presence. For he certainly was no longer the same rather robust, hearty-looking man he had been when he had first entered the hospital, and Mrs. R. painfully admitted that she simply no longer had the emotional strength to endure the agony of seeing him in his present condition. Consequently, I spoke with her on the phone at least twice every day to appraise her of his current condition, and it became increasingly difficult to sound optimistic and hold out much realistic hope for any eventual recovery.

In addition, there were three teen-age sons in the family, two of whom were away at college at the time, and I increasingly began to dread the sound of my beeper going off and the operator informing me of an incoming call. Even though I knew it would be best in the long run, I nevertheless found it extremely difficult and upsetting as I would attempt each day to inform Mrs. R. of the harsh reality of her husband's deteriorating condition, and it became even more distressing when she began wanting a definitive answer as to when her husband was actually going to die. It was naturally impossible to make any predictions of any sort, and I could only comfort her by emphasizing that he was in a coma and not consciously suffering and that we were doing everything possible to make him as comfortable as possible.

It would be an understatement to say that as the weeks went by, the situation became quite an emotional drain on myself, as well as on the patient's family. Mrs. R. felt it best that the older children not visit either so that they could remember their father as the strong, loving man they once knew and not the unresponsive person whose only signs of life were a direct consequence of the elaborate life-support systems to which he was attached by the innumerable tubes and other paraphernalia which seemed to come out of every available orifice of his body. On those mornings when I had not been on call the previous evening, it became impossible not to rush to the ICU immediately upon arriving at the hospital, covertly hoping that the now inevitable catastrophic event had occurred during the time I was gone, yet only to find that Mr. R.'s great reserve of strength had somehow managed to keep him alive, although just barely, and I would then anxiously await the inevitable phone call.

The situation remained unchanged for another week to ten days, and finally after consultation with our attending physician, the cardiologists and the renal specialists, a conclusion was reached that all evidence indicated that such widespread, irreversible damage had occurred it would serve no one's best interest, be it the family or, most importantly, the patient, to prolong the ordeal by any heroic measures. It then fell upon me, after a lengthy, open and difficult discussion with Mrs. R., to write the order *not* to call for the pacemaker team when Mr. R. would suffer an arrest. I remember the moment quite vividly, and even the precise location on the order book page where I wrote the actual order and how I also attached a "flag" to the same effect on the front of the chart. Intellectually, I could tell myself that the ultimate course of events was not under my control and that I had worked as long and as hard as I possibly could in an attempt to help this man, but despite all the logic and sound reasoning, I was still extremely upset and distraught. To add to my uneasiness, I was torn between a desire to see the ordeal ended as soon as possible for everyone involved (myself included) and, as much, by a wish not to be present when the actual event occurred.

Yet it seemed inevitable, even appropriate, that not only was I physically present in the hospital when Mr. R. ultimately expired but that I was actually at his bedside, preparing to draw blood for additional studies. And despite my ambivalent feelings, I was truly relieved and thankful that I was present and was able to be the one to notify Mrs. R., as well as comfort her when she arrived at the hospital, and I knew that she felt the same way.

All in all, it was quite an upsetting experience to undergo in my first month and a half of being a doctor, and although it did not make the next time a similar situation developed hurt any less, it certainly gave me a much greater insight into my own fears and doubts, especially about death.

And as those first two months drew quickly to a close, I began to realize, with a great deal of personal pride and satisfaction, how much overall confidence and skill I had acquired in such a relatively short period of time. I suppose this reflects well on the "firing line" type of training I was receiving.

This meant I did not have the luxury of being able to sit back and observe what course of action would be undertaken by a fully trained, practicing physician in each new clinical situation I would encounter while contemplating and speculating on an intellectual level how I would have responded. It was therefore imperative that I quickly and properly acquire the necessary skills and knowledge required to conscientiously provide for the best possible care for my patients at the current moment; this would also be in my own best interest from an educational point of view. Of course, this was far from an overnight process, and involved much trial and error, and there were still occasions when I felt a high level of anxiety, especially at those previously mentioned times when my resident might not be readily available, and I alone would be the one called upon to make a critical decision or take a definitive action.

However, even though such potential was literally present all the time, for the most part the vast majority of situations began to become more and more routine as the amount of my exposure to varied clinical situations became greater. Quite importantly, I had also begun to acquire the necessary skills to be able to assess what was a true emergency and demanded immediate intervention and what could wait for another more experienced opinion or even be looked up in an appropriate text before taking any action. Therefore, as time went by, not only did situations that had originally scared the shit out of me the first few times I had to deal with them on an emergency level, such as cardiac arrest or an epileptic seizure for example, become much less frightening and anxiety provoking, but in addition I also found myself much more comfortable with my developing ability to assess the condition of a newly admitted, nonemergency patient presenting certain complaints and physical findings. I became more and more aware of my developing ability to be able to appropriately decide what diagnostic tests or studies were called for immediately and which others could be most efficaciously performed over the course of the following day—and what precise medication or other form of intervention was indicated at that exact moment.

It therefore became quite gratifying not to have to call upon the resident as frequently as I had to in the beginning, as particular situations would begin to arise that I had previously dealt wth successfully (but I certainly don't want to give the impression that after only such a brief amount of time, I considered myself a real hotshot, able to handle almost anything that would come my way). I still continued to rely heavily on my resident and others to teach and point out my errors in judgment or technique, which still occurred with rather frequent regularity, but the general feeling of growing competence and skill, so dearly paid for in terms of time and emotional investment, was extremely self-satisfying. Of course, there were also frequent times when I became extremely discouraged and could have kicked myself for not having remembered something I had just read about or had been similarly involved with on another patient only the week before, and there were moments of utter frustration, when I felt there would be no way I could ever know even as much as my resident, much less an attending. Yet despite the demands, the chronic fatigue, and inability to read as much as I wanted, I somehow managed to amass a considerable amount of practical expertise and knowledge.

I tried very hard to keep everything in perspective and to be aware of my own limitations, which quite often became blatantly obvious in retrospect. The awareness of this aspect of the situation (and again, more importantly, the *acceptance* of it) made it much easier to swallow my pride and not hesitate to ask for help or guidance when I felt I needed it, despite the concomitant feeling that it might make me appear even more ignorant and less knowledgeable than I was. Good judgment and common sense rather quickly superseded any misplaced hubris when I recognized that, at least at this point in my training, there was a highly competent individual readily available for help and guidance, and it would be pretty silly not to use this to my best advantage and then find myself at some later date in a similar situation with no one to whom I could turn. Several of my colleagues seemed to have great difficulty in being able to ask for any kind of help or assistance in this respect, be it from a resident, an attending or even a peer, as if to display the existence of even the slightest doubt or limitation in almost *any* area or situation, even those in which a neophyte intern could not possibly be expected to have any prior knowledge or experience, was still somehow a horrible admission of inadequacy. As a result, these individuals surely made a difficult experience even more difficult than it had to be.

Just as importantly, I also began to realize that I was a good intern, and a good doctor, and I mean this not only in the sense of becoming knowledgeable as to what was expected of me in a purely functional sense but also the manner in which I went about doing my job as well. Although I knew there were times I failed, and sometimes to much more of a degree than at others, I felt truly good about the way I at least attempted to relate to each patient as a human being. I knew I was doing something right because not only did I feel good about myself and the quality of care I was able to give to them, but just as importantly, I knew by the way they spoke and related to me that the patients felt pretty good about having me for their doctor. And even more astounding and gratifying, most of them were actually getting better!

CHAPTER / 31

IN THE interest of receiving the broadest medical training within the given resources, we were obligated to divide up our internal medicine rotation between the VA Hospital and Martland, as each patient population varied greatly, not only in regard to makeup but in the type of problems and situations that prevailed as well. One obvious advantage that Martland offered was the opportunity to care for female patients, which was so severely limited at the VA Hospital as to be almost nonexistent. In addition, being in a large, inner-city hospital, with an active (what an understatement!) emergency room and clinic operation, and functioning almost in the capacity of a family doctor for a large segment of the general community, the training doctor would be exposed to a much greater variety and assortment of disease entities than a VA hospital could afford. Not only was there a much greater opportunity to see and manage many more emergency and critical short-term situations, but as importantly, the physician would also be able to learn to properly manage the more mundane, ambulatory walk-in type of patient, presenting such symptoms as a common cold or diarrhea for example, who would comprise the vast majority of patients he would ultimately see on a day-to-day basis in a general private practice. On the other hand, as a general rule the VA patients represented more chronic and long-term management problems, and naturally, there was a certain amount of overlap between the two institutions as well. The point I'm trying to make is much more clearly illustrated by considering the general surgical service. At the VA Hospital there existed a greater opportunity to develop skills with regard to a great many more elective, nonemergency procedures, such as hernia repairs, and removal of hemorrhoids, pilonidal cysts, and even varicose veins (which generally represent a large portion of a general surgeon's average case load), whereas at Martland, the surgeon was much more likely to be faced with many more varied and acute situations, such as a gunshot and knife wound, for example, which obviously necessitate immediate intervention. Add to this the other forms of trauma and emergency situations seen routinely in a city hospital (automobile accidents and "hot appendixes" pop quickly into mind), where the approach and evaluation of the patient's condition are naturally much different, and it can be seen that the training surgeon is thus afforded the opportunity to develop somewhat different surgical techniques as well.

Although perhaps not as obvious as on the surgical service, there was nevertheless quite a noticeable transition in my own medical experience as I switched hospitals. However, although the change in patient population, with the ramifications of having to deal with the wide range of problems and situations that exist in the inner city and which have such a profound influence on the general health and well-being of the community as a whole was striking, the most significant difference seemed to be one of attitude. The general pervasive atmosphere of the institution as a whole, from the patient level, to the administration, to the house staff, and even to the larger number of paramedical and auxiliary personnel, seemed to be that of resigned frustration.

On the house staff level the frustration seemed most focused upon the issue of performance of nonmedical functions. This is hardly unique to any city hospital, and it appears to be a chronic, on-going source of controversy, as evidenced by its being one of the two pivotal issues involved in the "doctors' strike" by the house staff of nineteen municipal hospitals in New York City last spring and by the fact that the issue still remains fundamentally unresolved.

The frustration is especially intensified at an institution like Martland, where the house staff officer quickly finds that all too often, he has no alternative but to function in a nonmedical, strictly service-oriented capacity or that particular job simply will not get done, and unfortunately, it is the patient who would ultimately be the one to suffer. This situation exists as a result of a multitude of factors, the most apparent and obvious being the generally overcrowded conditions within an inadequate, outdated facility that does not even have call buttons at the patients' bedsides, so that the individual must literally shout at the top of his lungs or throw a soiled bedpan on the floor to alert a nurse that he is in need of care. In addition, the paramedical personnel are chronically understaffed and generally poorly motivated, and I regularly found myself, both as a student and even more so as an intern, personally wheeling a patient to X ray, wasting valuable minutes on the phone with the dietician attempting to change a particular patient's diet when a simple written order should have sufficed, and making literally hundreds of little side trips each day to the supply rooms or wherever because more often than not, there would be no one available, or even willing, to assist me in any capacity, even one as simple as gathering needed material I had requested for a particular procedure.

Another very crucial factor contributing to the overall situation is the fact that although the overwhelming majority of patients and paramedical personnel are black or Puerto Rican, the house staff and attending physicians are predominately white or foreign born and trained. This inevitably has profound implications and repercussions, and the all too obvious consequences are the deep-seated racial overtones emanating from both sides, which permeated practically every interaction, from doctor-patient, to doctor-nurse, and even to doctor-orderly or cleaning man. It is a very real issue, and sadly, my experience in this regard was that its existence was not acknowledged to any significant extent, especially by the hospital administrators, and it was quietly swept under the rug whenever possible (the "maybe if we shut our eyes, the problem will go away" school of thought) or dealt with rather poorly if an overt incident occurred that could not be overlooked. It is possible that perhaps very little could have been done to significantly alter the situation, since the problem is surely societal in scope and not simply one confined to an inner-city hospital, or even to a city as polarized as Newark, but very little effort seemed to be expended, and the racism was so blatantly obvious and intense at Martland that it played a very significant role in the overall poor quality of patient care, as well as contributing to the unpleasant working conditions in general. It should not be so surprising, then, that there was generally such a low morale among the hospital personnel as a whole and the house staff in particular, especially among the more perceptive and talented parties involved on both sides.

Another somewhat frivolous but nevertheless annoying circumstance that helped contribute to the general atmosphere of tension and frustration was the seemingly all-pervasive attitude of the women manning the switchboard and page systems, who felt as if they were doing you a great personal favor if they complied with a request to either connect you with a party you were attempting to reach within the hospital or give you an outside line so that you could dial out of the hospital directly. Only doctors were given the privilege of using the house phones to make local outside calls, and the procedure involved was to simply identify yourself and then be given an available line. However, regardless of the time, more often than not it seemed that the operator would frequently say that no outside lines were free at that moment. Now this may or may not have been true at any given time, but I found it hard to believe that it was always legitimate since it happened with such regularity and at such varied intervals. To add further insult to injury certain operators were so incredibly rude that they wouldn't even have the courtesy to inform you if a line was free (even when you were positive there had to be one available—like at midnight) and would simply hang up on you before you could even finish your request without even as much as extending the courtesy of an explanation or an apology.

An additional aggravating feature contributing to the general tone of frustration concerned the elevators, and after experiences in other institutions and talking with other house staff officers trained elsewhere, it, too, seems to be a problem endemic to almost all large municipal hospitals, and hardly unique to Martland alone. This fact, however, was of minor consolation during the countless minutes I spent each day waiting for elevators, and I was able to read an entire small novel that I carried in a pocket of my white coat for just such purposes in the intervals I spent waiting for the elevators over a time period of less than one month.

There was one elevator, manned by an operator, which was supposedly designated for only emergency and routine transport of patients and hospital personnel, but due to the volume of traffic, it was not uncommon to find yourself with a patient, either in a wheelchair or on a stretcher, whose condition could run the gamut from highly infectious to being near death; a drunken visitor who somehow slipped in; perhaps a visiting professor; and the inevitable maintenance man with his bucket and mop. Needless to say, and rugby notwithstanding, I used the stairs whenever possible, and I rarely hesitated, except perhaps on the last leg of a thirty-six-hour shift, to walk up or down as many as nine flights just to save myself the even greater wear, tear, and aggravation that would be involved in fighting the elevators!

CHAPTER / 32

In an attempt to convey as much as possible what it was like to be an intern on the medical service at an institution such as Martland, I'd like to present a log of one typical thirty-six-hour tour of duty. I offer this accounting in the hope that it may make it somewhat easier for the reader to conceive what is involved in serving as a "frontline" doctor in a large, municipal hospital, as well as gain a greater awareness not only of the profound mental and physical stresses involved but the depth of the emotional involvement as well. I choose this particular day out of all the experiences incurred while working such a schedule—where I was "on duty" every fourth night—not because it is particularly exciting, stimulating or dramatic but because I feel it to be illustrative of my experiences in general.

7:45 A.M.—I arrive on 12 North, which is my assigned unit, or home base, for the two months I'm on the service. As a consequence of the physical limitations of the hospital itself, the general medical floors are divided into a north and south section, or wing, with each side being comprised of one large thirty-six-bed ward, and two smaller rooms containing eight beds in each. Since there is only one large bathroom to service all the patients on any one side, it is necessary that the wings be segregated by sex. 12 North happens to be all male; however my resident and I are also the primary physicians for female patients and other males not on 12 North proper who have been previously admitted to our team but who have had to be placed on other wards or medical floors wherever appropriate space was available. Therefore, the particular wing or side to which you are arbitrarily assigned is not that critical in itself, except in that one vital regard of the quality of teaching which is available. This, you will recall, is dependent on the degree and differentiation of style and knowledge of the individual attendings and chief residents, who are similarly responsible for all the patients admitted by their respective teams regardless of their exact location in the hospital. The individual ward assignments for the house staff are done for administrative and logistical ease, and although not always achieved, hopefully to effect as equitable a division as possible of the work load, especially with regard to floor coverage at night.

My resident is already present; he is from Pakistan and is quite knowledgeable and fluent in English. He is also an excellent all round doctor and teacher. Our plan is to first make quick work rounds on all our patients; I will keep a list of all that needs to be accomplished for each patient for this particular day. This might entail expediting or following up on procedures or diagnostic techniques previously ordered and hopefully done, as well as to remind ourselves of other chores that we ourselves will have to perform. We will then divide up the work wherever possible in an attempt to organize and make the best use of our time.

It will be especially important to be as efficient today as possible because we are both well aware that we are on duty tonight and will most probably have several new admissions during the day as well. There is one other scheduled long team, as well as several short teams, with whom both of us on "long" will alternate admissions until 5 P.M., whereafter all subsequent admissions will be divided between the two long teams until 8 A.M. the following morning. We will also be responsible for taking care of any problems that might arise through the night involving any of the other medical patients already in the "house"—another example of medical slang, referring to those current in-patients previously admitted.

7:50 A.M.—We first go to the ICU, which is located one flight up and on the south side of the hospital, where we will see our two most critically ill patients. Both of them are in a coma and require a great deal of time and attention. Mr. K. is a twenty-one-year-old recently returned Viet Nam veteran who had attempted to commit suicide four days before out of despair after losing his job and his girl friend. He had ingested several ounces of turpentine, along with twenty pain killers and approximately forty tablets of a long-acting oral medication used in the treatment of diabetes. The latter was an important factor contributing to his current poor condition because this particular drug, which remains active in the body for a long period of time, was the cause of a persistent lowering of his blood sugar to critical levels. To make matters even worse, two evenings before, while in his comatose condition, he had vomited and then inadvertently "swallowed" some of the vomitus down "the wrong pipe" into his lungs. The resultant aspiration pneumonia was a serious enough condition in itself, but it became even more so when compounded with a low blood sugar. It had become necessary to perform a tracheostomy when he began to have difficulty breathing, and the tracheostomy tube was attached to a mechanical respirator that regulated not only how often he breathed but also the percentage and pressure of oxygen as well.

However, when we arrive in the ICU, Mr. K., as often happens, was making an effort to breathe on his own, and consequently struggling in an attempt to override the machine. This added factor means that the percentage of oxygen and carbon dioxide in his blood will have to be monitored even more frequently than before, which means that repeated samples of his arterial blood will have to be obtained.

The procedure involved is not what most people visualize when they think of a routine blood test, because here the blood must be taken from an artery and not a vein. This is necessitated because if blood was taken from a vein, it would have already circulated and thus would have given up oxygen and picked up carbon dioxide from whatever tissue or organ through which it had previously passed after leaving the heart and lungs. The arterial blood sample must be drawn up into a heparinized syringe, since the heparin will prevent the blood from clotting in the syringe as it would normally do. The syringe is then sealed airtight by plunging the needle point into a rubber stopper, and it is then put into ice to stabilize it and sent off to the lab with as little delay as possible. If I had a dime for every trip I made to the ice machine, which was naturally located way down the hallway, I could probably have retired for life at the end of two months.

By definition then, to obtain the sample necessitates entering an artery, and this is somewhat more difficult (often a lot more difficult, especially at 4 A.M.) than to puncture a vein, since the vast majority of veins are located much closer to the surface of the body than the arteries. The most easily accessible sites are the femoral artery, which is quite large and located in the groin, and the brachial and radial arteries, which are most easily located and entered in the inner aspect of the elbow and wrist, respectively. There are fewer potential complications in the brachial or radial approach as there are fewer structures, such as veins or nerves, to inadvertently injure, but the femoral artery, which carries blood to the leg, is obviously much larger and therefore easier to penetrate successfully. The procedure is accomplished by first palpating (the fancy medical term for feeling) with your fingertips for the pulsation of the artery, carefully cleaning the area and then gently directing the needle through the surface of the skin in the region of greatest pulsation. You know when you have successfully entered the artery and not a nearby vein because the blood from the artery will be cherry red in contrast to the darker, dusky color of venous blood, which occurs as a consequence of the respective oxygen contents. A second reliable guideline that you are in the artery is that the syringe should fill spontaneously because of the greater pressure, and you can actually see the blood entering in short, narrow spurts, which correspond to the heartbeats themselves.

After this was completed, I drew additional samples of venous blood so as to enable us to monitor his blood chemistries (such as the amounts of sodium, potassium, uric acid, and so forth), which should always be done regularly when a patient is on IV fluid therapy, and I also did a quick finger stick bedside lab exam, which gave me a rough estimate of his blood sugar level. The result showed that his blood glucose was quite low despite the constant infusion he had received through the night of a highly concentrated sugar solution. His urine output for the previous twenty-four hours was then tabulated (his penis and bladder having previously been catheterized for just such a purpose), his tracheostomy tube suctioned clear of accumulated secretions, and additional orders for the day were then written. The IV orders, however, specifying the quantity and composition of the fluid he was to receive over the next twenty-four hours, would have to wait, being contingent upon exact knowledge of his current blood chemistries, which were being formulated in the lab at that very moment. I also called the radiology department requesting that a portable chest X ray be done to help us evaluate the state of his pneumonia.

As we waited for the lab to call back the results of the blood gases, we turned our attentions to the patient in the next bed, a Mrs. W., a forty-eight-year-old woman who was also critically ill and also in a coma, secondary to being in an acute phase of chronic liver failure. The exact mechanism as to why a patient in this condition loses consciousness and lapses into a so-called hepatic comma is not fully understood, but it is currently believed to be related to a buildup in the body of certain toxic substances, ammonia being the one most frequently implicated. For, normally, the liver helps metabolize, or alter, ammonia so it can then be excreted from the body by means of the urine, feces or even the sweat and thereby not build up to any significant degree, especially in the highly sensitive central nervous system.

There is a peculiar, rather distinctive fetid odor to a person's breath in such a condition, and she also required the use of a respirator to help her breathe. An arterial blood sample had been taken by my resident at the same time I had obtained one from Mr. K., so the two samples were sent together to the lab. However, since the blood ammonia level is also more correctly assessed in the arterial blood, I was forced to draw an additional sample. Similarly, the ammonia must also be stabilized in ice during transport to the lab, and I knew it was going to be one of those days (and nights and next day probably as well) when I discovered that there wasn't enough ice left over from my previous sojourn to the ice machine, and I had to take another hike down the hallway. Venous blood was also drawn and sent to the lab for chemistries.

This will ultimately turn out to be the last of numerous admissions for this woman, who had a long history of chronic alcoholism and was therefore well-known to most of the senior

226

house staff members, many of whom had taken care of her in the past. As pointed out earlier, the liver is a remarkable organ in that it is able to withstand an incredible amount of abuse and yet retain an extraordinary capacity to regenerate itself. However, even this unique organ is capable only up to a certain point, and if repeatedly stressed by a combination of poor nutrition, alcoholism and chronic insult, it will ultimately fail. Remembering that one of its many functions is to help convert dietarily ingested protein into other forms which can be more easily transported and stored, one of the expected consequences of a failing liver is an inability to handle protein. People with poor liver functioning are therefore routinely placed on severely restricted protein diets, and if they do not pay scrupulous attention to what they eat, they can easily upset the delicate balance and throw themselves into hepatic coma. The amount of protein required can be as small as that contained in just one bite of meat, hence the derivation of the often-used expression, "the one-meatball syndrome." The only therapy that can be offered is basically supportive in the hope that if the liver is not stressed any further, it might recover at least partial functioning. There is currently a great deal of research being done employing baboons' livers, which are quite similar in form and structure to that of the human's, including the possibility of circulating someone's blood who is in liver failure through a baboon's liver, in effect a sort of combination natural kidney machine and heart lung device, but the work is still experimental and not yet perfected to any degree where it is reliable enough for use on the human clinical level.

It was frightening to realize that Mrs. W. had been apparently functioning well up until just four days before when she had started drinking heavily, and that in the two days since her admission, she had rapidly progressed from mild disturbances of consciousness, to rigidity in all her extremities, to her present state of deep coma, with intermittent seizures.

8:30 A.M.—I leave my resident to await the blood gas results, with which he will then be able to make any needed adjustments in the respirators, and I go alone to see another of our patients, who had only been transferred out of the ICU the previous day. He is a fifty-year-old man who was finally having a favorable response after a three-day siege of being in a condition known as status asthmaticus, where we had been unable to break his prolonged and sustained attack of asthma, and for a time it appeared he was going to be resistant to all our available therapies. He had truly suffered greatly over the previous seventy-two hours, and his chest was still puffed out as he tried desperately to move air in and out of his obstructed airways. He was extremely fatigued from his ordeal, and to be frank, it did not appear that we had actually done very much to relieve him. From having suffered through repeated attacks in the past, he knew we were not going to cure him but could only help him through this critical time period. Therefore, I was not at all surprised that when I approached him with the blood gas setup (after a third trip to a different ice machine), he literally cursed me and bluntly refused to let me draw the sample. Now this in itself is not a very uncommon occurrence in my hospital, and a patient naturally has the right to refuse any therapeutic procedure or diagnostic technique, and even leave the hospital, whenever he or she so desires.

However, for some reason I found this particular patient extremely difficult to deal with, and I guess I was frustrated and just plain tired of having to cajole or plead every time I needed his cooperation, especially since it meant more work for me and was for his benefit, not mine. So when he immediately started to give me a hard time, I simply turned away and left his ward, planning to meet up with my resident, who should have already finished in the ICU and begun to make rounds on the general female side, two flights below.

8:45 A.M.—I inform my resident as to what had transpired, and since the man had appeared clinically better, he says it is not imperative that it be done at this exact moment and that he would go up later and try his luck. We first stop at the bedside of one of our geriatric patients, who has been in the "house" for approximately three weeks. She is a ninety-year-old woman whose family was no longer adequately able to care for her, as she was not only senile but unable to feed herself or control her bowels or bladder. We had detected no signs or symptoms that signified the presence of any active disease process, and we were only waiting for a bed to become available in a nursing home that accepted Medicare patients in order to discharge her. Although the breakfast trays have been distributed almost an hour before, I notice that her food is cold and untouched, obviously because no one appeared to have either the time or inclination to help feed her. Her weight had been dropping steadily over the course of her hospital stay, and I therefore spend the next ten minutes at her bedside coaxing and spoon-feeding her, and yelling for an aide to come and change her soiled clothes and bedding.

While I attended to this my resident was checking the lab reports from the previous day on another of our female patients, who was also an alcoholic afflicted with liver disease, but who was not nearly in the same poor condition as Mrs. W. This woman had had several teeth extracted a few days prior to presenting herself to the emergency room with the complaint that blood had persistently continued to ooze from each of the extraction sites. Again, this is not an uncommon occurrence in our patient population since it often occurs as a consequence of the abused liver being unable to synthesize certain coagulation factors necessary for normal clotting. The situation is often complicated even further by the fact that the liver requires the presence of a certain minimal quantity of a specific vitamin, vitamin K, for their production, and this is generally in short supply as a result of the usual concomitant nutritional deficiency. I examine her and find no active signs of bleeding, and she appears to be responding well to vitamin and dietary supplements. As we leave her bedside to go and check on our remaining patients, a nurse suddenly runs over and interrupts us with the news that our ninety-year-old patient has apparently just expired while sitting on the bedpan.

We all rush over, although my resident and I both know we are not going to attempt any resuscitative measures at this point. It is no chore for me to lift her eighty-pound body off the bedpan. I adamantly refuse to lay her back down in the soiled bed and insist that a clean sheet be placed down before I leave her bedside. It naturally fell to me to then fill out the death certificate and notify the family. It is now approximately 9 A.M.

9:00 A.M.—I am on the phone with the patient's granddaughter, and I am growing more and more annoyed at her attitude as she seems much more upset by my insisting that she should come to the hospital to make the necessary arrangements than by the fact that her grandmother had just died. Rather than aggravate myself any further, I tell her to do whatever she wants and abruptly terminate the conversation. I inform the hospital administrator of what had transpired, make sure that all the papers are in order, and proceed to catch up with my resident, who by then is already on the male side.

9:30 A.M.—At this point we are due at morning report, where the previous day's admissions are presented to the rest of the house staff and several of the attendings. We had not admitted any new patients the day before, so it was not critical that we be there exactly on time. However, it happens that I am scheduled to give the daily ten-minute article presentation, which had recently become part of the protocol, where a current article dealing with new advances in medicine is brought to the attention of those attending. The article is generally presented at the end, and usually there are only a few minutes left for a rather brief presentation. Occasionally though, if the admissions had been light for the previous twenty-four hours, time was available for questions and discussion, with an occasional "roasting" by several of the attendings who were notorious for "ball busting." I had my notes ready, and since it was therefore imperative that I be present at a reasonable time, it was agreed that my resident would finish rounds on the four male patients we hadn't yet seen and I would go to morning report.

Two of the patients are located in the fourteenth-floor isolation ward. One is a twenty-four-year-old male with active tuberculosis, who has subsequently developed kidney failure secondary to his antituberculous medications. He was being followed closely by the renal department and the infectious disease group as well, and at that very moment he was in the operating room having his shunt revised. A shunt is a mechanical device that is inserted between an artery and a vein, usually in the wrist so that it is easily accessible, in order that a person's blood supply can then be shunted out of his body and through the dialysis (kidney) machine. The blood can then be filtered and potentially harmful waste products removed before the blood is returned to the body, again by means of the shunting device. The procedure must be performed at regular intervals until such time, if ever, when the kidneys have recovered sufficiently to perform their function.

230

Unfortunately, the shunt has a tendency to become clotted with blood, and that was the reason why the patient was presently in the OR. We also currently have a thirty-year-old male patient who is recuperating in a separate room of the isolation sector from acute, infectious hepatitis. He is doing quite well, and as we do not feel he currently presents a danger of spreading his infection, we are considering early transfer to the general medical ward.

In addition, there are also two male patients in the general medical ward, both of them suffering from congestive heart failure and each responding well to treatment and due to be discharged soon.

10:00 A.M.—Morning report—this a welcome respite simply because I know I will be able to sit down for at least fifteen minutes. However, I become just a bit uneasy when I notice that two attendings from the renal department who are not usually in attendance at morning report are present this morning; I had chosen an article reporting on the toxic effects to the kidneys of certain of the antituberculous medications (which I would have read anyway because of my patient). I am wary that they might ask me some tough questions, but as things work out, my anxiety proves unwarranted since I have only seven or eight minutes in which to make my presentation, which is rather straightforward, and there is only enough time left over for one doctor to make a comment and not even put me on the spot.

10:30 A.M.—Fortunately, I am not scheduled to present a case to the head of the department on morning rounds, as I planned to slip out and go down to the operating room where a former patient of mine was scheduled to have part of one lung removed. She was suffering from a chronic lung abscess that appeared to be resistant to medical therapy. Although she was now a thoracic, or chest surgery, patient and I was no longer her primary physician, I wanted to be present if only as an observer, especially since I had been the one who had spoken at length with her and her husband about the apparent need for such an operation. I had told them that without surgical intervention, she would continue to be plagued with chronic fatigue and shortness of breath, as well as the intermittent episodes of coughing up blood and large quantities of foul-smelling sputum that had made her seek medical attention in the first place. Both the husband and the patient trusted me, and I liked them as well, and they consequently gave their consent for the surgery.

As soon as I can get away, I quickly duck down to the OR, get into a set of greens, and proceed to watch as the surgeons "cracked her chest," a term the thoracic people love to use in referring to the necessity of having to break or crack several of the patient's ribs in order to properly expose the lungs.

11:15 A.M.—My beeper goes off, and since I am not scrubbed, I can answer. I am informed by a nurse that I have an admission waiting to be seen on the detoxification unit. These drug abuse patients are not usually a problem, but they can occasionally be quite time consuming, and since there is usually little that can be learned, if there are no concomitant problems, they are therefore rotated evenly amongst all the teams. It generally requires at least an hour to an hour and a half to take the history, perform the physical exam, draw the necessary bloods (more on that later) and write up the findings and orders. The saving grace here is that the nurse can administer the first dose of methadone without a direct written order, and you therefore don't have to drop everything immediately and tend to the patient.

11:30 A.M.—I run down to the cafeteria to grab a quick sandwich, because although there is a scheduled twelve noon conference on electrocardiograms, I would much prefer to use the time to work up the new admission. Besides, I hate EKG lectures to begin with and I know my resident wants to attend, and if there are no complications, he will not even bother to see the new patient. It is therefore totally my responsibility, and as such, I want to get it out of the way as quickly as possible.

CHAPTER / 33

12 Noon—I arrive at the detoxification unit, and the first thing I do after introducing myself to the patient is to prepare to draw the required amounts of blood. The ten tubes used for collection are already labeled according to the protocol of the unit. The patient is a thirty-year-old male, and after finding out that he has been a junkie for the previous twelve years, I know it means potential trouble for me, for the odds are good that I will be unable to find a vein that has not previously been probed and scarred beyond use. My fears turn out to be justified as it takes a full fifteen minutes to get all the required blood and, at that, I still have to use several small veins on the top of his hands.

At first, whenever I attempt to enter a vein that is scarred or thrombosed, the patient shakes his head back and forth knowingly, until finally he is unable to contain himself and proceeds to tell me point-blank not to even try several others I have been considering because "they'll just roll right out from under the needle, Doc, believe me. Even I couldn't get blood out of them." After twelve years of multiple daily needle insertions I have to respect his judgment, and he reciprocates by pointing out a small vein on the inner aspect of his left wrist that he "had been saving for a rainy day," and as I began to successfully get blood back, he shouts in glee, "It's a hit, Doc. It's a hit!"

His exuberant reaction is not all that unusual in light of several of the current hypotheses which postulate that a part of the so-called euphoric rush described by many intravenous drug users may be intimately related to the actual penetration of the skin by the needle.

I like to talk with the drug abuse patients if I am not overly pressed for time both to try and get a feel for what's going on "in the streets" and in the drug subculture in particular and also, as would prove to be the case in this particular instance, because it can be entertaining as well as enlightening.

I thought I knew a great deal of the street jargon already from my previous experiences with drug abuse patients and alcoholics, and my glossary of frequently used slang terms and expressions relating to drugs and alcohol was becoming quite extensive. For instance, I already knew that wood alcohol (chemically known as methanol and used quite frequently in the manufacture of antifreeze and paint remover, and which if ingested in sufficient quantities may cause blindness and even sudden death) was referred to frequently on the street as smoke, whereas home or commercially produced whiskey (chemically ethanol, the type of alcohol prepared for general human consumption) could be either iron, or white lightning.

If someone was starting to go into early alcoholic hallucinosis, a condition where the drinker may visually hallucinate and imagine he is seeing objects and figures that are not physically present, he is often referred to as havings a case of the rams. I have heard various stages of intoxication referred to as being lit, stiff, plastered, loaded, stewed, blotto, pie-eyed, crocked, potted, and my favorite, three sheets to the wind.

An injection of any drug is a "bang," and a packet of heroin, in addition to the more traditional expressions, such as "lope" or "nickel bag" (referring to the fact that most heroin is sold in five-dollar quantities—at least preinflation—which usually come packaged in a glassine envelope), is also known as a "bindle," so that if someone "copped a bindle," it meant that they had made a purchase of drugs. However, if the narcotic purchased was of poor quality or low grade (much of the heroin dealt on the street level is generally less than 5 percent pure and is most often diluted, or "stepped on," with milk sugar or quinine, both of which are white powders that physically resemble heroin), it was a "blank." Poor-quality heroin has its own specific slang term, "lemonade," and I learned that a "bambita" is an injection of both heroin and amphetamine. "Chipping" describes someone who uses narcotics only occasionally and is therefore not addicted in the true physical sense, and even with the trend toward poorer-and poorer-grade heroin, the existence of fairly large numbers of such "weekend junkies" surprised me.

Cocaine, an up-and-coming abused drug among middle- and upper-class whites, but long popular and widely used in the black community, at least until the prices began to skyrocket, is most often referred to as snow. The list could literally go on and on, including such items as "yellow jackets" or "reds" (barbiturates, so called because of the color of the outside covering of the capsules themselves) and which are also referred to variously as downers, barbs, and goofballs, while their opposite counterpart uppers, or pep pills (amphetamines), are also known as dexies and jolly beans.

Yet all the above notwithstanding, my lessons in this regard were far from complete as I was to vividly find out as I begin to interview this particular patient. He turns out to be quite articulate, and after telling me he is a practicing Black Muslim, he goes on to freely admit that he has had his last "fix" at approximately 10 A.M. and is still pretty high, or "mellow," as he puts it. As our discussion progresses, I begin to have serious doubts as to whether he is putting me on or is the original Mr. Malaprop masquerading as a patient.

For example, during my review of systems, in which I routinely inquire about the various areas of body function in order not to miss something that the patient perhaps does not think important enough to mention but may be an important clue to an underlying disease, I ask him if he has ever had VD. He looks at me somewhat quizzically, so I confidently, and more than a bit smugly, rephrase the question into the vernacular and ask him instead if he has ever had "bad blood" (syphilis) or a dose of the clap. I think he understands when he finally answers in the affirmative, until he goes on to add that he once had the last thing I had mentioned "up in my chest." This time I have the quizzical look on my face, and with just the slightest hint of a smile, he explains that he had been in a car accident the year before in which he had struck his chest against the steering wheel, and after examination in the ER, the doctor told him he was suffering from "col-lapse of the lung."

I can't help but laugh, and when he laughs along, I still am not sure whether I am being "had" or not, but I give him the benefit of the doubt (actually it really doesn't matter either way as I am enjoying it as much as he apparently is) and plunge ahead in an attempt to be more specific and graphic. So I ask him if in the course of passing his water, did his urine ever burn? With a valiant attempt at a straight face, he looks me in the eye and deadpans, "Doc, you know, I'm not really sure. I mean I never tried to light it," and proceeds to completely convulse with laughter. After he calms down, he levels with me and says that he knows what I had been referring to all along and has "just been messing around" and feeling me out at the same time. Apparently deciding that I am all right, he proceeds to contribute to my education. He says that in the future I probably will have better success in obtaining information in this regard if I ask the patient if he has ever had the "gleet" or the "strain," since they are the more common street expressions for a penile discharge of pus.

As my history-taking continues (by the way, just to satisfy the prurient curiosity of anyone really interested, it turns out that he had contracted both gonorrhea and syphilis in the past, but had been sufficiently and properly treated), I am surprised to learn that, on the other hand, he has never had hepatitis or any other serious infection. This is unusual enough in itself, since infectious disease is a quite frequent concomitant to intravenous drug abuse, resulting most often from the widespread practice of using unsterile syringes that are usually shared or "passed around." I am secure that he trusts me to a certain extent when he confides that the primary reason for his good fortune in this regard was the fact that a close friend of his works in a surgical supply house so that he always has an ample supply of sterile syringes.

Besides being lucky, an additional factor contributing to his success in avoiding serious complications in the past is his strong affiliation with the Muslim movement; consequently, he has watched his diet carefully, and on physical exam he proves to be quite well nourished and in rather good shape (track marks notwithstanding) not only for a drug addict but for any person living in the inner city. As I am finishing up the exam, he tells me rather proudly that in his twelve years of living off the streets to support his habit he has never been arrested. This is not generally the case with the majority of the people that pass through the unit, as a large percentage have been offered treatment as an alternative to jail, and these people are usually poorly motivated and quickly return to their habit. Yet somehow, I have the feeling that this won't be the case here, partly because the patient has chosen to voluntarily come in for treatment and, also, because he has told me point-blank that he is just plain tired of having to hustle each and every day to raise the seventy dollars it takes to support his daily habit. The clincher comes when he tells me he really isn't even getting all that high, since his tolerance level has become such that he is forced to shoot all that junk into his body just to stay "physiologically normal" and therefore not suffer withdrawal symptoms.

At this point I complete the examination, and although I very much want to continue to talk and find out, for example, how he reconciles his drug habit and concomitant sociopathic behavior (the imputed criminality is speculative, but you don't just find seventy dollars lying in the street each and every day, so someone, somehow, has to be getting ripped off) with his religious beliefs, I realize the time and know that I had better get the write-up completed before something urgent comes up. Furthermore, I always feel it a priority to make certain that each patient thoroughly understand the protocol of his three-day detoxification program. I therefore carefully explain how he is to receive gradually decreasing amounts of methadone each day (it is important to remember that the goal of a detoxification plan is for the patient to become completely drug free, and not be stabilized on a maintenance dose) and that he will also be given sedatives if he should become overly agitated. A sleeping pill is on order to help combat the almost invariably present sleep disturbance, and similarly, medication will also be available for the diarrhea that is also generally a problem of heroin withdrawal. The latter, by the way, is a rebound consequence of one of the inherent physiological properties of the drug itself, as heroin will generally produce constipation in the user. As a consequence of this, morphine, which is a synthetic heroinlike derivative used most frequently for its analgesic effect (for the relief of severe pain), is also widely used for the treatment of severe cases of diarrhea as well.

When I have finished, the patient asks if I can order a special porkless diet, and I then spend the next half hour writing up the history and results of the physical exam, as well as the orders. I note with some satisfaction that I am on schedule, and my sense of well-being is definitely enhanced by the knowledge that one of the benefits of working up such a patient is that when the initial work-up is completed and there are no unforeseen complications, the patient generally requires relatively little subsequent attention, and since the drug counselors were actively engaged, he therefore will only need to be checked on once a day.

1:30 P.M.—As I start down the stairwell on my way to the twelfth floor, my beeper goes off, and from the phone number of the extension given, I realize that my resident is up on the isolation ward, across the hallway from where I had just been. I hurry back upstairs and find him with the renal doctors, discussing our TB patient and his kidney problems. The patient is finally being dialyzed, and is presently hooked into the artificial kidney machine in the renology department downstairs, and I proceed to present the latest lab data on the chart. Unfortunately but certainly far from unexpectedly, the results of the lab work ordered that morning by my resident have not yet been reported. Twice during the course of the general discussion that followed I had to excuse myself in order to hound the lab for the results, and I really resented this unnecessary, time-consuming chore not only because of the frustration involved but more importantly because it meant I would be cheated out of some valuable teaching.

While on the phone, I get two of the standard, most classically employed responses. First, I was told that the blood chemistry analyzer was on the blink, and second, they went on to say that they had not received *any* specimens whatsoever on the particular patient about whom I was inquiring. Since I know my resident has drawn the blood himself and since I had been subjected to this runaround many times before, I immediately track down the supervisor, report what has happened and am subsequently told that he will "look into the situation" (a third classical response!). This was not going to do our patient any good since there is now no way to know his present status. Fortunately, the renal doctor has had the foresight to utilize the patient's newly revised shunt to obtain his own blood samples before the patient was connected to the machine in order that he can compare the pre-

and postdialysis results and thus evaluate the effectiveness of the treatment. He says he will get both sets of figures as soon as possible, and write the appropriate orders based on the findings. The attending then turns to me with a "request" that I go through the literature and find out if there are any other reported cases of renal failure secondary to the medications the patient has received.

2:00 P.M.—My resident and I go back to the ICU to check on our patients and reevaluate their current status. A major adjustment had been made in the morning in respect to the amount of oxygen the respirator was delivering to Mr. K., based on calculations from the results of the earlier blood gases. It is now time to draw another arterial sample to see if the proper corrections have been made, and this necessitates another trip to the ice machine.

2:30 P.M.—I am off on my own to the surgical recovery room on the sixth floor to see how the woman with the lung abscess is doing postoperatively. I am informed by a nurse that she is back in the OR because of a bleeding complication, and I am upset to learn that they are actually going to have to open her up again to attempt to locate the exact source of the continued bleeding. I knew this sometimes occurs, but somehow I had bad vibrations about the whole thing, although I made an effort to keep my unfounded fears in check when I spoke to her husband, who was nervously pacing in the corridor.

2:40 P.M.—I am beeped again. My resident informs me that he is back on the fourteenth floor and about to present our TB patient to the infectious disease specialists. The patient himself was in the process of being transferred back to the isolation ward, and ironically I get on the same elevator. As we both arrive, my resident is detailing the situation and explaining that we were in a real bind because despite the patient's apparent renal sensitivity, he still requires some form or new combination of antituberculous medications to treat his moderately severe TB. After a brief discussion we take their suggestions about initiating a new drug regime. As the infectious disease group turned to leave, I had my fingers crossed, but the attending stopped in the doorway and asked me to research the renal toxicity of the various drugs discussed. At least I will be able to kill two birds with one stone.

3:00 P.M.—My beeper goes off. Another admission for our

team, even though it's fairly early in the day, but this time we're lucky. It's a renal patient with chronic kidney problems who has come in for her biweekly dialysis, and I am familiar with her case, having taken care of her during a prior hospitalization. This will therefore be a relatively easy work-up since I already knew her history, and only a quick cursory physical exam is indicated to ascertain if there has been any change in her general condition since her last admission. She is scheduled for peritoneal dialysis, which is a procedure that predates the kidney machine and which operates by making use of the fact that the internal covering of the abdominal cavity, the peritoneum, can function quite effectively as a filter. This means that the normally occurring breakdown products of metabolism, which are usually disposed of by the body by "flushing" them out through a functioning kidney, can instead by diffused out from the blood across this abdominal covering into a special fluid that will be introduced directly into the cavity by means of a long plastic catheter, or tube.

The procedure involves leaving the fluid in place anywhere from twenty minutes to an hour, draining it out along with its absorbed impurities, and then replacing it with fresh fluid. It requires anywhere from thirty to forty repetitions before the desired results can be achieved, and although it is obviously· much more time consuming than using a kidney machine (forty hours of total treatment compared to six to eight to ten on the machine) and although there is an added danger of infection, pain and bleeding, it is a much less expensive proposition than the machine, with its large initial cost outlay and need for specially trained personnel. Another important factor is that there are only just so many machines available to go around; also, in certain chronic conditions the patient may even benefit more from peritoneal dialysis than from being on the machine. For whatever the reason, this was the treatment the patient was to receive.

Due to the chronic nature of her condition, and the fact that she comes in regularly for biweekly treatments, the patient has an indwelling catheter already in place. This is a piece of plastic tubing that has previously been inserted, and which serves as a passageway from the outside into the abdominal cavity. My physical exam satisfies me that there has been no appreciable change in her condition since her last admission, and I draw the necessary base-line studies. She will have to stay in the hospital only until her treatment is completed, usually no more than two days. Here she will be watched carefully by the renal people, who will write the actual dialysis orders, although I will be responsible for any emergencies or complications that might arise during her hospital stay.

3:40 P.M.—After a somewhat cursory write-up, I arrive late for a scheduled X-ray conference, and I basically doze in the back of the room for twenty minutes.

4:00 P.M.—My resident and I go down to the X-ray department to look at films that have been taken on our patients both today and yesterday, and our luck continues to be good in that we are able to find all but one. Mr. K's pneumonia appears to be resolving, and although it is now primarily academic, we review an upper GI series done the day before on the ninety-year-old woman who had expired earlier in the morning. It appears normal. However, another portable chest film taken on our patient in hepatic coma reveals that a catheter inserted through a blood vessel in her neck and threaded close to her heart in order that her blood volume and pressure can be monitored as accurately as possible is not exactly where it should be, and a note is made to check it later. There is no change noted in a chest film of our TB patient, which is gratifying in one sense because although there has been no obvious improvement, we naturally are concerned that there might be a spread of the disease as a consequence of our having to temporarily discontinue his medications.

5:00 P.M.—My beeper goes off, and upon dialing the digits that I know all too well will connect me with 12 North, I am informed by a nurse that a patient under treatment for acute pancreatitis has pulled out his naso-gastric tube, which had been connected to a suction machine. The rationale behind this mode of treatment is that if the stomach is suctioned out, you therefore cut down on secretions that would normally be evoked by the presence of anything in the stomach, as the pancreas is normally stimulated to secrete by this mechanism. Thus, by stressing the inflamed organ as little as possible, recovery is thereby facilitated, and the patient is definitely more comfortable.

I arrive on the ward, and the patient immediately begins to protest about having the tube reconnected. However, I tell him that although it is unquestionably uncomfortable to have the tube in place, it is certainly a hell of a lot better than the terrible knifelike pains in his abdomen for which he had been admitted the night before. I then go on to strongly, albeit somewhat dramatically, warn him of the distinct possibility that they most likely will return if the tube is not reinserted; it is the latter part of my "sales pitch" that apparently gets through to him, and he agrees to cooperate. It thus appears that my luck is still holding out since I will not have to become engaged in a lengthy debate, but my mood quickly turns sour when I discover that not only hasn't the nurse gotten together the materials I will need but, in addition, I have to go over to the south side of the hospital to hunt up a suitable tube. I then have to look elsewhere for the lubricating jelly, and finally after all this by the time I get back to the bedside, the patient has to be reconvinced about the need for the tube. By this time I'm in no mood to quibble, and I resort to the scare tactics that had been effective earlier; the patient is soon "reconnected," and I leave the ward hoping to get at least a few minutes of peace and quiet as I go off for a quick meal.

5:45 P.M.—Down to the cafeteria on the first floor for dinner, where the selection consists of either a tuna fish sandwich or pork chops, which not so coincidentally were also the same items offered at lunch. In the middle of my meal I am beeped again, and a nurse informs me that it is 6 P.M. and time to administer the IV medications, which are only permitted to be given by an M.D. in my hospital. I tell her that I will be up shortly, and no sooner do I hang the phone up when the damn beeper immediately goes off again; this time it is a nurse from another floor I'm also scheduled to cover for the night telling me the exact same thing. I start upstairs to give the required medications, and arrange to meet my resident in the ICU when I have finished.

6:15 P.M.—I find my resident again drawing blood gases on our two critically ill patients, and hallelujah, he has already gotten the ice. My momentary joy is soon dissipated, however, when I notice the time and realize that in order to get the results as quickly as possible, I had better run the samples down to the lab myself. I know I should do this after many experiences in trying to obtain emergency lab results at this time. This was so because of a combination of several factors, the first being that the sample could easily sit at the nurses' station until the ice melted, simply because the only person available to take it down to the lab would either be at dinner, on a break or else is just nowhere to be found. And even if you are somehow fortunate enough to find someone willing to take it down, the same situation usually prevails regarding the lab personnel. The laboratory staff has the added advantage of being physically removed from the ward by ten long flights of stairs (or two interminable elevator trips).

All of which is the reason I find myself, blood and ice in hand, on my way down to the lab, in order that I can personally hand the sample to the technician and wait for the results, knowing in the long run I will ultimately be saving myself both time and aggravation, although surely not any shoe leather!

CHAPTER / 34

6:30 P.M.—I arrive back at the ICU with the lab results, which indicate that our corrections on the respirators made earlier in the day were correct and the changes were apparently well-tolerated by the patients, especially Mr. K., who is presently not "fighting" the machine any longer. I am also able to write the IV fluid orders to cover the patients through the night, calculated upon results from blood drawn earlier in the day, which I had the foresight to pick up in the lab along with the blood gas results.

6:45 P.M.—I finally have a chance to write my formal daily progress notes on each of the patients on our team, which entails checking on those people I hadn't yet seen myself. My luck holds out, and I am just about up-to-date on everyone when my beeper goes off. It's funny, but when your beeper doesn't go off for any appreciable length of time, instead of enjoying the respite, you begin to worry if it's functioning properly. Consequently, I had developed what might best be described as a nervous habit, as did many of my colleagues, whereby I would almost unconsciously push the receiving button on my receiver every ten or fifteen minutes, just to be reassured by the sound of static or another doctor's message coming through that things were in working order and someone hadn't died because I couldn't be reached!

8:00 P.M.—The incoming message was from the doctor on duty in the emergency room. He wanted me to be aware that since we were next up for admission, a patient had just been brought in by ambulance in a semicomatose state. The patient's sister had informed him that she was an insulin-dependent diabetic who had not taken her injections or eaten properly for the past two days. She appeared to him to be in pretty poor shape and would definitely have to be admitted.

I quickly page my resident to inform him of the situation, and we agree to meet in the ER. We both arrive simultaneously, and it is quickly obvious that the woman is seriously ill, and that we will soon have a third patient in the ICU. The ER doctor has already drawn the initial blood work, as well as passed a catheter into her bladder, which is essential in situations such as this because the content as well as the volume of the urine would have to be checked frequently. Our initial impression is that she appears to be in a critical state known as diabetic ketoacidosis, where the patient is suffering the ill effects of a grossly elevated blood sugar while at the same time her vital organs are paradoxically starving for this nutrition. Most people are unaware that one of the mechanisms by which insulin works is through facilitating the blood sugar's uptake by the tissues, where it can then be utilized, or to put it another way, the circulating sugar is essentially worthless (and harmful, as you shall see) to the rest of the body if the mechanism for its uptake and utilization is deficient. Her condition is then further complicated in that her body in an attempt to continue functioning and literally stay alive attempts to use other pathways to burn up whatever other materials *are* available, such as fat and protein. But although these pathways are active and functioning to a certain degree in healthy individuals, they are stressed here beyond tolerance, and soon the body finds itself unprepared and unable to deal with the rapidly accumulating toxic waste products that are the end result of such efforts. The patient's condition is even further aggravated by the marked degree of dehydration present, which is the result of the body's vain attempt to deal with the grossly elevated blood sugar levels by allowing large quantities of the circulating sugar to be extracted from the blood by the kidneys and thereby excreted via the urine. However, not only is this ineffective in decreasing the blood level to any appreciable extent but it creates a grave consequence in itself, for in order for the kidneys to excrete such large volumes of sugar, they must pull out water with it, thereby leading to a rapid and potentially life-threatening state of dehydration. The unfortunate sequence of cause and effect continues as the resulting chemical imbalance triggers off a further compensatory effort by the body to get as much carbon dioxide into the body as possible. This is done because the carbon dioxide is converted by the body into certain forms that can then act as buffer bases to neutralize the acids that are building up. Consequently, the woman is strenuously laboring to suck in as much air as possible, and someone in this condition is appropriately referred to as being "air-hungry."

While still in the ER I start an IV, and an initial bedside lab test reveals a hugely elevated blood sugar as well as the presence of the aforementioned breakdown products, all of which documents our initial impression of the seriousness of her condition. We immediately give her insulin, both intravenously so that it can work as rapidly as possible and also by injection under the skin so that it will be absorbed more slowly and therefore maintain itself at a higher level. As we push the stretcher onto the elevator to transport the still-unconscious woman to the ICU, my resident and I exchange glances which indicate that we both know we have a very sick woman on our hands and that we are in for a long night. She will require constant monitoring initially, including blood work and urine studies, with a subsequent follow-up every two hours or so as she hopefully improves, until she is finally stable.

As we are in the process of transferring her from the stretcher to the bed, my beeper goes off, and a nurse informs me that I am required in a certain medical ward as soon as possible. It turns out that there had been a nursing oversight, and I had not been informed of the fact that a certain female patient was on heparin therapy. This is the drug I've already mentioned in another context, and it is a powerful anticoagulant that must be administered intravenously to be effective. The patient in question turns out to be an elderly, bedridden woman who had previously been transferred from a nursing home for evaluation and treatment of what appeared to be a case of thrombophlebitis. She had initially complained of severe calf pain, which along with other criteria strongly indicated the presence of blood clots in the deep veins of her leg. The heparin is employed here in the hope that its anticoagulant property will "thin" out the blood and therefore make it more difficult for new clots to form, as well as hopefully dissolve those that have already formed. The presence of these clots is significant, not only because they are quite painful—and if large enough, they can occlude, or block off, the vessel altogether and cause serious problems in the leg itself—but more importantly, because these clots, or thrombi as they are called, can actually break loose from the walls of the blood vessel in which they initially formed and are thus free to travel through the rest of the circulatory system. Since the vast majority of these clots form in veins, rather than arteries, and since the veins get larger and larger the nearer they get to the heart itself, the traveling clot, now referred to as an embolus (again from the Greek, where it means a wedge or stopper) has very little to impede its movement even through the opened valves of the heart itself until it leaves the right side of the heart and enters the pulmonary artery. It is at this critical point that the heart then attempts to force the clot through the progressively narrower arteries in the lungs, and the pulmonary thromboembolus, as it may now properly be called, inevitably becomes wedged in a vessel. If the embolus is large enough, it may actually become a life-threatening situation, since no blood can get around it to travel to the lungs, where it can become oxygenated, and the heart can rapidly fail from the tremendous pressure and effort it exerts in an attempt to keep the blood circulating.

The best level for treatment purposes is to keep the heparinized blood's clotting time from two and one-half to three times longer than it would normally take without the presence of the drug, and this is determined on the basis of base-line studies conducted before the heparin is first administered. This is not nearly as complicated as it may seem, and is easier to grasp if you consider a concrete example. Let us say a patient's blood is found to clot in eight to ten minutes under normal circumstances, in which case enough heparin would then be administered to make it take twenty-eight to thirty minutes for a clot to form.

It may become even clearer if you keep in mind that under normal circumstances, freely circulating blood does not spontaneously form clots. If the formation of a clot is then indicated for survival, such as in the case of a cut, it is achieved by the existence in the body of a rather exquisitely sensitive system comprised of both clot-forming and clot-dissolving elements. It is essential that this system be in a fine balance, as the body needs to have the ability to both keep the blood fluid and mobile under most circumstances in order to function properly but also retain the ability to form a clot if it should become necessary.

Ideally, a patient's clotting time should be monitored rather frequently if he is on heparin therapy. This can be accomplished rather easily right at the patient's bedside by simply obtaining some of the patient's blood in an unheparinized tube and then actually timing how long it takes for a clot to form. For standardization purposes the procedure actually involves three separate tubes of blood, but it is basically fairly simple, although time consuming. Since the woman had been scheduled to receive her heparin at 6 P.M., it was therefore imperative to conduct the testing so I could then calculate the quantity of heparin to be administered. Since not unexpectedly, the tubes needed for the study were nowhere to be found, the procedure ended up consuming about forty minutes and additional shoe leather.

10:00 P.M.—I return to the ICU and find that our newest admission is slowly beginning to respond. I start to compile a "flow sheet," which will enable us to see at a glance what medications the patient has received, including the quantity, at any given time, as well as her clinical response and any available lab results, thereby permitting us to keep a running tally. It is just about up-to-date when my beeper goes off. It is now . . .

10:30 P.M.—This time my worst fear is again realized as it is the emergency room physician. It appears that we are again next up for an admission, and I am told that there is currently a male patient brought in by the police who is a known alcoholic and who had been picked up at Pennsylvania Station after reportedly exposing himself to an entire trainload of commuters. He is currently profoundly confused, tremulous, extremely agitated and apparently experiencing visual hallucinations. He is also sweating profusely and has both a rapid heartbeat and fever, and this evidence, along with his history, makes it almost certain that he is in frank dt's, which constitutes a true medical emergency as there is a 15 percent to 20 percent mortality rate if untreated.

It takes three of us to hold the patient down, and I am somehow able to insert an IV line, which is often difficult enough to accomplish on a cooperative patient, much less a moving target. I also manage to draw some blood and a catheter is passed and an injection administered in an attempt to control his agitation.

It is critical that the agent employed for such a purpose be quite specific and not simply a barbiturate or some other similar-acting sedative, as alcohol itself is a central nervous depressant and, if combined with another depressive agent, can precipitate a deep coma along with respiratory depression to such an extent that there can be a complete cessation of breathing.

Despite the relatively large dose of sedative I have administered in the ER, the patient is still grossly agitated when we finally get him up to the ICU, which would now seem a more appropriate home base for us than 12 North in view of the fact that four of the six beds in the unit are currently occupied by our patients.

My resident, upon noticing that the patient was still quite agitated, asked how much medication I had given him in the ER, and upon noting the man's size, he promply doubled the dose. This is a good illustration of the desirability of having someone available with more experience and confidence, for I would have been quite hesitant at that point in giving double the dose of the drug, especially so soon after administering the initial amount. However, my resident, having had much more experience with both this type of patient and the particular effects and potential adverse side effects of the drug, and to what extent it can safely be pushed, was quite confident that the patient was undermedicated and that additional medication was definitely indicated. He turned out to be right on all counts as the patient soon grew groggy, and it was then possible to examine him much more easily and thoroughly.

From his soiled clothes it was obvious that the patient had been vomiting, and our initial studies correlated this and confirmed our clinical impression that he was moderately dehydrated. This may seem paradoxical in that someone who has been drinking heavily may nonetheless be water depleted, but it makes sense if you are aware that alcohol is a potent diuretic, and since it therefore causes excessive urination (just ask any beer drinker!), the drinker can soon become depleted in water volume, along with a loss of other vital elements, such as potassium and sodium.

My only consoling thought at this point is the fact that the last two admissions have been unable to give any sort of history, and I will therefore save time in my write-ups, but it is only a very minor consolation at best.

12 MIDNIGHT—I am beeped by the floor nurses to remind me that IV medications are again due to be administered. I decide to hold the heparin on the one patient since I have given her the last dose only several hours before, and I wanted to wait an hour or two so I could better reevaluate her status. Everything proceeds smoothly so that I am back in the ICU by 12:20 A.M.

1:30 A.M.—Things are finally beginning to settle down as both new admissions seem to be responding favorably to treatment. The diabetic young woman is now fully conscious, and a blood and urine analysis recently completed showed vast improvement, and the Penn Station "streaker" has also responded favorably to the dosage of medication that my resident had pushed, and was sleeping comfortably. His subsequent laboratory studies have revealed that his degree of dehydration was not as severe as we had originally thought, and the IV fluid therapy currently being administered will soon correct the deficit. We proceed to draw another set of blood gases, as well as blood work on the diabetic, hoping that if the results are favorable, we might be able to get in a few hours' sleep.

2:00 A.M.—I am beeped by a nurse on the male side because a middle-aged man, who had been admitted earlier in the day by a "short" team, is actively vomiting. He had warranted admission because of a rather severe attack of gout, and was in the process of being treated by a drug that is quite effective for an acute attack of this nature but which unfortunately must be taken orally and is quite an irritant to the gastrointestinal tract. It is routinely given in hourly doses until the painful symptoms of the gout subside, or unless, as in this instance, GI symptomatology develops. Fortunately, both processes were occurring in this patient at the same time. His swollen ankle was much less painful, and I could thus discontinue the offending medication and switch to another anti-inflammatory agent that is much less caustic to the GI tract. At the same time I order an antiemetic to relieve the vomiting.

Just as I'm about to leave, the nurse informs me that an IV on a particular patient who had been on the floor for many weeks was found to be clotted and needed to be restarted. As I spend ten minutes attempting to find a suitable vein that had not been previously scarred beyond use, I'm not sure who I am feeling most sorry for—the poor old man who has to endure the futile stabs and probes of the needle or myself, as I grow more and more exasperated and frustrated thinking about all the work I still have to accomplish before I can even think about grabbing any sleep. I finally resort to inflating a blood pressure cuff around his calf, after having no success at all with either arm or hands, in the hope that this increase in pressure will force the smaller veins to remain filled up with blood and therefore become visible. My ingenuity pays off as I find, more by touch than sight, a small but suitable vessel on the inner aspect of the ankle, and I gratefully, and quite carefully, insert a small-gauge needle into what certainly qualifies as an "intern's vein." This would at least assure that a pathway remain open through the night through which he will continue to receive fluid and medications.

2:30 A.M.—Upon returning to the ICU, I find that my resident has gone across the street to try and get some sleep, as he was obviously satisfied with the condition of the two newly admitted patients. He has left word with the nurse that I am to draw blood at 6 A.M., when I am again scheduled to give IV medications, in addition to drawing blood gases on the respirator patients, so that all the results will hopefully be available at 7:30 A.M. when we can then reevaluate their condition. I still have to finish the write-ups on the two new admissions and also bring the flow sheet up to date, and when I have finally gotten all caught up, I beep my fellow intern to see how things are going for his team. More importantly, however, I want to hear him say that they have not gotten an admission after our last one so that when I am finally able to go over for whatever sleep I can manage, I can rest a little easier knowing that we were not "up" for the next admission. No such luck, however, as he tells me that he is just finishing his write-up of an apparent case of pancreatitis that had been admitted shortly after our patient in dt's. So it appears we are "on deck" again, and believe me, it's a much better feeling if you know there is a "buffer," since the odds at this late hour are slim, although far from improbable, that there will be two new admissions before 8 A.M.

3:10 A.M.—I check in with the nurses on the respective wards I am covering to see if there are any new problems that may have arisen, so that I can quickly deal with them and, hopefully, still manage to sneak in three hours of uninterrupted sleep before having to get up at 6 A.M. to give medication. I have gotten into this habit of "bedtime" rounds because of previous experiences where I would be called for some minor problem that could have been easily taken care of several hours earlier if I had taken just such a precaution as I was now doing. It proved to be fortuitous this time, as a patient had just come to the nursing station demanding a sleeping pill for which his doctor had neglected to leave an order. I leaf quickly through his chart to make sure he is not under treatment for any condition that could make the taking of a sedative a risk, but upon seeing the lateness of the hour and taking into account the fact that the patients are generally awakened at 6:30 A.M. for early morning blood work and other ward functions, I decide it would be unwise to sedate the patient at this time and therefore order a placebo instead. A placebo is an inert compound or substance, which can be administered in pill or liquid form, or even by injection, and which does not contain any active pharmacologic agent whatsoever. The important thing is that the patient believes he is receiving medication, and it is sometimes quite startling just how effective this can prove to be. The effect is obviously purely psychological, yet I don't feel I'm trying to "put one over" on a patient but rather am helping him to accomplish something without having to add another drug to his body. It is a rather widespread and commonly accepted medical practice.

This task completed, I ask the nurse to call me at 6:30 A.M. to give medications, even though they are scheduled to be given a half an hour earlier. This way I can get in a little more sleep, and the lag period would not be critical or harmful to the patients.

3:30 A.M.—I sign in with the receptionist at the desk and go upstairs and slip into the room where my resident is sleeping. I strip to my underwear and get into bed, but I find it difficult to fall asleep immediately, even though I am exhausted. This can be extremely frustrating when you know what little time you have available in which to sleep. There is also the added psychological factor that you know that the phone can ring at virtually any moment, and it is also possible to hear phones ringing in nearby rooms as the doctors on other services are awakened as needed. Despite all this, I nevertheless fall asleep fairly quickly.

4:45 A.M.—The goddamn phone rings. I am awake instantly

as my resident answers, and I quickly curse to myself again when I hear him ask if blood has already been sent for a type and cross match, since I just know, both from the conversation but more so the tone and inflection in his voice, that it is most probably a GI bleeder who is actively bleeding. As I pull my pants on, my resident tells me that the patient currently in the ER had been discharged from the medical service just the morning before. I was correct in my assumption that he was a GI bleeder, and at the moment, he is vomiting up fresh blood. I see that it is still dark outside, and I realize that I must now make a very important decision. The burning question is whether to decide if I am going to put back on my still wet, smelly socks that I had only just so recently peeled off and gamble that I might be able to get back before 7 A.M. so that I might at least be able to shower or whether I should put on the fresh pair I customarily brought and reserved for the next "day." Sizing up the odds, I come to the conclusion that it is most likely already morning for me and that my "new day" has already begun, so I put on the clean socks.

5:00 A.M.—My resident goes directly to the ER while I go to the medical records department hoping to find the patient's old chart. I am lucky and spot it on a pile that the night crew is just starting to file away.

5:15 A.M.—The naso-gastric tube has already been passed by the time I get to the ER, and I hand my resident the chart and relieve him at lavaging. The water return is bright red, with large clots, and I see that this must be a fairly massive bleed.

5:20 A.M.—My resident is fuming as he reads through the old chart in the elevator on our way up to the ICU with the patient. He says that the patient was in such obviously poor shape that he should never have been discharged in the first place.

5:30 A.M.—I continue to lavage. The resident is on the phone with the GI doctor who is on call at home. He reports that he is quite familiar with the patient, and that he had been "scoped" (short for esophagoscopy, where a tube with its own light source had been passed down the esophagus into the stomach so that the exact site of bleeding or other pathology can be determined by direct viewing) just four days ago, at which time it had been demonstrated that the patient had massive gastric and esophageal varices. They were observed to be actively oozing at the time, and the consensus was that they were capable of bursting at any given moment. It appears that the GI doctor had strongly advised against the discharge, even though the active bleeding had apparently stopped, but it appeared that the patient had been insistent upon going home. Although the prognosis now seemed extremely poor, the GI doctor said he would be in as soon as possible.

5:45 A.M.—The sun is beginning to rise, and it is one of the clearer mornings over the New Jersey meadowlands, as the combination of smoke from burning garbage, haze and fog that seems to almost always be invariably present to some degree is almost nonexistent, and the New York City skyline looks beautiful in the soft, early morning light. I am still lavaging, and despite his ordeal, the patient is conscious, cooperative and noncomplaining, and I try to reassure him that everything will be fine, but I don't think I am very convincing.

6:30 A.M.—I have just finished hanging a unit of blood when the GI doctor arrives, and the nurse is telling me at the same time that the ward had called in regard to IV medications. I leave the unit and quickly give the medications, and upon my return I proceed to draw the blood samples on our new admissions, as well as blood gases on the respirator patients. By now it is . . .

7:15 A.M.—The GI doctor has gone off to get the equipment required for the insertion of the balloon-type apparatus I have previously described, and I take the opportunity to do a bedside finger stick so I may arrive at a gross approximation of how much blood the patient has already lost. This necessitates a trip to the laboratory on the next floor where the equipment required is located, and I take the opportunity to give the ice machine a symbolic kick on my way by. After getting the results, I return to the unit and relieve my resident, who is still lavaging. I notice that the nursing shifts have changed for the third time since yesterday morning.

7:45 A.M.—The other teams begin to filter in, including the resident who had discharged the GI bleeder the morning before. I make quite a scene insisting that this patient rightfully belongs to his team, and after conferring with the chief resident, it is agreed that the other team should assume management at this point. Naturally, they are still quite resistant, but I am even more insistent, and the chief resident, who has the final say in such matters, agrees. I breathe a sigh of relief.

8:00 A.M.—We remain in the ICU to reevaluate our patients. I spend a not-unexpected frustrating twenty minutes on the phone with the lab trying to get results on the 6:30 A.M. samples that I damn well know were sent. It dawns on me that the personnel in the lab must have also changed, so that the night shift has most probably left some samples for the day shift to complete. Fortunately, they have done the blood gases, and after threatening to go to the supervisor, I am finally able to get the results for the "supposedly lost" other samples.

8:30 A.M.—We spend the next hour writing new orders and getting the charts themselves in order so that my resident can present the new admissions at morning report. I then go round up the admission X rays of the new patients, which I had "squirreled" away, and make sure the flow sheet on the diabetic patient is up-to-date. She is doing much better and is alert and comfortable, and I also look in quickly on our asthmatic, who is also much improved. Mr. K. is still basically unchanged in that he is still comatose, but his blood sugar is finally holding steady at an acceptable level. However, the woman in hepatic coma is having more frequent and generalized seizures, and also appears to be bleeding both internally and at each of the puncture sites from which we have drawn our all-too-frequent blood samples. I speak to the chief resident about whether we should consider blood transfusions with additional added clotting factors, and after consulting with my own resident and also the liver specialist who is familiar with the case, it is decided that it would most likely only be in vain.

9:30 A.M.—Morning report (again), and there is a rousing and spirited debate about the protocol to be followed in future instances if and when a situation should arise similar to what had just transpired with the GI bleeder. The decision is finally reached that any patient readmitted less than twenty-four hours after discharge is the responsibility of the original team, although the team on duty will naturally administer any necessary emergency care.

9:45 A.M.—After apparently dozing off while listening to my resident present our admissions, I am startled awake by the sound of my beeper going off. It is the ICU, and Mrs. W. has apparently just expired. I am still a bit groggy when I get to the unit, and I recognize that vaguely familiar sense of relief I had when Mr. R. had finally died. An attempt to notify the family proves futile, so I go ahead and complete the necessary paperwork. At that moment the GI bleeder expires as well, and the GI doctor and intern make no attempt at resuscitation. It seems that I am more emotionally affected by his death than by Mrs. W.'s, partly because of the three-hour effort I had just expended but also partly because of a resentment toward the other team, not only on the somewhat petty level of the lost sleep but for exercising poor medical judgment. Rationally, I knew that the patient had been insistent upon going home, that most probably nothing more could have been done and that a man should be able to choose where he wants to die, but nevertheless my sleep-deprived mind finds it just too difficult to reconcile that harsh intellectual reality with my current emotional state.

10:30 A.M.—I present the diabetic patient to our attending on rounds, and receive an infrequent "well done." I was complimented on the flow sheet especially, and except for some rather minor points regarding the specifics of treatment, which are somewhat controversial to begin with, as well as being academic at this point since the woman had obviously responded well to our particular treatment modality, it was generally agreed that the case had been well managed. It is quite important to receive these "positive strokes" from time to time, because all too often an attending will come in, after spending the previous evening with his family and sleeping in his own bed, and proceed to spend an hour making trivial and often picayune points without ever acknowledging any of the hard work and good judgments that might have been made. However, this wasn't the case this time, and it was appreciated.

11:30 A.M.—I realize I haven't eaten since 6 P.M. the night before, and I'm starved. I have to settle for another tuna sandwich, and then go off to a conference with the comfortable knowledge that we have all afternoon in which to see our remaining patients and that we cannot possibly get another admission. I immediately fall asleep even though the topic is interesting, but I simply am unable to keep my eyes open.

1:00 P.M.—We make rounds on our patients that we haven't yet seen (since it had obviously been impossible for us to conduct our routine early morning work rounds). At one point I tell my resident that I am going to be totally unavailable for the next twenty minutes or so and won't respond to my beeper at all. He gives me a knowing smile as I grab a magazine off a patient's table and trot off for twenty minutes of solitude and bliss in the bathroom. However, I don't even take the full twenty minutes because I find myself dozing off repeatedly, and I decide that I don't want to risk a concussion by falling off my precarious perch or what would be even worse, run the risk of falling so soundly asleep that I end up sleeping in the bathroom for the next twelve hours. I therefore go and draw one last set of blood gases, as well as some miscellaneous blood work required, so that we can write fluid orders for the period through the night. I then contact the team that is scheduled to cover the ICU this night and explain the situation regarding our more seriously ill patients so they have an idea what is going on. I also ask them to draw blood gases sometime later in the evening whenever they got a chance.

I had recognized earlier that afternoon that I was entering into my manic stage of exhaustion, which is where I find that I overcompensate for the effects of the fatigue and sleep deprivation. I know when this is occurring because I start getting short-tempered with people and generally flit about. I have gotten to the point where I can recognize when I am approaching this situation, and although I am not able to prevent it, I am at least aware of it to the extent that I know to walk away from any potentially explosive situations if at all possible.

5:15 P.M.—I go out to the parking lot and breathe a sigh of relief. I get into my car, and ritualistically tune into an all-news radio station because I literally have no idea what has gone on in the rest of the world for the previous thirty-six hours. I look at myself in the rear view mirror as I back the car out, eyes bloodshot, with deep circles underneath, and a two-days' growth of beard. I am of the school of philosophy that if you work thirty-three straight hours, you should look as rotten as you feel, and besides, I also haven't had the time or the energy to shave. I shudder when I realize I have to be back at 7:30 the next morning, and would have to do it all again in just three nights. I have been on duty for the previous thirty-three hours, during which time I had gotten one hour's sleep, eaten three crummy tuna fish sandwiches, declared five people dead, learned some medicine and had experienced moments of self-satisfaction as well as moments of despair and futility. I had had tremendous demands made of me, and I felt I had responded well. Despite the exhaustion and utter fatigue, I smiled as I realized that at the very least, I could put two big X's on my calendar and that there was one less night in which I had to be "on duty" as an intern.

CHAPTER / 35

"OH, SHIT, they're playing our song again. That's definitely an ambulance and not a fire engine."

Although it was the second week into my final month's rotation as an intern in the surgical emergency room, I was still amazed at the uncanny ability of the surgical resident to distinguish the slight difference in pitch between the two sirens. Of course, it didn't necessarily mean that the ambulance was transporting a patient who required immediate surgical emergency treatment, as the person could potentially be anyone from a child in the throes of an acute asthmatic attack to a heart attack victim or even possibly a woman in labor, which meant each would be seen and treated by the house officers on duty in the other emergency rooms, be it medical, pediatric or obstetrical. However, we immediately knew we were "on deck" when the nurse at the front desk shouted to us that a police call had just come through reporting a shooting of two patrons of a nearby bar during an "altercation."

"This one caught it in the chest, Doc, and he's in pretty bad shape," the ambulance attendant called out as the first stretcher was soon quickly wheeled in. Even though it was almost 2 A.M. the head nurse still found it necessary to transfer two patients from one treatment room to another so that we would not only have more room in which to maneuver but also so that the two of them, one of them being only a four-year-old youngster, would not be exposed to the gruesome scene that would almost certainly ensue.

"I'll put in the chest tube, and you get as many IV lines in anywhere you can," the resident barked as soon as he saw the location of the wound and listened to the victim's chest. At the same time one of the nurses was quickly and efficiently cutting away the blood-stained clothing, as well as pulling off his trousers, because even though it was obvious that the chest wound was life threatening, it was standard ER practice to ascertain if the patient was injured or bleeding elsewhere. For it would be absurd to work vigorously for any length of time in an attempt to keep the patient alive only to find out later that he had actually bled to death from an unseen wound in the thigh or elsewhere.

The patient had already lost consciousness as I started an IV line in each arm. I watched out of the corner of my eye as the resident swiftly and confidently made an incision with a scalpel above one of the ribs, and then, with gloved finger, probed bluntly until the blood that had been accumulating in the thoracic cavity was given an exit way and began to spontaneously spurt out. A tube was then quickly inserted, with one end actually in the chest cavity itself and the other end under a level of water contained in a large bottle on the floor in order to permit the blood to be drained, but simultaneously allowing for the cavity to remain airtight in order that the lungs could continue to expand. The blood flow in the tube was so rapid, however, that it was obvious that one or more major vessels had been damaged severely, and my resident shot me a quick glance that immediately and succinctly conveyed his feelings that the patient would most probably not make it to the OR alive. Nevertheless, we naturally continued our emergency procedures.

In the midst of all of this, a second ambulance pulled up with its siren wailing, and the other participant in the fight was also brought in on a stretcher, but fortunately for him he was only shot in the thigh. I quickly turned my full attention to him, and was somewhat taken aback as I cut through the makeshift bandage on his leg and discovered it to be a bra strap, with one "cup" stuffed with a wad of bar napkins that were acting as a compress, and each and every one emblazoned with the message, "Drink Heavenly Hill Bourbon. It's out of this world." By this time things were so hectic that I was unable to pause for even a second to appreciate the irony, as my resident suddenly shouted across the room that it appeared the first patient had suffered a cardiac arrest. Quickly making an assessment on my patient, I instructed an aide to clean the wound, and I dashed over and began external cardiac massage as the resident applied the ambu-bag.

We were soon joined by the surgical team on call who had been alerted by the nurses, and they quickly assumed management of the other patient. After five minutes it was obvious to all of us that the first patient was not going to respond to our resuscitative efforts, as blood continued to pour out of the tube in his chest faster than we could pump fluid into him. By this time the room was filled with policemen and detectives, as well as doctors, nurses, and orderlies, and as the patient with the leg wound was being brought up to the OR by the surgical team, my resident and I both stopped our efforts at the exact same moment.

The entire scenario lasted no more than fifteen minutes, but it was nonetheless exhausting. My white ER outfit was covered with blood, and as I sat on a stool filling out the death certificate and attempting to unwind, I suddenly realized that my wallet was missing from the chest pocket of my scrub suit. A quick search of the room, which was naturally quite a shambles, proved fruitless, and I went out to the main desk to ask the head nurse if anyone had possibly picked it up amidst all the confusion. She said that nothing had been reported to her, and she went back to the treatment room to enquire. I sat there for a few seconds to catch my breath and compose myself, when I overheard a Newark patrolman on a nearby phone asking the hospital operator to connect him with a certain number that immediately rang a bell. And well it should as I suddenly realized that it was my parents' home phone number, and I gingerly grabbed the phone out of his hands before the startled cop could say one word. With one hand over the mouthpiece, I managed to stammer that he happened to be calling *my home* at this ungodly hour, and I sure as hell wanted to know why. The policeman had naturally been taken aback by my abrupt actions, as well as by the somewhat hysterical quality of my questions, and it was probably fortunate that I hadn't given him time to react. After a few hectic, rapid-fire questions, it was quickly determined that during our frantic efforts, my wallet must have fallen on the floor in the vicinity of the now-deceased patient. The policeman, after being unable to find any identification on the victim's person, had simply assumed that the wallet on the floor was his, and without even double-checking he had gone ahead in an attempt to reach the next of kin who were listed to be notified in case of emergency.

After I had quickly hung up the phone as soon as I heard my mother's sleepy voice on the other end of the line, the somewhat chagrined patrolman embarrassedly handed me back my wallet; to this day I'm not sure what might have happened if my mother had actually received the message from a Newark cop that her son had just expired from a bullet wound in the chest. Thankfully I never got the chance to find out, but subsequently, I sure took a lot of ribbing from the nurses about it, and from then on I made quite sure that my wallet was safely tucked away in my back pocket!

Things had already quieted down in the treatment room when I returned, as the police had left to question the other victim before he went into surgery, and the nurses were busy checking on the other patients who had previously been herded in the back room, in addition to several newcomers. It was at times such as this that I was most often struck by how quickly events can unfold in a surgical ER, wherein an area that may be virtually deserted at any given moment can suddenly be filled to the brim with hectic activity almost before you can say "they're playing our song," and then almost as quickly be emptied.

As the door shut behind me, I was somewhat startled to find my resident bent over the now-lifeless body of the victim, completely absorbed in the process of attempting to insert a tube down the dead patient's throat and into his lungs. However, I quickly realized that he was "practicing" his technique for intubating, since this is definitely a skill that must be perfected firsthand and which cannot be learned from a textbook or even from practicing on a simulated model. Furthermore, since the speed with which it is successfully accomplished is so vital, in that the patient should naturally be deprived of oxygen for the shortest amount of time, possible, it is therefore imperative that the training physician perform the actual procedure as often as possible.

The resident was somewhat startled as well when he heard the door shut, but upon seeing it was me, he quickly motioned for me to come over so that I could also gain some valuable experience. I realize that to an outsider this type of "practice" may appear macabre, sacrilegious, or even simply in bad taste, but it is important to understand that it is not done in any way to defile the body, but is simply in the interest of the doctor's education, who will then be better skilled in emergency procedures and will perhaps use that very skill to someday save a life. As it happened, we spent only several minutes at this because we didn't want to risk any potential incident if someone was to observe and misconstrue our intentions, and the number of patients who still had to be treated was steadily continuing to mount, even at this late hour.

It was sure one hell of a way to end up my year of internship, but the two months I spent in the surgical and medical emergency rooms, or "in the pits" as they were commonly called for reasons which will soon become obvious, were certainly a necessary and integral complement to my general medical training, and if nothing else, certainly capped the year off with a bang rather than a whimper. As the ER physician it was my responsibility to make the final determination of whether or not a patient was sufficiently ill to warrant immediate admission to the hospital, and with no one to pass the buck to, I was necessarily forced to develop a different aspect of my medical judgment and acumen.

Not only that but this also afforded the aforementioned opportunity to learn how to properly evaluate and treat many of the more mundane ailments and complaints that would ultimately make up a large portion of a general practice and to which I would not have been exposed if I had only dealt with the care of hospitalized, more seriously ill patients.

This latter aspect, however, is a dual-edged sword that can quickly and easily turn a potentially good experience into a nightmare, both from the patient's point of view, as well as the training physician, and is the result of a combination of several interrelated factors. Probably the foremost element contributing to the chronically overstressed conditions that prevail at most inner-city hospital emergency rooms is that of education or, more properly, a lack of education. An ER is set up to function as just that—a facility to handle the most immediate (and true) emergency situations. Granted, and rightfully so, if the proper facilities existed to provide the necessary care for the incredibly large number of people that present themselves for nonemergency care at most city hospitals (50 percent, according to one study), the figures would certainly be drastically reduced. However, other studies have shown that even in those situations where the general health delivery system is adequate for the population served, if the public is not properly educated as to what does, or does not, constitute a true medical emergency, and thereby warrants a visit to a hospital ER, then the same overcrowding will still prevail. If this aspect of education is overlooked, there can be no hope for change from the frustrating, although hardly unique, situation in which a harried ER physician must attempt to deal with a true crisis, like a heart attack or severe asthmatic attack, which might come in while someone is taking up valuable time and space complaining of a headache he has had on and off for the previous three months.

Of course, there is much more than just this involved, as the situation is further perpetuated, for example, by the absurd structure of the Medicaid system. At the time of my internship, the state of New Jersey would pick up the entire fee for an ambulance, whether a true emergency existed or not, but there was absolutely no provision wherein that person could get reimbursed for bus fare, much less cab fare, if he used his discretion and elected to have his problem evaluated on a nonemergency basis. There are many other factors and variables operating as well, which go far beyond the scope of this book, but just in light of the above, the incredible volume and number of nonemergency ER visits is somewhat more understandable.

As the final months progressed, I was constantly exposed to the terrible things that can happen to the human body, whether by accident or by design of one person on another. Yet somewhat surprisingly, I found myself becoming less and less repulsed and nauseated by the actual disfigurements and horrible physical presentations I observed and more and more upset by a growing awareness of the overall human condition, which not only made such occurrences possible but commonplace. The more I recognized that the perpetrators of the horrendous crimes and assaults on others were those very same people who seemed to have the least amount of self-respect, the clearer became my understanding that if a person is consistently treated as if he is worthless for his entire life, he naturally has very little recourse but to believe that it must be so. For if someone has never been shown the proper consideration and respect that every human being so desperately needs, both by those closest around him and by society in general, he consequently has no real chance of ever developing any true respect for himself, much less for anyone else, and when someone arrives at such a point, then it is not very difficult to see how and why certain situations subsequently evolve. As simplistic and somewhat obvious as this may sound, my experiences and observations along these lines have been so reinforced and crystallized that I feel they must be emphasized.

Accordingly, it almost seemed as if there existed an unwritten, but nevertheless widely accepted, code of behavior in the inner city, wherein any argument, even the most superficial and seemingly minor of disputes, would almost invariably lead to physical acts of violence, especially, but far from necessarily so, if the parties had been drinking. What was most frightening to me was the implicit understanding that even if one person was successful in his attack upon another, even to the point of killing him, the perpetrator would then become the target for revenge by someone connected to the victim. This could be anyone from a family member to a close friend, and the retaliatory act would occur without any seeming regard for the consequences resulting from the perpetuation of this vicious cycle.

I had become chillingly aware of the existence of such a "code" as early as my junior rotation on general surgery, when I had admitted a rather young black man who had been involved in a fight in which his two older brothers had been killed. Although he, too, was beaten and shot, he was fortunately wearing a heavy leather outercoat that had served to slow the bullet up to the extent that it had just barely penetrated his body and had become imbedded just under the surface of his skin. He had been placed under observation, and the bullet removed rather easily, without even necessitating a trip to the OR. I was present on several occasions when the young man was being questioned by the police, and I was taken aback not only by his seeming composure in the midst of all of this but even more so by his reluctance to give any hard data to the officers and detectives, and their subsequent attitude of resigned acceptance. "What do you mean you can't describe any of them? They killed your brothers, for Christ sake. Oh hell, you know these people, he's not going to talk even if he knows anything!" Three days later the patient asked to be discharged so that he could ostensibly attend the funeral, and since there was no medical reason for keeping him hospitalized any longer, he was released. There had been no charges filed against him, but the police were nevertheless notified well beforehand of his impending discharge. Less than twenty-four hours later the young man was in the custody of the police after openly confessing to fatally shooting the two men who had obviously been involved in the earlier incident.

One very unexpected consequence of working in the ER was my acutely increased sense of awareness and frank appreciation of how tough it is to be a policeman, especially in an inner-city situation like Newark. If anyone spends any time at all in an ER at a hospital such as Martland, one of the first things he will be struck by is the omnipresence of a great many policemen and detectives. The hospital itself, in addition to private security guards, employs a uniformed off duty Newark patrolman for additional security, and at almost any hour of the day or night there are usually several patrol cars present. After completion of whatever business had brought them to the ER, the policemen would generally hang around for a cup of coffee and some small talk, and I consequently learned a great deal about what it's like to be a cop, not only from their narratives and reminiscences but from actually seeing them in the performance of their duties.

I was particularly struck by the similarities in what is required of an officer in order for him to execute his job with its wide range of demands and the varied personalities and situations involved and how I, as a doctor, was expected to react and function on a great many occasions. A good illustration is the not uncommon situation (especially in Newark!) in which a patrolman finds himself in a tense crowd situation. All too frequently someone will try and provoke a confrontation, and may even go so far as to bait the officer by calling him a name or actually spitting at his feet. Whereas the cop's first instinct as a man would be to strike out or retaliate in some fashion, in this instance he cannot follow his natural inclinations because to do so would most likely not be in the best interest of the general public. Quite similarly, from having to deal with the large numbers of drunk, hostile and abusive patients who passed with such regular frequency through the ER, I could very much appreciate how very difficult it is to be in a position where you are not able to react spontaneously to the most blatant and obvious provocation but instead must exercise an enormous amount of self-control so that you may continue to function as best as possible under the circumstances.

There were several occasions when I was actually struck by patients in the course of attempting to treat them, several of my colleagues have had knives drawn on them, and there have been instances where shots had actually been fired during the course of a scuffle in the ER itself, which is an extremely dangerous situation because of the presence of the tiled walls off of which the bullets can so easily ricochet. Naturally, I *always* tried to protect myself in any situation, but sometimes there is a very thin line between a protective stance and the attempt to restrain or control an assaultive person without succumbing to the overwhelming impulse to strike back as forcefully and effectively as possible.

To illustrate further, my fiancée brought me dinner one evening while I was on duty and then stayed on and observed. When I later had the opportunity to ask what had affected her the most, I pretty much expected a response concerning the blood and gore. After first commenting on the presence of all the police, she somewhat surprised me by saying that she had been particularly struck by the manner in which I responded to each of the patients and how I had addressed them respectively as "Sir" or "Ma'am," no matter what their condition or degree

267

of drunkenness or abusiveness. Although I did make a particularly conscientious effort to treat each person with as much respect as I could muster under the circumstances, I certainly do not want to leave the impression that I was any sort of saint in this regard. I can honestly say that I never struck a patient back, but on those occasions when I found myself in a situation where a person was in a position to do me real harm, I found myself employing more force or strength than might have been indicated in order to achieve the desired effect, and having absolutely no qualms about doing so.

More often than not, it was usually the case where the person would not actually strike out at me per se, but would grab at my hands, which were gloved and sterile if I had been suturing, thereby requiring a change of both gloves and instruments. At those times when my patience would ultimately give out, I would just remove my gloves and walk away rather than continue to struggle to the point of frustration where I wouldn't have been able to function at all. Then, if the other doctor on duty also found it impossible to work on the patient, he would either be left untreated and be free to walk or stagger out if that is what he desired, or more unfortunately, if the wound or injuries appeared so severe as to be life threatening, the patient might then have to be restrained until he either lost so much blood or became so exhausted that he could then be safely and effectively treated.

I realize that this situation must seem inconceivable to most people who have not actually had the experience, and how difficult it must be to comprehend how or why a person who is severely cut, injured or hurt to such a degree can be abusive or even assaultive to the person who wants to help. Again, I found that one of the largest contributing factors in such situations was most frequently the degree of drunkenness of the patient. However, this does not alter the intensity of the frustration of being a doctor in such a paradoxical situation, where you are literally torn between your own instincts and training, wherein on the one hand you want to reach out and attempt to help someone in pain, and on the other your own pride and self-respect make you want to respond by telling the person to go to hell and quit wasting your time. It is obviously very tough to try to deal with such situations on a personal level, and although it is difficult to grasp how such a situation can even exist, the fact is that it does, and this was the reality that I found myself being forced to somehow deal with as best I could.

Although at certain times, especially Friday and Saturday nights but also during any holiday period, it seemed that at least every other patient seen in the surgical ER was slightly tipsy if not frankly drunk, the general situation was actually such that the majority of patients treated in any given twenty-four-hour period had not been drinking at all. Yet for obvious reasons, when reflecting back on the overall experience, it is usually the drunken patients that stand out most vividly, and not necessarily just the abusive and hostile drunks. For thankfully, these obnoxious types were basically in the minority of "drinkers" that were there for treatment, and there was quite a large, distinct catagory of "fun drunks" who would appear regularly. They were not only generally pleasant and cooperative (oftentimes they were so "self-anesthetized" by the alcohol that if they did require suturing, you often found that you didn't have to administer any local anesthetic) but were often quite funny, and therefore provided comic relief at those times when it seemed you most needed something to help break the generally prevailing overall pervasive atmosphere of tension.

For instance, one evening two women were brought in to the ER both drunker than hell, who had gotten into a squabble in the kitchen of one of their apartments, and in the course of the argument, one of the women apparently picked up a glass jar of white house paint that was lying about and proceeded to smash it over the head of the other. Fortuitously, the "attackee" had a bushy "Afro" hairstyle and suffered only two relatively minor scalp lacerations (which ultimately required suturing), and she made quite a sight as she paraded about the ER, hair almost entirely coated with thick white paint, and with two areas of distinct, gradually increasing red blotches, which, set off by the numerous rivulets of white color, made a striking contrast to her ebony black face. She was laughing and carrying on, and flirting with the orderlies, doctors and any other male in the immediate vicinity, including other patients, and each time I attempted to approach her in order to evaluate the extent of her injuries, I had to break out in laughter along with her and everyone else in the room, as she looked like a Felliniesque version of a female Al Jolson turned inside out!

As if this weren't enough in itself, when she had calmed down enough to answer my questions, I found I had another Moms Mabley on my hands, as exemplified by our following dialogue.

"What brought you to the hospital today?" (OK, a seemingly silly question, but it was standard protocol, and of some importance, since she might have twisted her ankle or incurred some other injury that might have been overlooked, especially in her condition, if I would have proceeded to treat only her scalp wounds and failed to ask.)

"The avalanche brought me here, honey. It's the chauffeur's night off," accompanied by peals of laughter from her and everyone else in the room.

"The what?"

"The avalanche. Man with that siren going, *everybody* got the hell out of our way. Whoo, whoo." (The latter was a remarkably good imitation of a drunken siren.)

"Have you ever been a patient in this hospital before?" I stupidly pressed on.

"Yeah, a couple of years ago my old man knocked me upside my nose pretty good, and I needed an operation to fix a deviate symptom, or something like that," followed by what may be best described as general chaos!

Somehow, I was finally able to suture her scalp, and as she waltzed out of the ER, I decided that I had earned a little respite, and I went to the refrigerator to get my snack that I had brought in earlier that day, but lo and behold it was missing. I began to rant and rave and was just about to start accusing the ER personnel of stealing my food when I spotted a very intoxicated, somewhat elderly man propped up on a stretcher in the far corner of the back treatment room. He was contentedly munching on my salami sandwich, and was passing around the dill pickle that I had so carefully picked out the day before. I stormed over to confront him, but since he had already shared the pickle with two other patients and I couldn't be sure who else might have bitten into the sandwich, I ended up with the proverbial tuna salad from the cafeteria; not unsurprisingly, the incident seemed a lot funnier to the rest of the staff than it did to me at the time.

CHAPTER / 36

As THE final weeks went by, I began to notice that many of the patients began to look vaguely familiar. At first I thought this might be some form of "combat fatigue," since by this time I felt as if I must have already seen the entire population of Newark pass through the emergency room doors at least once. However, in mentioning this to the resident and head nurse, I was reassured that I was not suffering from shell shock, as they went on to inform me that there was a whole army (just to continue the military analogy) of "regulars" who were rather intimately known to the emergency room staff because of their frequent and almost daily visits. These malingerers and hypochondriacs presented themselves most often to the medical emergency room, and the vast majority were neither alcoholics nor drug users. It was fairly obvious from the general tone of the discussion that these people were not held in very high regard by the hospital personnel, which is not all that unreasonable since there were times, especially when it was particularly hectic, when I definitely felt much the same way. However, an incident had occurred when I was on duty in the medical emergency room which taught me a very important lesson, and serves as another good example of how much can potentially be learned from almost any type of patient.

This particular "regular" was a grossly obese woman who was brought in by ambulance (naturally) complaining of chest pains. She was a particularly demanding and unpleasant woman to deal with, and the nurse informed me that she was, indeed, seen rather frequently for the very same complaint, which had always turned out in the past to be nothing more than gas pains and acid indigestion. Even though I was made aware of her pattern, I somehow didn't like the way she appeared, as she was quite agitated and sweating profusely, and although initially tempted, I did not want to simply brush her off as a "hypo" by doing a cursory physical exam and then sending her home with antacids, as had generally been the case on numerous previous occasions. Since I was not pressed for time, for a change, I elected to do an electrocardiogram.

I detected a definite abnormality as the rhythm strip of the EKG machine streamed out, and upon doing a complete cardiogram study and discussing the findings with the resident on duty, as well as a cardiologist consultant, it was unanimously felt that the woman had most likely suffered a recent myocardial infarction, and she was immediately admitted to the coronary care unit, where she was subsequently treated and closely monitored for several days and eventually went on to recover. Needless to say, I proudly strutted about like a peacock for the next few days, for there was a strong possibility that the woman might well have died if she had been sent home, but more important than my ego gratification was the fact that I vividly learned a very crucial and important lesson, which is that even malingerers and hypochondriacs actually do get sick on occasion, and although it's like the little boy who cried wolf, as a conscientious physician, you are obligated to approach each "cry for help" as legitimate until proven otherwise.

The opportunities for learning were therefore not only numerous in the emergency room setting, but, as you have seen, were quite varied as well, and it seemed that almost every situation, no matter how mundane or routine the circumstances might initially appear, had something of value to contribute to your education and in the furthering of your skills. This was true even in the case of the suture removal clinic, which took place each weekday from 8 A.M. to 9 A.M. in the surgical emergency room. This was the time specifically set aside for anyone who had received stitches in the preceding four to six days to have the progress of his wound recovery evaluated, and if there were no complications, such as infection for example, the sutures could then generally be removed. This was usually quite a painless procedure in itself, and in one sense was almost a form of "busy work" in that the amount of skill required to perform the actual task was not all that great. More importantly, however, it afforded an excellent opportunity for the doctor to follow up on his own judgment and technical expertise as he was able to see firsthand the results of every aspect of his prior treatment. This included his selection of which of the different suture materials to employ, whether or not the proper number of sutures were administered, and if the sutures themselves were "pulled" too tightly or left too loose, all of which go into not only determining the success of the wound closure in regard to cessation of the bleeding process but the probable degree and size of the subsequent scar involved as well. This is obviously a very important aspect of the training experience, since you are actually able to "see the fruits of your labors" and, basically, is the only way to really learn which technique and procedure to employ in any given situation in order to accomplish the best results. This time involved some of the most gratifying hours spent in the emergency room, or anywhere else in the hospital for that matter, because you were able to see firsthand that as a direct result of your skill and training, someone would not have to carry around a jagged, disfiguring scar on his body for the rest of his life.

This is especially important if you consider not only the great number of facial lacerations that are treated every day, but that a large proportion of these cases involve young children and toddlers. A great many of the injuries are incurred in or around the house (as are most accidents of all nature across the nation in general), but a strikingly high number are unfortunately the result of a youngster having been struck by an automobile. I was unprepared and somewhat staggered by the high incidence of such occurrences, which appeared to stem from a number of varied factors, the most obvious being that there are oftentimes simply no safe, convenient places for inner-city youngsters to play. Contributing as well is the general overcrowding of the city itself, lack of proper supervision and the unfortunate natural tendency of young children to dart out recklessly from between parked cars.

The most commonly seen injury to toddlers just beginning

to walk, and who are naturally somewhat unsteady on their feet, is a gash on the point of the chin or on the forehead. This is quite understandable as these are the obvious areas that would tend to be struck when a child falls, since he has not yet learned how to use his hands to break his fall, and they also happen to be especially vulnerable to injury. This is so because the skin in these regions is normally stretched quite taut, with almost no cushion of underlying fat and connective tissue between it and the bone, which therefore greatly increases the chances that any fair-sized blow to the chin or forehead will cause a split or tear, which will often require suturing.

Naturally, you would most especially like to do the best possible repair on a youngster so that he or she will not have to be burdened with an unsightly facial scar for the rest of their lives, but unfortunately, this is not often easily accomplished. Obviously, because of their age and general state of fright, they cannot be reasoned with on a rational level, and as a rule they are usually crying and extremely agitated. It helps a great deal to wrap the child tightly in a sheet, with his arms pinned to the side, and have someone hold the body still while someone else securely holds the head.

On the surface it would appear that the best person to assist would be one or both of the parents, as they could hopefully quiet and reassure the child at the same time. However, as my experiences mounted, I soon realized that this would prove to be more of a headache than a bonus in approximately half the cases. For it became all too obvious that although some of the children would become completely panic stricken if their parents left their sight, just as often the parent would turn out to be more upset than the child, and naturally if the mother begins to cry and carry on, the child is going to do the same. Consequently, there were many occasions when I would be forced to ask the parents to leave the treatment room when they appeared to be getting more hysterical than the child. It is difficult enough to attempt to perform a somewhat delicate task on a "moving target," even when the child is being held as securely as possible, but it becomes even more so when the mother is screaming and reaching out for her child and the child is naturally attempting to reach back.

Occasionally, this would lead to a confrontational type of situation, and on more than one occasion I had to summon a guard to physically escort the parent from the treatment room, although this was rather infrequent. There is one incident that particularly sticks out in my mind, which although not dealing specifically with the precise circumstances just described, is nevertheless quite analogous, and serves as well to illustrate further some of the difficulties encountered that were not covered in any of my textbooks or lectures.

It all began routinely enough when a four-year-old youngster was brought in by ambulance after being struck by an automobile. Upon examination one leg appeared to be broken, and we suspected that there might be additional damage to the internal organs as well. The child was obviously in pain, and soon after our initial examination began, her parents came dashing in, having been alerted by a neighbor as to what had occurred. Upon seeing his youngster in extreme discomfort, the father insisted that we immediately give the child pain medication, which would have been in poor medical practice. I attempted to explain that to do so would be doing his daughter a grave injustice, for if we treated her symptomatically with an analgesic, it would surely have made her more comfortable but might possibly have then prevented us from early detection of an even more serious life-threatening injury. For example, if we had "doped" her up before completing our examination, when we got to the abdomen and went to push down on her belly, the child would most likely not have winced and cried out in pain, as she actually did when examined, and we might not then have proceeded with the haste we did to further investigate the strong possibility of a ruptured spleen. This turned out to be the case, and the youngster could quite possibly have bled to death internally while going up for X rays or while her leg was being casted.

Unfortunately, the father was so distraught by this point that he was unable to listen to reason, and in his blind rage he accused both the resident and myself of being racists, shouting that if his daughter had been white, she would have already received a pain-killer. It required two security guards to remove him from the treatment room, and they, along with several black nurses, were able to finally calm him down. The youngster ultimately went on to recover completely, although she did have to undergo emergency surgery to have her spleen removed, and surprisingly enough, her father actually came back and apologized two days later.

One comment he made in particular really helped put things into perspective, as he related that in the vast majority of his previous experiences with emergency rooms, including those of several other hospitals and not just Martland, no one had ever taken the time to *explain* exactly what was going on and the reasons why a particular procedure was being performed or not being done. Part of this may be attributed to the communication problems and cultural differences resulting from the large numbers of foreign born doctors (which has already been discussed), especially in light of the large volume of patients that are generally seen and treated each and every day. An additional factor at work relates to the fact that *all* house staff members are generally chronically fatigued as a consequence of the overwhelming work load, pressure and long hours, and therefore are often overtired to the point of irritability. I offer this not as an excuse for the doctor per se but to inform the general public of the totality of the situation, and I hope that in some way such an awareness *on both sides* can, at the very least, help defuse somewhat similar situations in the future.

The "fatigue factor" to which I have just alluded is an inevitable by-product of working a straight twenty-four-hour shift, which was the policy in the Surgical Emergency Room. About the only "fringe benefits" of working a twenty-four-hour on-duty, twenty-four-hour off-duty schedule was that you could basically throw away your calendar for the month. All you really needed to remember was that when you left the hospital at 8 A.M. after working the previous twenty-four hours, you had the following twenty-four hours off, until 8 A.M. the next day, when you had to return to begin another straight twenty-four hours on duty, regardless of whether it was a holiday, weekend day or whatever.

As if the experience involved in dealing with the daily horrors and wild and hectic events that would occur with such regularity was not enough in itself, it was accentuated and punctuated by the incredible strains and demands involved in simply working such an arduous tour of duty. Personally, the toughest time for me was in the late afternoon, around 4 P.M. to 5 P.M., when I would generally find my energies sagging, and then that long stretch from approximately 4 A.M. to 7 A.M., when everything seemed to take on an almost surrealistic quality. The volume of patients would drop off to only a trickle, the resident would usually attempt to sneak in a little sleep on a stretcher in the back room, and I would be left "alone" to handle whatever came in. There were certain blocks of time when the volume could generally be counted on to be fairly heavy, especially weekend evenings, but one of the fascinations involved in working at an institution like Martland was the omnipresent potential that just about anything and everything could happen at virtually any time, and you therefore were always in a constant state of tension and readiness, as you never knew what might come bursting through the door at any hour of the day or night. In addition, as previously explained, there was the added uncertainty of not knowing whether a true emergency life-threatening crisis would suddenly drop in your lap or if it might simply turn out to be someone who decided to have a sore tooth checked out; the possibility even existed that the situation might turn out to be incongruous, unusual or even humorous.

For along with the drama, blood and gore, there were many instances similar in nature to what had occurred one early morning at approximately 3:30 A.M. when a man was wheeled in on a stretcher, semiconscious and completely naked under the ambulance blanket. I was informed by the driver that the patient's wife was filling out the emergency room form, so I was forced to begin the examination before any information or clues as to what happened were available. The gentleman was lapsing in and out of consciousness, and in the course of my initial examination, I discovered only a rather large bump on the top of his head; it seemed most probable that the man had received a blow of some sort and had been knocked unconscious. The neurological examination did not reveal any signs of gross pathology or possible brain injury, although the possibility could surely not be definitely ruled out as yet, and the man was now almost fully conscious, although still somewhat groggy. It was important to rule out anything more serious than a probable mild concussion, and I was therefore in the process of filling out an X-ray form when a woman, who hurriedly identified herself as the patient's wife, dashed into the room to find out his condition. I told her at this point it didn't look like there would be any serious problems or aftereffects, although I could not make any guarantees, and she was greatly relieved when she found him to be alert and responsive. Naturally, I then proceeded to ask what had happened, and when the wife became somewhat flushed and embarrassed, cynic that I was quickly becoming, I jumped to the conclusion that there had probably been a family fight and that she let him have it with a frying pan or something. I couldn't have been more wrong.

It seems that the two of them had not had any altercation at all and had actually been home in bed for several hours. However, it seems that the wife had difficulty falling asleep because of a leaky, dripping faucet in the kitchen. Her husband on the other hand was sleeping quite soundly, but she awakened him to ask him to attempt to fix the leak, and he groggily complied, padding downstairs dressed in nothing but his "birthday suit." He was thus still half asleep and fully naked as he squatted under the sink and began to fiddle around with the pipes when, at that very moment, the family cat happened to chance by. Apparently being in a playful mood and spying the two "family jewels" dangling freely between the husband's legs, the cat approached from behind and proceeded to take a healthy swat at one of the testicles with his claws. This came as quite a painful shock, needless to say, and the husband instinctively responded by jerking his head upward, which soon brought it into direct contact with the overhanging kitchen drain pipe with apparently more than enough velocity and force to knock him out cold.

The husband grinned rather sheepishly as he corroborated her story and filled in the details, and sure enough, on further examination several deep scratch marks were discovered on his right scrotum. The skull X rays turned out to be normal, and after a short observation period and a prophylactic tetanus shot, as well as instructions as to what potential signs to be on the alert for that might be indicative of the development of something more serious, the two left the emergency room, with the husband wearing a pair of borrowed pants and a hospital gown and slippers and suffering from no more than a mild concussion, a moderate headache and a large case of embarrassment!

From a broader viewpoint, the experiences involving the hostile and belligerent patients were more than balanced by the larger number of patients who were genuinely appreciative of your efforts, especially if you were at all considerate and did a good job, and it was especially nice to receive such positive feedback. This was somewhat dramatically reinforced in the situations involving two specific conditions that are commonly seen in a surgical emergency room, wherein as a result of the doctor's intervention, the patient enjoys immediate and almost complete relief. They represent a striking illustration of what to me is one of the more appealing aspects of surgery in general, which is the frequent opportunity to see the immediate fruits of your labors. There are very few "guarantees" in medicine, but one is when a surgeon removes a "hot" appendix and predicts to his patient, who might have initially come to him in excruciating pain, that he will *never* again suffer an attack of appendicitis.

The first of these conditions is most often typified by the patient who presents himself doubled over in pain with the complaint that for some reason he has not been able to void, or pass, urine for a period of anywhere from a matter of hours to even several days. This condition, medically referred to as acute urinary retention, may come about from a wide variety of causes, but most commonly occurs as a side effect of several types of medications or as a consequence of an enlarged prostate gland in men. The bladder is an organ specifically designed with many sensitive nerve endings, so that as it begins to fill, the person is made subjectively aware that it is time to voluntarily void. However, if for some reason the urine continues to accumulate, and thus distends or stretches the bladder, the subsequent sensation is that of pain, which may become so severe that it can virtually incapacitate the patient. Except in certain specific instances it is a relatively quick and painless procedure to insert a catheter and drain off the urine, and most often, the catheter is removed when the bladder is emptied, although the patient must naturally be given the earliest possible appointment for a thorough work-up so as to determine the cause of the retention. You could almost plot a graph showing the correlation between the quantity of urine removed and the broadness of the smile of almost ecstatic relief that is evoked as the urine passes out.

Similarly, there are those patients who present themselves in extreme discomfort resulting from hemorrhoids, which you will remember are nothing more than enlarged, tortuous veins, but which may bleed upon defecation and can be quite painful at times. The situation can become even more painful on occasion if a complication develops wherein the blood that normally circulates through the vein becomes completely clotted; in such instances the pressure in the vein increases, and the hemorrhoid is stretched even further, until the pain may become almost unbearable. You must be fairly certain of your diagnosis, however, before you attempt to surgically intervene, because if the blood has not clotted, you may cause serious bleeding, even to such an extent that the patient might have to be operated upon to control the blood loss. However, if you adhere to certain very specific criteria and are fairly certain of what you are dealing with, it then involves only a relatively minor procedure to anesthetize the hemorrhoid, make a small incision and if everything is as you expected, the blood clot will then almost literally pop out of the vein. The minor bleeding that occurs can be easily controlled, and the patient experiences immediate relief. These patients are also most effusive in their thanks, primarily I think because they won't have to ride home leaning on their side, as they most likely had been forced to do on their way to the hospital, and the most frequent comment is the excited anticipation of not having to sleep on their stomachs that night.

Working such a shift, especially in an active emergency room where your physical presence is basically required at almost all times, naturally plays havoc with your diet and digestion, and one of the more important lessons to be learned for survival in this regard was where and how to get the type of food that you would be able to eat and digest, much less enjoy, especially at 3 A.M. Again I wish I had a dime for every White Castle, Gino's or McDonald's hamburger I ingested over the three-year period I worked at Martland as both a student and an intern; I would still be way ahead of the game if I only included the time spent in the emergency room. For some people the smell of the antiseptic cleaning agents that seem to pervade every hospital corridor is enough to evoke memories of their hospital experience, but for me, I still can't eat a "Big Mac" or "Gino Giant" without being instantly reminded of Martland. In addition it is important to understand that the hospital cafeteria (lousy as it was) was only open from 6 A.M. to 7 P.M.; at all other times you were completely at the mercy of an orderly or whoever else might be on a break and willing to go out and bring back some food.

There are obviously not too many eating establishments in the Central Ward that stay open all night, and if they do, they usually cater to a very specific segment of the population and, consequently, usually feature a very ethnic menu. This made things even more difficult for me, having been raised in a kosher home, and although I did not adhere strictly to the dietary laws, heritage and cultural tastes are hard to overcome. I therefore found it quite difficult to adjust to a snack of broiled pig's feet or hog jowels, which was standard fare, most especially at 2 A.M. snack time. I will admit that home-style chicken necks were an interesting experience, and I was usually the one who could be counted upon to lobby most vigorously for either barbecued ribs or chicken. I rather enjoyed those meals, even if I did have to request the extra, extramild sauce because even the tamest of the traditional sauces would generally not only clean out my sinuses but blow out my taste buds as well, so that I usually couldn't taste *anything* for the next three days.

Needless to say, a month of such repeated insults to my abused GI tract in conjunction with attempting to cope with a new and completely alien and absurd sleeping pattern really put the finishing touches to the entire experience, and frankly, as the analogy with being pregnant so succinctly expresses it, you just can't have a real conception (pun intended) of what it was like unless you've been there. The matter of sleeping, for example, was a major adjustment that I was never able to make to any satisfactory degree. The first thing I invariably did after coming home at 9 A.M. was to immediately shower, which felt so good it was almost a quasi-religious experience, and then I would naturally go off to bed. I never had any appetite at that point, which is understandable after having filled up with all that crap through the previous twenty-four hours, and it was always fairly difficult at first to fall off to sleep. Nevertheless, exhaustion would soon win out, and I would drift off, but I tried to make it a rule not to sleep through to the late afternoon or early evening, although there were occasions I did find it absolutely necessary to do so. For if I did it as a rule, it would make it difficult to fall asleep at a reasonable time that same evening, and it was obviously imperative to get a good night's sleep because the next morning I had to again begin work for another twenty-four hours.

Therefore, I usually only slept until approximately 2 P.M., but the quality of sleep was generally poor, and when the alarm would go off, it would often take me several seconds to perceive whether it was 7 A.M. and I was being roused to go to work or whether it was really early afternoon and I should fight off the natural inclination to roll over and go back to sleep. Upon awaking fully, although usually still pretty irritable from not enough sleep, as well as often suffering from a whopping case of heartburn, I would nevertheless be hungry. However, at the beginning, I had a problem deciding if I wanted a breakfast-type meal, a sandwich, or an early dinner, but I soon began to eat whatever happened to appeal to me at the time and gave up attempting to give meals any of the standard classifications; I simply let my screwed up body make the decision.

I vividly remember my last day on duty as an intern, and not only because of the relief I felt or because of any particularly gruesome or sensational incidents but mostly because of the following patient and what ensued. It was a Friday, and we were in the midst of suture-removal clinic when an elderly little man wandered into the treatment room with a huge bandage wrapped around his head like some Eastern-style turban; he was not able to speak a word of English.

I recall immediately jumping to the assumption that somebody must have tried to cut the poor man's ear off in a mugging or else he was the victim of some other heinous assault or accident, and I thought that it seemed only appropriate to begin my last day having to treat a typical atrocious injury. The man, however, did not appear to be in any acute or even mild distress, and I could detect no signs of blood seeping through the makeshift bandage, and not being able to communicate, I began to unwrap the "turban." My suspicions were rekindled as the bandage must have been at least twenty feet long, and I expected to find something truly grotesque as I unraveled the last section, but all that was revealed were several gauze pads taped firmly over the ear. I removed them and was still surprised to find no blood or overt evidence of injury, and upon further investigation I discovered that there was a little cotton wick covering the opening of the ear canal, which upon removal revealed a small round white object that smelled to me exactly like camphor. Intrigued, I proceeded to remove it and look into the ear canal with my instrument, and lo and behold, lying right there in the middle of the canal was a small dead moth, which I proceeded to remove with no difficulty.

At this point, his wife who had been out front filling out the necessary papers came into the room and began to explain, in broken English, what had happened. It seemed that the previous evening she and her husband had been sitting outside on their porch when the moth somehow became lodged inside her husband's ear. She had the presence of mind and good judgment not to poke around in there with any sharp object in an attempt to remove it, and her simple and rather effective solution was to search out a small-sized mothball which would fit snugly in the ear, cover it with gauze and keep it all securely in place by the "turban" in the hope that the moth would thus be killed. It had obviously been quickly successful (probably the moth died more from asphyxiation than from the effects of the camphor), as the husband had not been in any discomfort, which he surely would have been if the moth had moved about, and the woman therefore did not feel it necessitated a visit to the emergency room that late in the evening. The man and his wife then went to bed and slept undisturbed until the morning, when they proceeded to come to the hospital.

The woman, noticing my smile, wanted to know if she had done the proper thing and I quickly assured her that she had handled the situation like a real professional. She smiled back, asked if anything further needed to be done, and when I announced that everything had been taken care of, she thanked me, proceeded to gather up all the bandages along with the mothball, and the two of them walked out of the emergency room hand in hand, animatedly chattering to one another in their native tongue.

And although I would hardly call it representative of my experiences of that last month in the emergency room, or the internship in general, it was certainly a nice image to carry over as my last vivid recollection of the year.

EPILOGUE

ALL IN all, it was certainly quite a five-year period in my life, to say the least, from that first moment I was approached by Larry Peerce in the Plaza Hotel to that early Saturday morning at 8:30 A.M. when I dropped my blood-stained emergency room outfit in the laundry chute and walked out of the hospital as a licensed M.D.

I had spent the first two years of medical school studying the basic sciences, 50 percent of which I have subsequently forgotten as a natural consequence of rarely having been called upon to use much of it, and had put in innumerable hours poring over text-books and sequestered in various laboratories either cutting up a cadaver, getting a headache from squinting through a microscope or spitting out a mouthful of urine.

I then began my introduction to the practice of clinical medicine and learned how to diagnose and care for sick people, and somehow managed to amass a great deal of knowledge in that regard in addition to learning a great deal about myself as a person as well. There were situations in which I was stimulated, challenged and enthused, and there were others that left me discouraged, disheartened and extremely frustrated. I experienced the exhilaration of delivering a new baby into this world and was simultaneously exposed to the squalor and hopelessness of the inner-city culture to which the infant would most likely become a victim.

As an intern, I finally understood the true meaning of responsibility, and the unique implications that this has for a doctor, and which, to my mind, distinguishes a committed physician from the vast majority of members of other professions. I learned to care for people.

Simultaneously, in my excursions into the world of "show biz," I was fortunate to have the opportunity to be able to step back from the Central Ward on occasion and view everything from a totally different vantage point. I was placed in the rather unique position of being able to juxtapose that Central Ward of Newark, where I was expected to learn and grow in order to become a competent, conscientious "professional," with the sound stages of Hollywood, where I was also expected to "perform," but on a wholly different level, and with the investment and stakes involved being drastically different.

I would not think there are too many doctors who can say that over the course of their training they have also "masqueraded" in commercials as a jogger, a basketball star, a football bench-warmer and a bike rider with bad breath, as well as a "BMOC" (Big Man on Campus), a swinger at a cocktail party and a dogged suitor. I have played the parts of a recent college graduate about to be married and a newlywed on his honeymoon. I've portrayed a doctor (art imitating life imitating art), a greaser, a grocer and a flipped out Viet Nam war veteran. I've opened shopping centers and closed amusement parks, judged beauty contests and a battle of the bands. I've been a four-time loser on the *Dating Game*, and repeatedly invaded the sanctity of people's bedrooms as a late-night talk show guest, and I very nearly asphyxiated a TV crew in Cincinnati by overdosing them with garlic fumes. I have had my name and picture in magazines and publications I never before even knew existed, as well as found myself on the same pages with the likes of soap opera stars and Jacqueline Kennedy Onassis.

I look back upon the entire experience of both medical school and internship and my "other life" with a variety of emotions, both positive and negative, and although there were times I think my medical training might have gone along a bit more smoothly without my show business involvement, I can honestly say I wouldn't have missed any of it for the world.